HANDBOOK
OF
Trailer
Sailing

HANDBOOK

OF

Trailer
Sailing

by
Robert F. Burgess

A TRITON BOOK

DODD, MEAD & COMPANY
NEW YORK

Published by Dodd, Mead & Company, Inc.
79 Madison Avenue, New York, N.Y. 10016
Distributed in Canada by
McClelland and Stewart Limited, Toronto
Manufactured in the United States of America
Designed by Stanley S. Drate/Folio Graphics Co., Inc.
First Edition

Library of Congress Cataloging in Publication Data

Burgess, Robert Forrest.
  Handbook of trailer sailing.
  Includes index.
  1. Sailing. 2. Sailboats. 3. Boat trailers.
I. Title.
GV811.B86 1984   797.1'24   84-8007
ISBN 0-396-08302-1
ISBN 0-396-08303-X (pbk.)

*To Hutch, Gerry, Buck and Clarkie
Who Made It So Much Fun*

CONTENTS

Preface

This book is about trailerable sailboats. It tells how to select one to suit your needs, how to outfit it, how to trailer it, how to sail it, and how to have fun with it. It also tells how to handle some of the problems that might arise. I have tried to combine this information into a compact handbook for those who enjoy sailing the size sailboat that can be towed behind the family car.

Most of what you will find here has been learned by trial and error. Since I started sailing before trailer sailing became popular, I may have had more chances than most to make mistakes and to learn what I could from them. The first boat I ever sailed single-handedly had a mast no taller than I was at the time—about five feet. I was six years old then and size was not so important. My father and I had built the marvelous thing by sawing the top off a wooden flagpole and shellacking it. The sail—a triangle of heavy gray canvas—was lashed to this flagpole mast with clothesline. It had no boom to support, it needed none. Age had stiffened the canvas into a permanent flatness. We had built it to fit my father's fast outrigger kayak with its big lateen sail, which we often sailed together. But this smaller sail was to be my very own. Since I would be sailing alone across a large Michigan lake with it, I suspect that my mother may have had something to say about how large and powerful it would be. No matter, this sail was my passport to adventure.

A couple of years later it was another boat and another sail, this one a large square sail of unwieldy canvas stepped aboard my grandparents' heavy wooden rowboat. With it I sailed down the lake at a nice clip, steering with an oar, blithely unaware that square sails were made to do only one thing really well: sail downwind. Luckily, my parents' motorboat caught up to me just as I sailed over the horizon.

From then on it was always sailboats—no matter what kind—just so they could ride the wind and carry me and my boyhood buddies off on never-to-be-forgotten voyages of discovery. Gradually we progressed to a small armada of sailboats so leaky and disreputable that their owners often gave them to us just to haul away. In those pre-fiberglass days we worked wonders with bucketsful of caulking compound, ropes and rags, wood plugs, copper patches, tar, and plenty of paint and perseverance. Indeed, it seemed that the worst dry-rotted hulls imaginable were not beyond our unflinching belief that we could salvage, restore, and make them sailable again.

This we did with several sailboats from twelve to eighteen feet long. None was ever put on trailers then. The boats were propped upside down on sawhorses beside the lake, repaired, repainted, and refloated as soon as possible, ready for sailing. At summer's end they went back atop their sawhorses on shore. When winter came the lake froze solid. Several feet of snow turned our sailboats into just so many lumps on that white landscape. We boys could hardly wait for spring when the ice melted, our sailboats sat steaming in the sun, and it was time to go sailing again.

On summer nights we sometimes slept below deck in our boat's narrow cockpit, two of us fitting into an enclosure barely wide enough for our feet, the sailboat lying to anchor on the still, misty lake with a railroad brakeman's lantern glowing brightly from her masthead. It was all pretty basic but we loved it then, forty years ago.

Since then we have seen many changes. Wooden boats are still popular and are being sailed by those who cherish the memories. But today, fiberglass boats have largely taken over the market. They have no frames to clutter up the interior of their hulls. Their curves are so magnificent that one has difficulty imagining them in wood. And what incredible silkiness to the touch; what permanence. To own a hull that never has to be scraped, caulked, sanded, or painted, seemed almost a sin. To be able to maintain a fiberglass hull for years with little more than soap, water, and wax, was surely most unseamanlike and certainly unethical, I once thought. But along with the modern boats came equally modern trailers to support the streamlined shape whether they are single-hulled or monohulled, some of the latter so beamy they must hinge and fold to fit legally on our nation's highways.

With these changes came the more mobile small boat sailor. Towing his sailboat behind his car, truck, or recreational vehicle, he ranges far and wide. He is a seagoing gypsy, a trailer sailor. He can go anywhere on the continent, wherever there is enough water to float his sailboat.

Today, the northern trailer sailor need no longer watch his boat disappear beneath a winter snowdrift if he chooses not to. He can hitch it behind the family car, trail south, and sail tropical waters as long as he wishes. Lakes, rivers, bays, and oceans are his for the choosing. He can pick his water, his weather, and where he wants to sail from day to day any time of the year. Only the trailer sailor has this option. Compared to its big boat brethren, his sailboat is small and compact. So are his needs. All he really requires is mobility. His sailing thrills aboard his sixteen-foot trailerable are just as big as those aboard a sixty-foot nontrailerable sailboat. Often bigger. The trailer sailor has it all; it just comes in a smaller package behind his car. Moreover, en route to his sailing vacation, his pocket cruiser on wheels becomes a self-contained land yacht. Living and sailing aboard these sailboats on land and sea is what this book is about. If it does nothing more than save you a few trials and errors of your own, it will have accomplished its purpose.

I would like to take this opportunity to express my appreciation to those friends and associates who have contributed in some way to this project: to our long-time friends and cruising companions, Carl and Nancy Zillmer, who were often the target of my camera and whose sailing tips, from their sloop *Sea 'n Zee,* proved so helpful; to Harley Sachs and his family who know all too well what it is like to sail with ice off Michigan's Upper Peninsula, for their equally valuable suggestions; to Stan and Marie Thomas for their input despite having lost their sailboat not to the perils of the sea but to the greater perils of the road; to naval architect Bruce Bingham, who shared with us his insights on Flicka; to Robert F. Murray who showed us an easier way to navigate; to Andrew Dossett who helped speed things up, and to Nat Bishop who made it a reality; to Art Bandy who pointed the way, then helped us steer there; to Howard D. Irwin who helped us keep track of our progress; to Frank R. Ahlbin who shed some light on shady subjects, and helped us find ourselves when we went off track; to Paul A. Dennis who kept the project charged; to Keny Kenyon for our fine fondues; to Belinda Sanda who taught us the value of light provisions; to Bill Hefner who twice made it easier for us when the going got hard; to Peter E. Flood who saw that the project was kept Bristol fashion; to Richard G. Nicholson who gave it a name; to Com-Pac 16 sailor J. Bruce Siff for his tips on mast-stepping; to the National Marine Manufacturers Association for permission to use their trailer illustrations; and to the Hutchins Company for their assistance in all phases of this project—to all of you, thank you.

Happy trailer sailing!

Robert F. Burgess

1

How to Decide on the Right Boat

Trailer sailing offers the best of both worlds: using your boat as a land/sea yacht, living aboard it at campsites or living aboard it on the water. Both options are yours if you are willing to put up with certain limitations. The main limitation is size. Trailer sailors are generally small boat sailors, if you consider everything up to twenty-eight feet as small. That is not to say that larger boats cannot be trailered. It is just that one reaches a point where bigger is not better for trailering, especially frequent trailering.

Boat and trailer size then become the first decision you must make. For the sake of some arbitrary limit in boat length, I would say a twenty-eight-foot sailboat is as much boat as anyone would care to trail. Most are smaller and more easily managed. But for you and your family, how small is small? How big is too big?

For starters, ask yourself: Who will be sailing your boat most of the time? Just you? Just you and your wife? Or a family of four or more? The fewer the people the less boat you need, the easier it is to trail, rig, and sail. Before you even start looking at potential buys, understand right now that no

One of the nice things about trailerable sailboats is that they can be used as live-aboard campers on land.

With the addition of a bimini top and an aft sun curtain, this Com-Pac yacht provides comfortable living for her crew on water.

sailboat will *ever* seem big enough for your needs. No matter how big a one you get, sailboats are simply not shaped that way. If you want roominess, choose a houseboat. There you have the floating box—lots of room but none of it shaped for seaworthiness. Whereas even the tiniest of sailboats are hydrodynamically shaped for water, which means a pointed front end, a squared-off rear end, and lots of seemingly useless slants and curves in between. Useless, that is, only to the uninformed landlubber. For those slants, curves, and point are what will keep the boat afloat and safe in virtually any condition of water it is likely to sail in. So at very best, even on the largest of sailboats, living room is at a minimum. Your choice is just how little can you make do with.

Many small boats designed especially for day sailing are rather easily convertible for overnighting. Many devotees prefer this arrangement, stowing their supplies wherever possible and relying on nothing more than a light waterproof ground cloth or piece of colored polypropylene plastic for fitting over the boom to form a kind of pup tent over the cockpit. Other sailors simply sail ashore and set up camp there. This is the way most trailerable catamaran overnighters do it. More on this later.

After the completely open sailboat, there are those with cuddy cabins, small deck-covered areas far forward usually used for stowing sails, anchors, lines, and yourself scrunched up when the rains come and the cuddy is the only dry place in reach.

Most cuddy cabin boats were designed for day sailing. Their cockpits and seating capacity are large, comprising most of the upper deck space. Older models of one popular line, however, offered a cuddy large enough for an inflatable mattress and adequate shelter if one chose to sleep aboard.

Better, however, to consider the many different pocket yachts that are actually miniaturizations of big cruising type sailboats. In length they run from about fifteen to a little over seventeen feet. There are at least a dozen manufacturers of

Some forty years ago, family and friends helped the author *(far right)* launch one of his first sailboats—a Snipe—in which he and a sailing companion often overnighted in its narrow cockpit, sleeping in a space barely large enough for their feet.

these vest-pocket cruisers in the country. All the boats feature tiny cabins, two full-sized berths, and a small space for stowing gear. Cabin interiors are spartan but enthusiasts have managed to squeeze in such comforts as a miniature galley, chemical toilet, cockpit awning, a library, cookstove, electric fan, stereo radio/tape deck, and a freshwater shower. Not to mention such other amenities as self-steering devices and a one-man inflatable raft with oars and foot pump that all fits into a single backpack.

How much comfort does one need?

That's for you to decide. Another question is: Just how seaworthy are these small minicruisers? Well, probably one of the smallest of the lot is the West Wight Potter at fifteen feet. While her cockpit is too short to lie down in, she makes up for this by giving you more cabin space and quite an impressive performance record for so tiny a cruiser. Having originated as a wooden hulled boat in England, she is now produced in this country in fiberglass. Her owners have proved her seaworthiness with a long list of voyages from such places as England to Sweden, New York to Florida,

At fifteen feet long, the West Wight Potter is one of the smallest of minicruisers, yet this pint-sized sailboat is large enough to sleep two comfortably.

Seattle to Alaska, and Mexico to Hawaii. Not too bad for the tiniest of her gender weighing out at a scant 475 pounds.

These days, when sailors are trying to break records by sailing across oceans in boats no larger than six and a half feet, one questions not so much the safety of such endeavors as the sanity of them. The length of a boat has little to do with its seaworthiness and safety. Hull shapes, displacement factors, amount of ballast (or lack of it), sails carried—these are some of the considerations. Really lightweight cruising sailboats can be expected to be tender sailers: they will respond more quickly to wind gusts by tipping. Small multihulled boats such as catamarans that usually lack any kind of ballasted keels use this feature to advantage to gain speed. One hull may lift entirely clear of the water so that in effect a large sail is powering a slender hull with low wetted surface and consequently minimal drag. While the smaller cats are thought of more in their capacity as day-sailing racers, they need not be entirely ruled out as trailerable cruising type sailboats. For inshore protected waters, catamarans, coupled with basic camping necessities and a lightweight boom tent, can provide all the pleasures, if not all the creature comforts, of bigger boat cruising. And of course the larger catamarans such as the twenty-seven-foot Stiletto and trailerable trimarans are specially designed for a certain amount of live-aboard comfort as well as speed.

While looking over all the different kinds of sailboats and trying to decide which kind will be best for you, keep firmly in mind this thought: bigger is not always better.

The highly intoxicating illusion that a bigger boat means more safety, more comfort, more prestige, more of all the other good things one thinks about, must also be balanced by the other side of the coin. A bigger boat can also mean more initial cost, more weight to trailer, more maintenance, more launching and loading problems, perhaps more sailing problems. Some of these things will be immediately obvious.

Multihulled boats such as catamarans are fast and responsive to wind changes. Coupled with a boom tent, these easily trailered sailboats can provide overnighting capabilities on a beach.

Some large trailerable multihulls, such as this twenty-seven-foot Stiletto, are designed both for speed and live-abord facilities on the water.

Others may not be until you have made your purchase and have had to learn the hard way.

Friends of mine who had long enjoyed sailing a Com-Pac 16 minicruiser decided that since it was so much fun, if they graduated to a thirty-foot Morgan, it would be that much more fun. Not to mention roomier and more prestigious.

They moved up. A couple of sailing seasons later they realized what they had sacrificed for that move. No longer were they able to sail carefree around the bays, gunkholing here and there, pausing to fish, dive, or go ashore and beachcomb. No longer was it simply a matter of dropping over the side to push their boat off a sandbar if they ran aground. Now, grounding was a serious problem. So they stayed well clear of the gunkholing areas, not even daring to sail the bay. Instead, they powered in and out of harbor and sailed back and forth over the ocean, regretting the variety of sailing experiences that had been deleted by their moving up to a bigger boat.

Perhaps the worst, however, was being restricted to a commercial marina where their ears were assailed by the thrumming of other boats' halyards night and day, their noses smelled the aromas of engine exhausts and decaying fish, and instead of being moored in a quiet cove where their eyes beheld sea birds and lavish sunsets, all they saw was a forest of masts. Nor was there much in the way of a reprieve. They had to stay because they were too big to trailer and too inexperienced at open ocean voyaging to risk wandering far from their expensive berth.

The kind and size of trailerable sailboat that will be best for you and your family is a decision you and your family alone must make. Not only does it depend on how much you wish to pay for a boat but on many other factors as well. List your needs so you can better decide whether you will be happier with a smaller boat with overnighting capabilities for one or two, or with something bigger with sleeping accommodations for three or four. Also, it will pay you to consider

The kind and size of trailerable sailboat you choose is a family decision. This Marsh Hen is easily trailered with a compact car.

On the water the Marsh Hen can easily accommodate the family and a boatful of camping gear if desired.

some of the advantages and disadvantages between small or large trailerables.

Here are a few to think about on the "pro" side of owning a small trailerable sailboat up to sixteen or seventeen feet:

• Initial cost is less
• Less powerful car needed to tow it
• Trailering to distant sites will be less expensive
• Launching will be easier; rigging and setting up the boat less complicated or time consuming
• Boat can be sailed on a variety of waterways ranging from ponds, rivers, and lakes to reservoirs, bays, and oceans within driving distance
• Smaller parking area required for boat and trailer
• Small boat faster and easier to clean up
• Minimal theft and vandalism temptation
• Smaller, more economical outboard may be used
• Lower insurance
• Sailing and sail changes are easier

The disadvantage of selecting a small cruising type sailboat with enclosed cabin for overnighting as opposed to the larger type cruising sailboat has largely to do with space. No boat ever seems big enough for all the stuff we try to cram aboard. Some points on the "pro" side for owning a large trailerable cruiser up to twenty-eight feet are these:

• Bigger and better accommodations inside. Entire boat better designed for family and friends to accompany you
• Larger stowage room for food and supplies, equipment, and head
• A less tender, stiffer sailing boat capable of handling more adverse weather and seas
• Generally less cramped and more comfortable
• Longer cruising capabilities and better live-aboard features
• Can be used as a family camper while on the road

- Doubles as a convenient guest room for children or adults while boat is on its trailer in your backyard

A few differences that must be considered in deciding between a large or a small trailerable sailboat are important enough to emphasize. If you purchase a large sailboat (the difference between a sixteen-foot and a nineteen-foot may be only three cubic feet but it could weigh almost twice as much) then:

- You must have a vehicle powerful enough to tow the combined weight of your boat, trailer, and everything aboard not only up and down hills but also up out of potentially steep launching ramps. While a compact car may adequately tow a sailboat up to fifteen or sixteen feet, a larger and more powerful car or truck will be required to safely tow boats in this category over sixteen feet long.
- You must have adequate space for storing your boat and trailer. Few things are worse than purchasing a big boat, then finding that it won't fit in your garage or driveway. Avoid this by taking measurements in advance. Otherwise consider marina storage, rental space at a friend's dock, or a permanent mooring for the season.
- You must plan on trailer as well as boat maintenance. This means licensing and registration where applicable, insurance, care of tires, brakes, bearings, and lights, along with general washing and touch-up painting if exposed to salt water.
- You must expect that towing a larger rig on the highway may increase driver stress as well as potential for an accident. Also be aware that launching and recovering the bigger boat may be more difficult and that some launching ramps for fixed-keel boats simply may not have water deep enough to float your boat.

While all such problems can be worked out, it is important to know they exist. Many are quite subtle. For example, a sixteen-foot-long full-keel sailboat on its trailer may be easily boarded by stepping on the trailer's wheel fender and climbing aboard. But a larger full-keel sailboat may require a full-sized stepladder in order to board. What do you do when you have to board this boat to rig it before launching and you have no stepladder?

The answer to this and other trailer-sailing problems will be discussed in the chapters that follow.

2

Finding Your Dream Boat

Once you have a general idea of how big a boat you want and roughly what it will probably cost, you now start refining your search for that boat.

Boat shows will give you a chance to look over the market's newest models. If you find something that seems to match your dream boat image exactly, don't be hasty. Learn all you can about it from the salesman and study the specification sheet that will be available as a handout. Unless you are absolutely sold on that particular model, don't be coaxed into a buy by the salesman's offer to fix you up with it at a special boat show discount. I say don't decide that this is the one and only boat deal you will ever have an opportunity to save on unless you have already explored all other avenues and have concluded that this positively is the best one for you.

Sailboats at boat shows are nice to look at but they are not necessarily the best buy. An older model of the same boat—a used boat—may be a far better buy.

Fiberglass hulls do not show their age as easily or as quickly as uncared-for wooden hulls. They age, but in a much slower, more graceful manner. Unless they have suffered

A sailboat show provides the potential sailboat buyer with the chance to appraise a wide variety of new boats inside and out. But a new boat may not be your best buy.

serious structural damage from cracks or some other accident that has weakened the glass, aging is usually only gelcoat or skin deep. It amounts to no more than slight crazing (hair-fine cracks) or chalking of the boat's surface. Nothing more than cosmetic breakdown.

Such things as sails, however, may show more signs of age. They can be torn and repaired, or simply blown out: stretched out of shape from years of use and misuse. But sails can be replaced relatively inexpensively. So can the boat's lines and standing rigging. No real concern here, but definite points that you might mention to the boat's owner if you hope to get him to lower his asking price.

Generally speaking, used boats provide potential trailer sailors with their best bargains. If it were a car you were buying with a hidden flaw, you might get stuck with a lemon. But with the smaller-sized cruisers that have no complicated inboard engines to be concerned about, you can pretty much see what you are buying. Naturally, if the boat is homemade or appears to be homemade, be especially wary. It may be so lopsided that it won't sail properly. If it's glass, look for any telltale waves in its hull, or seams that are poorly joined. Any obviously repaired places in a hull should be just as suspect as a crack near the keel. Similarly, a swing keel's inboard well that shows signs of major patching suggests that at some time or other it leaked and maybe still does.

In sizing up a used boat, take nothing for granted. If the price is right but you are a little in doubt as to exactly what kind of condition the boat is in, hire a marine surveyor to examine it for you. In the long run that's the cheapest way out.

The best time to shop for a used boat is at the end of the summer. Rather than bother with storing their boat for the winter, that's the time most people who want to sell their boat are most likely to give you the best of the bargain. When people sell they want to get rid of the bothersome selling bit as quickly as possible. So you may find you are getting lots of extras included in the price that you would normally have to buy separately when purchasing a new boat, such as an outboard motor, anchor, boat lines, cushions, life jackets, extra sails, compass, plus a variety of other nautical odds and ends former owners often throw in just to get rid of them. (All of which is money in your pocket if you don't have to buy them yourself.)

On the other hand, be aware that most sailboats over the years tend to appreciate in value rather than depreciate. Since most used boats are worth more today than they were when originally bought, you can think of a sailboat as a solid investment, fully capable of paying you back after a few years' use at the same price you paid for it.

One of the best places to shop for a boat is in the classified ads of your local newspaper. If you live in a small, inland

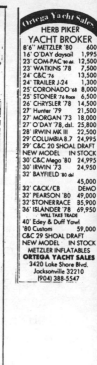
Comparing prices of used boats in your classified ads will give you an idea of the price of older model sailboats. Remember that these prices often include a wide variety of additional equipment such as extra sails, outboard motor, and other boating gear.

town, check out your nearest big-city newspaper, especially any along the coast. Most will offer columns of ads for used boats. A phone call will help fill in the specifics.

If the details make the boat seem to be what you are looking for and the price is right, go look at it. Be sure of what you are buying. Try to get the owner to take you out for a sail in it. Above all, don't buy a pig in a poke. You should be able to tell by looking whether a boat has been properly cared for, or has been abused. Take the time to haul those sails out of the sail bag and look them over. If the boat looks abused, you can be sure that everything else about the package probably is, too—the trailer, for instance. Has the owner been backing it into salt water and not keeping the wheel bearings greased? Or has he been conscientious enough to have installed well-greased bearing protectors and taken the trouble to mount his trailer lights where water won't short them out, or seen that any rust or corrosion was eliminated before it really got started? If he has done these things, then you will have reason to believe that he's probably taken similar good care of his boat.

Another place to find used boats is at marinas and boat storage lots. Drive around and check them out. Talk to people in the area who might provide leads. Have an idea of what size sailboat you are interested in buying and let others know you are looking. Leave your name and phone number where you can be reached by someone who hears of a boat for sale that might interest you.

If you have a certain stock boat in mind and would like to contact an owner of that make boat to learn more about it, *Cruising World* magazine offers just such a service. It is free and well worth using. This reader-to-reader service edited by Andrew MacLachlan is titled "Another Opinion." In each issue of the popular cruising sailboat magazine, available on most newsstands here and abroad, the column lists the makes of all boats involved in this service. The magazine requests that:

For a firsthand opinion of any of the [boats listed in this magazine], send a self-addressed envelope to Another Opinion, *Cruising World*, 524 Thames St., Newport, RI 02840, or call (401)847-1588. Please limit your request to five vessels. We will provide you with the names of owners willing to provide "another opinion" or we can add your name to the list of people to be contacted. (This is a *Cruising World* reader-to-reader service and is in no way connected with or responsible for the opinions provided by the owners.) We now list 1,013 boats. [As of this writing at the end of 1983.]

The above service will surely provide some unbiased opinions—both good and bad—on the stock boats in question. Few other sources will provide more accurate information about a boat than the owner himself. Naturally, most will be satisfied with the boat they own, but don't overlook the fact that they will also be aware of their boat's weaknesses, perhaps its inability to sail well to windward, or maybe a perpetual problem of leaking around the seals of its pop-top. Also, owners can pass on tips on how they corrected certain problems or perhaps added custom features that markedly improved their boat's comfort. All such bits of information are nuggets worth mining.

As time goes on and you look at more and more sailboats, your mind will begin to boggle by the seeming complexity of it all. Suddenly you become aware of the diversity of hull shapes—flat bottom, round bottom, clinker bottom, V-bottom; fixed-keel, spade keel, leeboards, daggerboards, or twin keels.

Help! you yell. *What does it all mean?*

In a word: stability.

No one design has so far proved capable of doing all things well. If a sailboat is designed for speed, it will not have a deep, full keel underwater unless it is a deep-water ocean racer with a skyful of sail designed for such things. Instead, it will be a flatter kind of hull designed for skimming and planing over the surface; or perhaps, as in the case of the racing catamarans, they will be knife-shaped, long and slender twin hulls made for swiftly slicing through the water at great speeds. Remember, in all these instances we are considering the hull shape bow on, not how it appears from its side, or beam.

Sailboat stability can be defined as that which enables the boat to resist being upset. A counterbalance to the wind's force on the sails has always been necessary, whether that in fact is the sailor's own weight hanging out over the water on his flat-bottomed boat, or whether it is a heavy lead keel under a round bottom hull that serves the same purpose. The key is weight stability.

Hulls that are less round and tend toward flatness with sharp angles where they touch the waterline (called the hull's chine) are so designed to resist being upset by their shape alone. This would be called leverage stability. Such hulls would have daggerboards, swing keel centerboards, or possibly even leeboards. In themselves, none of these boards would have the large amount of weight of a fixed-keel boat. They are used mainly to prevent a boat from sliding sideways (leeway) as it sails upwind. Sailing off the wind or straight downwind, such boards may be partially or completely lifted up into their centerboard wells to enable the boat to sail faster due to the reduced drag.

Since most cruising type sailboats are designed for as much live-aboard inside hull space as possible, their hulls will be designed more on the wine-glass configuration than on the flat-bottom pan shape. They are called displacement hulls. They push water aside rather than skim over it. Speed is not as important to the live-aboard cruising sailor as how much room he has to be comfortable inside his hull.

Still, he doesn't want a boat that is just going to barely wallow along in a brisk breeze. He wants something that will offer his family and friends adequate live-aboard space while still maintaining some semblance of a brisk sailing boat. Hence the diversity of hull shapes. It's all a compromise. And you, the buyer, must decide which style will work best for you and your needs.

Briefly, here are guidelines which may make your decision easier:

• Hulls with hard chines (angles) and flat areas such as found on V-bottom centerboard boats will pound harder than a smooth round or wine-glass-shaped hull of a keel boat.

• Flat-bottom boats have few virtues except that they are easiest to build. They pound and bounce.

• V-bottom hulls are modified flat-bottoms with hard chine and angled flat surfaces that correct problems of the purely flat-bottom hull. This style is popular with smaller sailboats and has proved to be a stable, fast sailing hull design.

• Round-bottom hulls tend to roll more than the V-bottoms but are fast and less likely to pound than the Vs. Such boats will not carry as much sail due to their tendency to heel, a characteristic that may be offset with the proper use of ballast.

• Clinker-bottoms that were popular in the past because their overlapping planks were thought to aid stability proved noisy with a tendency toward dragging and leaking between planks. Though the real clinker-built hull is seldom seen anymore, it still appears molded into some character boat hulls. At least this solved the problem of leaking.

• Arc-bottom hulls are more common to the inland small boat classes such as Lightnings, Comets, and Stars. Though more rounded than the V-bottom their sailing characteristics are similar.

• Wine-glass hulls feature more fullness in the chine line without resorting to flat surfaced angles. This, or a slightly squatter champagne-glass shape is most preferred in fixed-keel cruising sailboats with open ocean capabilities. Rather than being buffeted by the seas as a flat- or modified flat-bottom boat might be, boats with these hulls roll with the punch and are never jarring. But with a beam sea and the low ballasted keel, they roll wildly at anchor, thanks to the swinging pendulum effect of their keels. In its upright position at dockside, a boat with a fixed-keel wine-glass hull will tilt as one steps aboard, creating an illusion of basic instability. But under sail the more the wine-glass hull heels, the more stability it has from the weight of the keel counteracting any additional heel.

• Champagne-glass-shaped hulls tend to be more stable in an upright position with less tendency to roll with beam waves at anchor. Because of more flattened surfaces, they may seem more susceptible to harder rather than softer wave entries while sailing. One noticeable difference between a wine-glass hull and a champagne-glass shape is that the wine-glass hull will heel up to its rub rail before seeming to take a set and go no farther. With the champagne-glass shape, the heeling angle will not be as acute; the hull will stop heeling earlier and seem to take its set well below the rub rail.

Along with the different kinds of hulls to be considered are the centerboards or keels. There are but two types—centerboard and keel. Both devices are designed to provide sailboats with lateral resistance against the water to prevent the boat from sliding sideways while sailing. The simplest kind of centerboard is called a daggerboard. Most small sailboats use them. A slot in the boat's centerline allows the board to be inserted from the cockpit. It can be lifted out in shallow water. But down and in position while under sail, it performs like any fixed-keel. If the daggerboard strikes anything like a tree stump, rather than swinging up into its well, it remains fixed. The boat will feel the jar of the collision and the board may be damaged.

Some large multihulled boats such as catamarans and

trimarans use daggerboards. Their main disadvantage is the damage that can be done both to board and boat if they strike an underwater object plus the fact that raised boards must take up cockpit or hull space.

A centerboard is usually made of heavy metal that can be pivoted up inside a boat's centerboard trunk or well, or cranked down to perform its duty as a counterbalance and leeway brake. Since it swings up into its well if it collides with an underwater object, no damage is done to board or boat and the collision is seldom jarring. The advantage of a centerboard is that lifting it enables the boat to enter shallow water. Also, with the board up in its well, the boat can be easily trailered. The disadvantages of the centerboard are the wear and tear on the pivotal bolt and hoisting cable, and the leakage problems that sometimes occur around the centerboard trunk. Such boats also must sacrifice interior hull or cockpit space to the trunk. Some boards and their supporting cables develop bothersome wobbles and vibrations when lowered all the way. This condition can sometimes be corrected by taking up some tension on the lifting cable that raises the board a bit. A centerboard boat can be capsized fairly easily but one compensation is that if swamped it will not sink.

Leeboard boats have pivoting boards on their sides to minimize leeway when sailing upwind. These boards are more popular in Europe with large cargo carrying vessels operating in shoal waters. In this country leeboards are most often seen on sailing dinghies and canoes.

Fin keels resemble daggerboards with weighted bottoms. This, however, is a fixed keel. It cannot be raised or lowered. Most of its weight is in the torpedo-shaped bulge on the keel's bottom. The boat can sail in waters no shallower than that bulb. Because of its shape, it tends to collect fish lines, weeds, and kelp and hold on to them more than the smoothly contoured full-keel boats.

The full or deep keel of iron, lead, or cement is bolted to

Shoal draft boats can be easily beached but lacking heavy keels beneath their hulls they are more likely to be tender sailers.

Some trailerable open boats, such as this Marsh Hen, can be enclosed with a canvas cockpit "cabin" designed to provide weather protection and overnighting possibilities.

and molded onto the hull in a triangular shape that appears to be an integral part of the hull itself. The apex of the triangle is forward toward the bow; the base is aft, toward the stern. The longer this triangle, the easier it is for the boat to hold on course. But because of their length and lateral resistance, deep-keeled boats are not as quick to tack up narrow channels as are those with less keel. The major advantages of the full-keel, heavy displacement sailboats are their stability and their resistance to heel abruptly due to sudden wind puffs or shifting positions of the crew. This stabilizing factor is greater or lesser depending upon what percentage of the boat's overall weight (displacement) is made up of ballast. This ballast ratio should be as high as possible because it determines how much sail power can be carried for optimum performance. In the larger cruising/racing type sailboats this ballast-to-displacement ratio conventionally ranges between 35 and 50 percent.

The disadvantage of the full-keel boat is that if inadequate flotation material is carried inside its hull, when swamped, it may sink. However, if no water enters the hull, full-keel sailboats are self-righting. This means that if they are blown over, they will swing upright again due to the pendulum effect of the heavy deep keel. When crossing oceans such boats have suffered severe knockdowns and 360° rollovers before regaining an upright position and sailing on. For trailer sailors, the full-keel boat will be less easy to board on its trailer and will require deeper water at launching sites to get it afloat.

Short-keel sailboats are less heavily ballasted and there is less water resistance to their more abbreviated keel. They therefore sail faster than the full-keel boat and are more easily tacked. The disadvantage is that they will not steer as easily. If the rudder is no longer part of the keel, and is separated from it, it then is called a spade rudder. Spade rudders tend to collect fish lines, weeds, and trash much as fin keels do. But the most often mentioned main disadvantage is in the possibility of damage to the exposed rudder. Many trailerable cruising type sailboats designed with keels that are compromises between the full keel and the short keel feature stern-mounted "kick-up" rudders. Rather than being damaged if the sailboat grounds, or if the rudder blade is fouled, the heavy, usually cast aluminum blade, held in position by a tension nut, simply pivots up. After clearing an obstacle, it is lowered back into its original position.

Twin-keel craft are more favored by British sailors. Possessing two angled keels, this type boat can sail in shallower waters than the conventionally keeled boats can. Owners also claim more stability and less tendency to roll. Such boats are able to sit upright on their twin keels if caught aground on an outgoing tide and, due to their more lateral location, this style is lower profiled for easier trailering and launching.

The centerboard/keel is a compromise between a full keel and a centerboard. This popular combination for cruising sailboats provides some of the advantages of both designs. Like the pivotal centerboard it is easily trailerable and launchable. Centerboard/keel boats can sail into shallower waters than full-keel boats. When retracted the centerboard does not lift up into the interior hull but into a recess in the ballasted fixed keel. One problem with centerboard/keels is the old complaint about vibration, either from the swing keel or from its control cable.

The Lexcen winged keel that won the America's Cup in 1983 for Australia may well be the keel design of the future. In secret tank tests in The Netherlands, forty-seven-year-old naval architect Ben Lexcen developed a keel unlike anything ever used before. On its base are two stubby wings that give a boat added stability, more agility in tacking, and greater overall speed. With those advantages, you can be sure that it won't be long before some of our standard keels start sprouting wings.

No matter what style keel or hull design you choose, examine the boat inside and outside and judge its quality by the kind of workmanship you see. Are there unpainted patches inside that show light spots or bubbles in the laminated fiberglass indicating thin areas? Are chain plates, towing eyes, cleats, and any other types of deck hardware that will be stressed adequately backed up by reinforcing plates or blocks and substantial through-the-hull stainless steel fittings? When you look behind bulkheads and up under decks do you see a lot of rough edges hanging down to cut your hands on, or have they too been finished? When you try out the berths do you find the foam so thin and unsupportive that you hit bottom hard? Or has the manufacturer taken the care to provide comfortable berths employing high density foam and a durable covering material for the cushions? In the cabin are things that should be well attached simply stapled together? Are the bulkheads that appear to be fine mahogany actually that or cheap plywood with a synthetic or paper mahogany texture pasted over it? All these are small, unimportant things. But you can be sure if the builder scrimped on the insignificant details, chances are he did the same with the larger, more important things such as the structure and fabrication of the boat itself. It takes no expert eye to spot the difference between careful or careless workmanship, a quality boat or an imitation of quality.

Here are some additional points to remember:

- Don't fall for "Boat Show Special Price" announcements. This is simply a high-pressure tactic. Your local dealer will give you just as good a bargain—if not a better one—long after the show.
- One of the best times to bargain with a dealer for a boat is at season's end, before the new models come out. Then, not only will he make the price right but some will even throw in an anchor, lines, air horn, boat cushions, and other accessories that will, in the long run, save you additional money.

- Visit your local launching ramps, marinas, or parks on Saturday. You will see a variety of boats. Best of all, their owners won't mind telling you about their merits. Ask questions. Boating is a brotherhood of especially friendly people.
- Study all the boating magazines. They offer a wealth of information about sailing, sailboats, nautical problems, sail cruising, navigation, meals afloat, boating accessories, rules of the road, and lists of new and old boats for sale.
- Whether a big boat or a little one, consider the size of its cockpit. Ideally, and this is true also of a small (sixteen-foot) sailboat, it should have a cockpit long enough for you to lie down in. Remember that when sailing with a brisk breeze, your passengers should have room to sit on the same side of the boat with you. If they haven't, the cockpit's too small. Since most of your time sailing will be spent in the cockpit, be sure it is large enough for you *and* your friends.
- If you are concerned about the lack of headroom in the cabin—and most trailerables usually have only sitting room—you might consider boats featuring a pop-top (the roof of the cabin lifts up to provide standing headroom). But talk to those who own them. Some refuse to have pop-tops because they are constant leak problems.
- If you plan to do anything more serious than cooking meals in your cockpit while at anchor, make sure your boat has a safe, well-ventilated place for a stove along with adequate storage areas that are easily accessible for pots, pans, and food.
- If the boat is designed for overnight cruising, make sure it has room for a head, usually a chemical toilet. If its location is under a sleeping area, will this create a problem?
- Is there adequate room for block ice as well as food in the icebox? Is there space for a cooler so it won't be underfoot all the time?

Cabin roofs that can be raised (pop-tops) as shown on this Catalina 22, are popular because they provide full standing headroom and excellent ventilation.

Here is the same boat with the pop-top retracted. The Catalina can be sailed with the top up or down if you choose this style boat.

- Some boats feature a hide-away galley as an optional item. Ask about them.
- Remember: in deciding how much you can afford to pay for a sailboat, don't forget to also include the cost of a trailer. Some new boats are sold as a package with a trailer included. This deal is the best because the trailer will usually be custom fitted to your particular boat, especially if it is a full-keel model. Most used trailerable sailboats will also be sold with their trailers. Make absolutely certain that these are not so badly rusted out or otherwise deteriorated that they are inadequate for the job. No one wants to lose a boat, especially to a highway accident, because something like a rusty trailer frame broke.

If you choose a boat with cockpit long enough to lie down in, you and your crew will be comfortable. Note the tiller-tending block and line I am using here on our sixteen-foot Com-Pac *Nomad*.

- Demonstrator boats that a dealer has been showing for several months may be good buys. You may not have the pick of the color you want but most will come well equipped and ready to sail. Ask what kind of discount he would give.

By the time you have been to many dealers' showrooms, looked over dozens of used boats, plodded through boatyards full of old hulks, read reams of used boat ads, taken the time to climb aboard and thump the hulls of every likely vessel in various boat shows, you will have narrowed the field and come to a major conclusion. One of those boats will be just right. And that one will be your dream boat.

I reached that point in 1977.

3

Com-Pactly Speaking

Right from the beginning I knew I was looking for something that was practically nonexistent. I wanted a trailerable small sailboat with a cockpit large enough for four, a cabin big enough to sleep two reasonably comfortably, and maybe a place to do a little cooking besides. In my mind's eye I saw a sailboat with more freeboard than most of the day sailers I had seen or previously owned. Its hull ideally would be designed to take fairly stiff ocean breezes and sea swells. But too it should be capable of sailing in the gunkholing back-waters of lakes and bays. I wanted a vest-pocket cruiser that had more traditional rather than modern lines and came closer to my idea of a sailboat than some of the sleek, streamlined boats with weird-shaped bows, odd-shaped slop-ing cabins, and long glass windows that made them look as if they were intended to be speedboats until someone stuck a sail on them.

Looking them over, all I could think was, "Whatever happened to the just plain squared off low cabin? And where did portholes go?" Wasn't anyone making a sailboat that still looked like a sailboat? I wondered.

Of course I realized I was asking for a lot of boat in a small package. I didn't even like to tell dealers that the only car I had and the one I intended pulling my new sailboat with was a Ford Pinto. A compact. So, actually, what I was really looking for was a big little boat that could be towed satisfactorily with a small, compact four-cylinder car.

The boat that seemed to have what I was looking for was the West Wight Potter. It weighed under 500 pounds but incorporated many of the big boat features in a small boat package.

The other boat that caught my eye was Carl Arlberg's Cape Dory Typhoon. It had it all: the traditional lines, the quality workmanship, the large cockpit, the overnighting facilities, and the seagoing capabilities. But with a displacement of 1,900 pounds, towing it with the Pinto was out of the question. The Ford people advised me not to try towing anything over 1,000 pounds with the compact. There was also one other feature about the Typhoon that didn't quite match the picture I had in my mind. The boat, built in Massachusetts, carried more draft than I wanted for sailing along some of the shallow coastal waters of Florida where I lived and would do most of my boating.

So there the matter sort of got caught in limbo. After sailing the West Wight Potter with three aboard, it seemed a wee bit too small for what I wanted. Yet the Typhoon, with its 18½-foot length and rather deep draft, was just too much boat.

Both, however, had exactly the lines and characteristics I wanted. But one was too small; the other, too big.

The day I saw precisely what I was looking for at a Tallahassee boat show, I could hardly believe what I was seeing. It had exactly the features I wanted: the large cockpit, the traditional lines—right down to a couple of portholes on each side of the cabin—and a shoal draft keel. The boat had a bluff bow, lots of freeboard, and weighed only 100 pounds over the weight my Ford dealer said I could tow—sixteen feet overall with a displacement of 1,100 pounds. Even her name fit. She was called a Com-Pac yacht.

CAPE DORY TYPHOON WEEKENDER

SPECIFICATIONS

LOA	18' - 6"	SAIL AREA	160 sq. ft.
LWL	13' - 11"	DISPLACEMENT	2000 pounds
BEAM	6' - 3"	BALLAST	900 pounds
DRAFT	2' - 7"		

T$_Y$

E = 8'-9"

J = 6'-2"

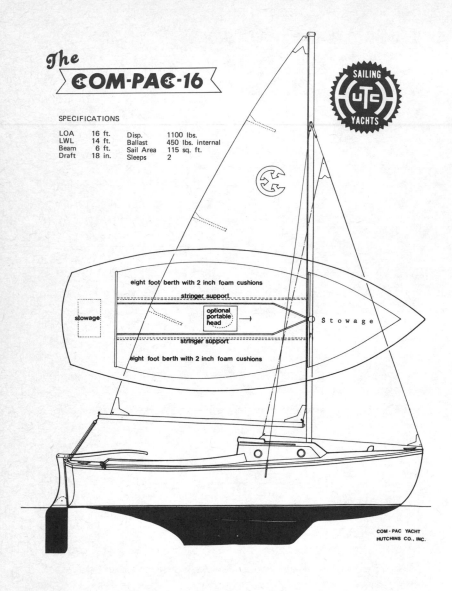

The
COM·PAC·16

SAILING HUTC YACHTS

SPECIFICATIONS

LOA	16 ft.	Disp.	1100 lbs.
LWL	14 ft.	Ballast	450 lbs. internal
Beam	6 ft.	Sail Area	115 sq. ft.
Draft	18 in.	Sleeps	2

eight foot berth with 2 inch foam cushions

stringer support

stowage

optional portable head →

Stowage

stringer support

eight foot berth with 2 inch foam cushions

COM - PAC YACHT
HUTCHINS CO., INC.

None of the literature I had been poring over for the last couple of years, none of the boat shows and sailboat directories I had examined had ever featured this little boat. I had never seen it before.

The dealer told me that the company was relatively small and new, as was the boat. It was being made by the Hutchins Company in Clearwater, Florida—in my home state! The boat and trailer came as a package. With the exception of a genoa sail, there were no other options. It came in basic white.

To say I swooned over it would be putting it mildly. The berths were a startling eight feet long, snug but comfortable. There was stowage space forward and under the quarter-deck; a lazaret aft. Between the berths but back under the step up into the cabin was room not only for a Thetford self-contained head, but enough space to hide a wet-cell automobile battery as well, one that would power all the running lights that I was already mentally installing.

For the amount of space in the cabin, the cockpit seemed amazingly spacious for only a sixteen-foot boat. I checked the specs and was pleasantly surprised to find that it was almost seven foot long. Plenty of room for at least four adults comfortably, not to mention a youngster or two. Unbelievable for a sixteen-footer!

Everywhere I looked I saw quality in the production of this remarkable big little boat. After looking at so many others, it was not difficult to detect. It sort of jumped out at me from the undercovered areas of smoothly finished and painted interior work to the long, smooth, and sturdy looking mahogany and ash-laminated tiller.

I clambered off the boat and stood looking at it from abeam. She had a mere eighteen-inch draft, just right for the kind of shoal water I enjoyed sailing over while ghosting around the isolated islands along the Florida panhandle in my Hobie 16 catamaran. There would be many times when my wife and I would want to go ashore to beachcomb, and the Com-Pac, despite its immovable keel, would not limit us to anything more than wading depth water.

Still, the 450 pounds of internal ballast meant that the boat would never be a pushover for gusty winds. She would be a stiff, stable sailer. She seemed to be the perfect package.

All that still bothered me was her weight and my fixation on towing her with a compact car. Ford had warned against towing anything over 1,000 pounds unless, of course, surge breaks were installed on the trailer. It was not the 100-pounds-over-the-limit boat weight that bothered me so much as the realization that this was just the beginning of any weight problem I might have. If the boat was 1,100 pounds, I could add to it probably another 450 pounds for the trailer, not to mention the additional weight of an outboard, live-aboard gear, and all the other odds and ends one tries to cram aboard a boat to make confinement to a few square feet of living space a bit more comfortable. All told, I figured it might run as high as 1,700 pounds. (In the end the total load actually weighed 1,900 pounds.) I was reluctant to put on surge brakes until I could determine how the Pinto handled what it had to tow. It was a stick shift transmission which I had purposely chosen not only for the extra economy but in the belief that when hauling such a load up out of a boat ramp, I would be better off with this, rather than an automatic transmission.

The uncertainty of this made it seem worth driving to Clearwater to talk to the Com-Pac people about it. Too, I wanted to see for myself how they were building the boat and maybe learn something about its seaworthiness.

Manager Buck Thomas was a tall fellow with an athletic build, black hair, and a wide, friendly smile.

"You shouldn't have any problem at all towing the Com-Pac with your Pinto," Buck told me. "Hutch pulls his all over in a Pinto with an automatic transmission."

Les Hutchins—or Hutch as everyone called him—was probably in his late middle age, full face, thinning white hair,

(From right to left) The key men behind the Com-Pac line of sailboats are the men with the idea, Les Hutchins, the man with the design, Clark Mills, and the man with the know-how, company manager Buck Thomas.

a man who, after a few moments of friendly conversation, left one with an impression of immense vitality. He looked less like a salty sailor than a friendly bank president. In reality he was a self-made man who had risen out of a rural farming background to become a successful inventor whose inventions ranged from automobile accessories to a cleverly designed fold-away high chair. He was the man who made the still popular "Ah-ooo-gah" horn, the kind that once commanded attention for all owners of Model A Fords. Now, he was an inventor turned boat manufacturer.

In the enjoyable couple of days we spent together, I learned more about the Com-Pac boat than I would have by talking to any number of boat dealers.

The company, which was small and only about four years old, was just then moving into an immaculate new factory with facilities for mass production reduced to an extremely small but highly efficient combination of people and materials. At the time, eight people were doing the fiberglass laminating and six were doing the assembly. This small group was industriously turning out eight complete boats a week.

Like the product it was producing, the company was so compact it didn't even have a secretary. Whoever happened to be in the office when the phone rang simply filled in.

"We're trying to build a small but highly efficient sailboat that will appeal to people who don't want to invest too heavily in a boat, yet one that they can easily trailer, easily rig, and easily sail," Hutch told me. "It's really made for the compact car people. We've tried to cut our costs by cutting out frills—one of the reasons we don't have a secretary," Hutch said chuckling. "Same with the lack of colors. We tell customers they can have any color they want as long as it's white." He smiled again. "By keeping everything simple, we're able to pass on the savings to the customer. That's why we're able to sell the boat so relatively inexpensively. Because our methods are proving successful, we're going to try to keep that price low as long as possible."

Touring the plant later with manager Buck Thomas, I saw some of that efficiency in action. In almost a hospital-like atmosphere of cleanliness and white light, white walls, and white parts of white boats, the Com-Pac crew diligently put together their boats. Several sailboats stood in different stages of construction: a propped-up hull here; a deck replete with cabin top there; a pile of masts to one side, rigging ready to be attached—what seemed a lot of boat parts for the six people responsible for putting them all together.

"It really moves along faster than you think," said Buck. "The forestays for example are all the same length. Like everything else, they fit quickly in place. All the masts will

In the white, well-lighted, almost hospital cleanliness of the Hutchins boat-building plant at Clearwater, Florida, Com-Pac yachts from sixteen to twenty-five feet long are assembled by a surprisingly small number of competent workers.

stand exactly alike. We don't have a variety of rigs to build. Same in the fiberglassing department. We're able to buy a better quality of gel-coat at a cheaper price because we are buying it in more volume than our competition. Since we're staying with white, the sprayers don't have to stop and clean out their equipment to change colors. All they have to do is turn and shoot another boat."

I liked the idea. By doing these things, not only were the Com-Pac people able to hold down production costs, but since they were turning out just one product, the time saved enabled them to polish the workmanship on that product until they ended up with a quality seldom seen in a stock production boat.

Later that evening at Buck's home I was able to learn more about how the idea came about and what kind of talented planning from several highly capable people combined to create this remarkable big little boat.

In the beginning it started with three key people: Les Hutchins, the man with the idea; Clark Mills, master boatwright and designer of the Suncat and Windmill, the man with the plan; and Buck Thomas, former builder of the Southern 21, the man with the know-how.

The idea of a sixteen-foot boat first came to Hutch because of an idea he had about shipping, Buck told me. "Shipping is a real problem and he has always been a person who believed in the easy handling of any product. His business in St. Louis, for example, which is the Ah-ooo-gah horn, is simplified by packaging. When a dealer gets his product it is all packaged and marked. This is the way you really market items. So Hutch felt that if the market grew, we could build a boat that would have a box to fit it. The boat would be built on a cradle and, when it was finished, the box would drop over it and be stapled to the cradle. Then it could be shipped.

"The sixteen-foot idea gave us the opportunity to put three boxed boats with folding masts in a boxcar to be shipped off to dealers. This was the original plan," said Buck.

With that in mind, Hutch went to boat designer Clark Mills, who was already well known for his traditional designs in the small sailboat class. Hutch told Clark to imagine a box five feet high, sixteen feet long, and six feet wide, then to trim it down and make a boat out of it.

The venerable Clark—or Clarkie, as he is known to all his friends—is alleged to have snorted and said, "Hell, that's no way to build a boat."

But he and Hutch started sketching until they came up with the design of the Com-Pac.

"Later, of course, we realized that the boxing idea was a little ridiculous," continued Buck. "But between the two of

them, Clarkie and Hutch put as much boat into those dimensions as possible."

Then they made the plug—the form of the original boat from which molds would be made. Shaping the plug was an art, one that involved sculpting it into Clark's traditional lines and compound curves while employing modern-day scientific knowledge for such things as the keel, which was no ordinary traditionally shaped keel. It was a hydrodynamically shaped keel that picked up lift as it moved forward because of eddies on the lee side. As a result it was a pretty scientific looking keel on a pretty scientific looking boat.

"The Com-Pac was not designed to be a traditional boat," said Buck. "It was not designed to be a contemporary boat. It was just designed along the lines of a good safe lifeboat, you might say, because it has the compound curves in the hull that provide strength and stability."

After two years of shaping the plug and getting it faired up perfectly, it took eight months to build the first boat that came out in 1974.

"We felt our market was the retiree," said Buck. "We had no idea that we would be selling it around the country as we are currently doing. Today we see young couples with a baby in our boat that were once buying Hobie Cats. We did not feel that these people were our market. We thought it would be the little guy who moved down here from up around the Great Lakes or the Chesapeake Bay areas who would appreciate the shallow draft, the seaworthy lines, and the stability of the Com-Pac. Initially, we were building it for the sixty-five-year-old who wanted a little sailing when he felt like it and didn't have a large amount of money invested in the boat. Since then we have sold a considerable number of boats to these people.

"It's a stable boat, a little on the short-rigged side because we have strange conditions on this coast as you have up in the panhandle. There is either light air, no air, or it blows like gangbusters. So you have to have a boat that will go in light air, shallow waters, and one that stands up in a hard blow and continues to be stable. It's difficult having all these things in the same boat. The deeper the keel, the more stable the boat, generally, but that keeps you offshore. The Com-Pac is a compromise there," said Buck. "Our idea was to take the middle-of-the-road approach. There is no way that the Com-Pac 16 is going to satisfy the big boat egoist. That just doesn't happen. Nor will it satisfy the first time boat owner who wants a boat that looks something like his bathtub toy. I'm talking about the twenty-plus-footers with the streamlined marketing approach, those strange looking boats that look as if they are going to be the first thing on the moon.

"We haven't been counter to these people in our approach to the boat and its sailing characteristics but we've gone back to a boat of older design with a more tried and proven shape, while still using some contemporary approaches—the hydrodynamically shaped keel, for instance. The hull has compound curves, there are no flat areas in it. We found that some of these old traditional shapes—the shape of the tradi-

Hutch, Clarkie, and Buck discuss some of the features they built into the
Com-Pac 16 Yacht.

tional boat with its compound curves—fit very well into the
theory of fiberglass. We can build our boat lighter, thinner,
and stronger because of the compound curves. It's like pushing on each end of an egg. You have an arch effect in every
direction. This is one of the things that make the Com-Pac a
strong little boat.

"Boat buyers are like car buyers," said Buck with a smile.
"They like to thump the product to see how strong it is. They
go along the sides of the boat and thump the hull and then
say, 'Wow! This is big and solid.'

"But the strength is really in those compound curves. A
flat-sided boat will slam into waves hard enough to make the
pop rivets fly out, but that doesn't happen on the Com-Pac. It
just seems to give with the blows.

"One of the reasons is the full bow design. If you look at the Com-Pac bow, or the bow of any good seaworthy boat, you will see that it is shaped like the pointed end of a football. If you lay a football on its side in a pool of water and heel it over, there is no change to its underwater shape. And this is what occurs to the bow of the Com-Pac, which is spoon shaped and, like a spoon when it is heeled over, the shape remains the same. This is not true, however, for the clipper bow that you have seen on clipper ships. This is a concave forward quarter section that looks beautiful as it enters the water, slicing its way through the waves. But somewhere there you have to pay the price. Somewhere you still have to push the mass of the boat through the water. Now you can start entering it very finely but you still have to get back to the mass. If you start off concave then you just get full a little farther back. Clipper ships were well known for their downwind performance, but you never saw them really beating to windward for when they were beating to windward they were laid over on their sides. When a clipper ship is laid over on its side, you've changed its attitude. You don't have that football bow. You have a differently shaped bow. It is concave, and when a wave smashes into that concave bow the tendency is not only to slam the boat but to slow its forward momentum. This might not be as critical on a large sailing ship as it would be on a sixteen-foot sailboat that lacks the mass to push itself through the seas. So even though the clipper bow was a beautiful sight on the old sailing ships, it doesn't work on every boat."

When beating into the wind, the full bow of the Com-Pac design is such that as the boat heels, the waterline actually increases, and therefore the boat sails faster at that angle, Buck told me.

To show me some of the sailing characteristics we had talked about, Buck took me out on Tampa Bay the next afternoon and we sailed one of the Com-Pacs up and down the coast in a brisk breeze. I was completely satisfied with the way she handled.

The next morning after I hooked up the long-tongued trailer and boat I had purchased, I was additionally pleased to see, in the next few hundred miles of trailering the Com-Pac, that the weight of the boat and trailer actually stabilized the compact car's ride.

After arriving home, my only explanation for why the boat trailed so easily was the Com-Pac's hydrodynamic shape and the trailer's well-balanced load. All told it seemed to be a beautifully balanced combination. A compact car coupled to a sturdy Com-Pac boat that trailed so effortlessly that my Pinto averaged twenty-two miles per gallon of gas when towing it.

I had found my dream boat!

4

The Com-Pacs: Economical Big Little Boats

The Com-Pac 16 that I bought in 1977 has hull number 396. By 1983, the Hutchins Company had built and sold more than 2,000 Com-Pac 16 boats—over 1,600 in the six years since I had bought mine!

In those years I learned a lot about the big little boat's uncanny sailing abilities. At least once a year I towed the boat that I named *Nomad* to the Florida Keys where a companion and I lived aboard it on land or sea for two weeks while sailing along the offshore reefs to dive, photograph fish, and catch whatever lobsters we could for food. More about this later.

As far as I was concerned, the Com-Pac 16 was quite sufficient for this kind of long trip. She more than filled our needs and proved more capable of handling a sea-sled and diver in choppy shoal waters where we hunted lobsters than a larger, less maneuverable boat would have.

Much of the comfort built into the Com-Pac 16 lies in the fact that it has an exceptionally large cockpit for the overall size of the boat. An almost eight-foot-long cockpit for a sixteen-foot boat! Try that on your slide rule. Prospective boat buyers are always inquiring "How many can she sleep?"

And generally they are more interested in this fact than in the cockpit's spaciousness. But when you consider how little time is spent inside a cruising sailboat and how much time is spent in its cockpit, you begin to realize which of these two areas is really more important.

As a new boat owner, I at first took many of these new features about the Com-Pac for granted. But over the years I began to question why this boat was doing things other boats I had owned before never did. Or so it seemed to me. For example, I began to wonder why, when the seas were exceptionally rough, or when we were caught in some exceedingly high waves coming from every quarter and smashing violently into any other boat they encountered in an ocean channel confined between stone jetties, the Com-Pac repeatedly sailed through this kind of turmoil without ever jarring any of us aboard. It seemed that no matter what kind of water she encountered the smoothly rounded hull never impacted hard against it. On my *Nomad* it was always the same: a steep set of waves would be rushing toward our quarter and passengers would always grab for something firm to hold onto.

"Don't worry," I would say, "she'll go through them like a knife through butter."

And she always did. Afterward my passengers would turn with surprised looks on their faces and say, "Gee, that wasn't bad at all!"

It happened often enough to become a cliché. Once, sailing through storm seas seven miles off the coast of Key Largo, friends who saw us from the upper deck of a sightseeing boat said that *Nomad* was disappearing entirely behind every other wave. To us it was an easy roller coaster type of sailing trip that was probably much more fun than it looked from afar. But there have since been times when *Nomad* has worked her way through some pretty steep-walled waves and taken them with such ease that I afterward quietly offered thanks to Clarkie's curves.

In time I learned more about how the boat was constructed and, since most prospective boat buyers are largely in the dark, as I was, about understanding the advantages or disadvantages of different kinds of fiberglassing techniques and the qualities that make up what is considered an outstanding fiberglass sailboat, I think it might be worthwhile if I detail some of that for you.

The Com-Pac is built using what is called the "hand-layup" method. This means that every square inch of the boat was made by placing template-cut pieces of controlled-thickness fiberglass sheets on a mold. This method differs from the more common "chopper-gun" technique by which chopped fiberglass is blown onto the mold. With this method one is never sure where there may be areas of thickness or thinness in the hull. This is not the case with the hand-layup method in which thickness and weight can be more easily controlled.

The Com-Pac is completely covered with at least one layer of twenty-four-ounce woven fiberglass roving. This assures a uniform degree of strength and protection. Often, prospective boat buyers ask a dealer, "How thick is the hull?"

Actually, because there is a controlled and intended variation in the engineering details of a boat, hull thickness intentionally varies from area to area, depending upon its location and the need for strength in that area.

Today, practically no commercially made sailboat decks are constructed of solid fiberglass and resin. This would make them extremely heavy. Instead, they are "cored" with a lighter weight material such as plywood or balsa wood. Unfortunately, most of these currently used interior coring materials are prone to two problems: deterioration with age and delamination.

The Com-Pac deck incorporates a core that will not deteriorate or delaminate. It is composed of a micro-balloon resin mixture that is applied in thicknesses varying from $3/32$ to $1/2$ inch. Micro-balloons are made from sand (silica) which is "popped" much like popcorn. This forms a tiny, hollow, spherical particle that resembles face powder. These microballoons are mixed with polyester resin to form the lightweight core material which is then sprayed onto the deck to the desired thickness.

The Com-Pac's finish is comprised of the highest quality gel-coat available. It is of a type known as NPG (neo-pentyl glycol) gel-coat. This type has a harder, brighter finish than the standard gel-coats. Laboratory tests prove that NPG gel-coats resist ultraviolet light, blistering, and corrosion better than other gel-coats.

The gel-coat finish is extremely hard as opposed to the fiberglass laminate beneath it. Under certain conditions, such as an impact or a buildup of internal stress, these opposite properties can cause tiny hairline cracks in the gel-coat surface. Over many years of exposure to the elements and use, these cracks, called crazing, are, as mentioned earlier, only cosmetic. They do not indicate any problem with the fiberglass laminate beneath it unless, of course, extreme impact or abuse has occurred.

It goes without saying that all sailboats should be assembled with noncorrosive stainless steel, aluminum, or brass fasteners, as is the Com-Pac throughout. While stainless steel fasteners and hardware, such as chain plates and mast steps, sometimes develop a slight rust condition, especially where runoff water may cause a rusty surface stain on the gel-coat, this is really nothing to be alarmed about. The stain can be easily cleaned off with an abrasive cleanser.

All hardware installed on the Com-Pac is through-bolted. Places where there may be extreme stress—the towing eye, mooring cleats, chain plates, etc., are backed up with wooden or metal plates, which are sometimes embedded in the microballoon core.

Few areas on fiberglass sailboats are more critical as to how they are joined together than the joining of the deck to

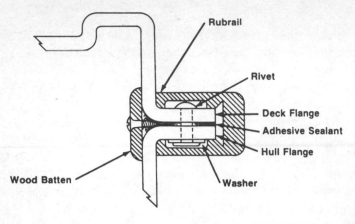

Rubrail

Rivet

Deck Flange

Adhesive Sealant

Hull Flange

Wood Batten

Washer

Courtesy Hutchins Co. Inc.

Called the "outside flange system," this drawing shows how the Com-Pac's deck is joined to the hull, then riveted and sealed to provide a strong watertight bond.

the hull. The method called "the outside flange system" is shown in detail in the accompanying illustration. Essentially, a strong marine adhesive sealant is applied between the flanges which in turn are secured with rivets that are bradded to form heads on both sides. The entire seam is then covered with a synthetic rub rail on the outside and a wood batten inside the hull.

The Com-Pac rudder is made of T-6 aluminum cast plate and is the kick-up type. A control line enables one to lift it when needed and a manual lever tightens it in any desired position.

All stays (shrouds) used to support the mast are made of stainless steel cables, the fittings swagged (pressed) onto the stainless wire.

As for the woodwork of the Com-Pac, the tiller is laminated mahogany and ash; the handrails, hatch drop board, hatch slides, are exterior teak wood; and the pressure post in the cabin directly under the mast step is mahogany.

The cabin has sitting room for two adults on the port and starboard berths which are covered with vinyl cushions. The forepeak of the boat could conceivably be made to accommodate a small youngster or two but this area is usually taken up with stowage of ice chest, food, and bags of sails. In the earlier model, which mine was, there was a small hatch in the forepeak which enabled me to stow a considerable number of small items such as toolbox, fishing tackle box, charts, medical kit, repair material, flares, navigation instruments, jumper cables (for grounding the mast in lightning storms), spare sail battens, cockpit side curtains, wind and rain dodger, ponchos, and even a collapsible condenser for converting seawater to fresh water in emergencies.

The present model of the Com-Pac, however, has eliminated this hatch and filled this space with more flotation material. Also, a low bulkhead in the forepeak was added to hold an anchor and rode. The cabin has four gold anodized aluminum ports. Hull ventilation is helped by a removable flexible ventilator in the foredeck. Space in the aft part of the cabin under the bridge is large enough for a self-contained head. Other items such as a small galley or one-man inflatable raft, dive ladder, etc., can be stowed in the after ends of the eight-foot-long berths. Additional stowage is in the stern lazaret.

All detailing and finishing both inside and outside are top quality for a production boat. Deck and mast hardware is made of marine grade materials and consists of three bronze mooring cleats, bronze anchor chocks, stainless steel chain plates and blocks, and cleats and fittings for the running rigging.

The bow pulpit which is well proportioned to match the size of the boat gives it a jaunty look while providing strong security for any foredeck activity such as anchoring. Additional safety features are found in the molded-in toe rail at the sheer and the molded-in antiskid design on the upper deck.

The standing rigging is ⁵/₃₂-inch 1 × 19 stainless steel with swagged fittings; open barrel stainless steel and chromed bronze turnbuckles. All halyards and sheets are braided Dacron. The mast foot is through-bolted to a stainless steel plate and the mast stepped easily by one person. All spars are anodized aluminum; the boom features spring-loaded roller reefing.

The boat carries 115 square feet of sail in main and lapper made of 3½-ounce Howe and Bainbridge Dacron cloth double-stitched with Daybond polyester thread. A 200 percent genoa is offered as an option.

Many of the Com-Pac 16's sailing characteristics are due to the nice lines in the Clark Mills–designed hull with its 450 pounds of glassed-in ballast and high-lift, low-drag shoal draft keel. With its eighteen-inch draft, the boat floats easily in wading depth water.

Two large throated hawse pipes in the aft end of the cockpit well guarantee swift emptying of the cockpit in the event it should take on any water. The twelve-inch step or bridge between the footwell and the main hatch means that the footwell (with hawse pipes plugged) would have to be full of water before any crossed the bridge into the cabin.

All cockpit coamings are exceptionally high and well contoured so that even with 2½-inch-thick cockpit cushions there is ample coaming to provide comfortable and secure back rests. Some Com-Pac 16 owners have successfully used the port and starboard seats to sleep two more passengers, an arrangement that becomes especially comfortable when the footwell is covered and an additional cushion is added between the two seats.

Probably the first thing noticed in sailing the Com-Pac 16 is its big boat feeling. This is part illusion, for the view across the low deckhouse, past the mast and out over the boat's bluff bow and jaunty bow pulpit, does indeed present the helmsman with a "big boat" appearance. But the bigness is not so much in what he sees as in what he feels under sail in a fairly brisk breeze, the boat well heeled over and being subjected to occasional sudden gusts. That's when one fully realizes that this little boat has a big boat feel because it is such a stiff sailer. When a sudden puff hits, the Com-Pac increases speed instead of swiftly leaning over more on her beam. The heeling tendency is gradual as is the tendency to move back on even keel once the pressure passes. The reason for this is the Com-Pac's well-ballasted shoal water keel.

I suspect this is why many Com-Pac owners mention this big boat feeling when they sail the 16 for the first time. She is not easily swayed by just any passing breeze, yet in light airs—the kind that barely ripple the surface of the water— she does not just squat down and refuse to move either. She responds to the lightest of breezes and once underway manages to hold her own in virtually any kind of wind, be it light or heavy.

My boat tends to have significant weather helm and needs to be restrained with a firm hand on her tiller, to keep her from heading up into the wind. This tendency, of course, is much to be preferred to a lee helm in which the harder the wind blows the more the boat wants to turn downwind with it. The Com-Pac 16's weather helm has never been a problem but you certainly cannot turn loose her tiller without expecting to immediately turn up into the wind.

I have used the boat's natural tendency to do this when beating by employing a simple block and line from the boat's tiller to one of her after cleats as an effective self-steering device. The boat will sail this way for miles on a steady wind, seldom wandering more than five degrees off course in either direction before the foresail loses its effectiveness and allows the bow to fall back on course.

Using this self-steering device on anything but a beat into the wind is less effective due to the gradual loss of weather helm. With this slackening, the boat wanders more off course and the self-steering device is no longer reliable.

Sailing downwind, the boat performs best when the main

and lapper sails are in a wing-and-wing (both let out on each side of the boat) configuration.

The fullness of the Com-Pac design keeps her full bow riding well up on downwind runs. As she gains speed, she virtually surfs up and down large waves running in the same direction, a rather uncommon performance for a displacement hull.

Tacking the Com-Pac is more like tacking a much larger displacement hull boat. She eases around with a certain amount of ladylike dignity rather than spinning about with the speed of a far less heavily ballasted hull. Yet she does not tend to override her tiller and continue turning with her momentum beyond a desired point as some heavier displacement boats might do.

In a strong, steady blow, the Com-Pac can be allowed to heel right on down to her rub rail where she seems to take a set as if refusing to heel any further. If conditions are gusty enough, she will go beyond this angle of sail. Interestingly, however, at this point, if struck by an additionally strong wind gust, rather than continuing to heel right on over the rub rail, the Com-Pac shows a natural tendency to respond instead by forcing her bow into the gust with the increased weather helm—an automatic response that luffs the sail and decreases her angle of heel.

In weather that might normally call for reefing, this natural tendency of the boat to head up into the excessively strong gusts acts as a built-in safety factor. Only when winds continued gusting to twenty knots have I reefed to maintain a more comfortable angle of sail.

For years, the only power I used with the Com-Pac 16 was a 1.5-horsepower Johnson outboard motor—a nice, lightweight, and economical power source when it was desirable to get in or out of harbors against headwinds. However, after twice having to motor the boat through ocean inlets against excessive headwinds and waves, I realized that under these extreme conditions the 1.5-horsepower was too small to do the job I was asking it to do. Though it always got me back safely, there were times when winds were so strong that had I allowed them to take the boat on her beam, it would have been very difficult to have powered her bow back into the wind again. So I moved up to a 4-horsepower Johnson outboard which has proved more than adequate in all wind and sea conditions with that boat so far.

A few years after the Hutchins Company sold me a Com-Pac 16, they turned out the Com-Pac 23—virtually a copy of the sixteen-foot model but on a larger scale. Again, the designer was Clark Mills and it is a pleasure to see his same traditional lines and curves expanded to the big boat layout. The Com-Pac 23 is twenty-two feet nine inches overall with a twenty-foot two-inch waterline. She has almost an eight-foot beam and carries 232 square feet of sail—120 square feet in the main and 112 square feet in the jib.

Despite a 3,000-pound displacement, and 1,340 pounds of molded-in concrete ballast, Mills has managed to retain the same type of high-lift, low-drag, shallow draft keel that draws only two feet three inches of water.

Spaciousness is the word for describing the Com-Pac 23. It can be seen both inside and outside the boat. As of this writing the company is now producing the Com-Pac 23/II which has far more live-aboard capabilities than its predecessor. Most distinctive of the topside features is the long but well-proportioned cabin with its six classic heavy duty bronze opening ports and hand-finished teak trim. The large seven-foot two-inch self-bailing cockpit has a gas tank storage compartment plus port and starboard sail lockers. The hull and deck of this twenty-three-foot eleven-inch boat are fabricated of hand laid fiberglass with the hull having longitudinal and traverse stringers integrated into it for stiffness. The deck has core material over 100 percent of its surface for rigidity and insulation. The large foredeck and wide side-decks make moving around and sail handling much easier of course than on the smaller boat.

From her bronze portholes to her bluff bows, everything about the twenty-three-foot Com-Pac yacht reflects Clark Mills' fine traditional lines.

The 23/II's stainless steel rigging has been substantially beefed up as compared to the 16 so that now instead of three stays on the mast, there are eight, including a backstay. Two bronze winches are conventionally located on the cockpit coamings for easy sheet handling. All the other deck fittings are also bronze.

The Com-Pac 23/II is intended for serious cruising. Some deep-water sailors may criticize the large cockpit and point out that skimpier dimensions might be better if she is ever pooped by a following sea, but quite obviously this boat is designed more for cruising comfort than for a steady diet of deep-water sailing. And in that respect, few things add more to life aboard a sailboat than a cockpit large enough to avoid cramping the boat's crew.

In the same way there is ample room below decks for live-aboard comfort. The space is divided into a two-deck cabin layout for privacy. The teak finished interior has three-inch, high density foam cushions for four, with filler cushions for the V-berth. There is space for an optional head in the forward cabin. All the upholstery is heavy-textured and top quality as opposed to the often found vinyl covered cushions. Along with the salty looking heavy bronze ports, there is

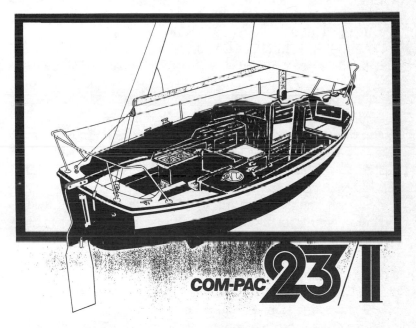

While still maintaining the traditional lines of the Com-Pac, this new version of the Com-Pac 23/II, by designer Bob Johnson, features an interior layout that promises even more comfort and convenience for the cruising trailer sailor.

enough teak and mahogany to warm the cockles of an aesthete's heart. No cold looking fiberglass bulkheads here. Instead there is lots of stowage space under berths, in lockers and shelves, teak hull cabinets in the main cabin with shelves and door fronts, a large divided chain locker with door in the forepeak, teak battened hull panels in the forward cabin and a teak and holly cabin sole.

In the galley there is a sliding hide-away pair of units for a two-burner alcohol stove on the port side with dish and utensil bins and a stainless steel sink with thirteen-gallon water tank on the starboard side.

The 23/II with its twenty-seven-inch draft and seven-foot ten-inch beam displacing 3,000 pounds rides astride its own custom designed tandem axle roller trailer which makes it practically a go-anywhere trailerable yacht.

Recently, the Hutchins Company built a Com-Pac model that might be considered a more logical size transition between the Com-Pac 16 and the twenty-three-footer. This is the nineteen-foot Com-Pac. While it features characteristics of both the 16 and the 23, it is distinctly different. There is no mistaking the 19 as a member of the Com-Pac line, but her designer was Bob Johnson, a well-known Florida East Coast designer who has incorporated some ideas of his own into this characteristic boat.

For trailer sailors wanting more boat than the 16 affords, but not wishing for as much boat to trail as there is in the twenty-three-foot model, the 19 is a nice compromise. This boat is three feet longer than the Com-Pac 16, but those three cubic feet make it almost twice as much boat. The displacement of the sixteen-foot Com-Pac is 1,100 pounds. The displacement of the Com-Pac 19 is an even 2,000 pounds.

Side by side the differences are enormous. The 19 looks more like a twenty-two-footer; indeed, its displacement is more than many of that size. Her freeboard is more and when seen out of water on her custom trailer alongside her small sister boat, she stands a lot taller.

SAILING
YACHTS

€ 19

HUTCHINS CO., INC.   1195 KAPP DRIVE   CLEARWATER, FLORIDA 33515
(813) 443-4408

The

€OM-PA€-19

Interestingly, however, there is very little difference in the size of their cockpits. But from this point on the differences are considerable. The longer cabin now contains four bronze opening ports. A large hatch in the foredeck provides easy access to a cabin forepeak chain locker. Six stainless steel stays support the mast. The spacious cockpit has port and starboard seat lockers that open into a large stowage area of the hull. The bow pulpit and tabernacle are standard equipment along with the usual items including a motor mount. Lifelines and a stern pulpit are advisable and available as optional equipment. The boat is nineteen feet overall with a seven-foot beam. Waterline length is sixteen feet four inches and the hull draws two feet, which keeps it well into the shoal draft depth of her sister boats. She displaces 2,000 pounds and carries 800 pounds of molded-in ballast.

Unlike the Com-Pac 16, the nineteen-foot boat is a masthead rig, her foresail going all the way to the top of the mast. She comes with standard Dacron sails—95 square feet in the main and 93 square feet in the jib, giving her a total of 188 square feet of sail, all of it 5½-ounce material.

The greatest noticeable difference between the Com-Pac 16 and the Com-Pac 19 strikes you at once as you step through the bigger boat's companionway. Again, like the 23, it is the sudden feeling of spaciousness. Careful workmanship and quality jump out at you all over the place. The tastefully well-upholstered berths have the same heavy duty fabric as the 23 does with the same quality bronze ports and the same quality woodwork. The mahogany paneling used on the inside of the cabin down to the deck line gives the boat's interior the same warmth and charm as that seen in the 23. The apparent beaminess of the interior is due, undoubtedly, to Bob Johnson's slightly less rounded hull design. There are four berths, each six feet four inches long with full sitting headroom. There is room between the V-berths for an optional galley that includes a mahogany drop-leaf table, sink, water tank-

Specifications and Sailplans

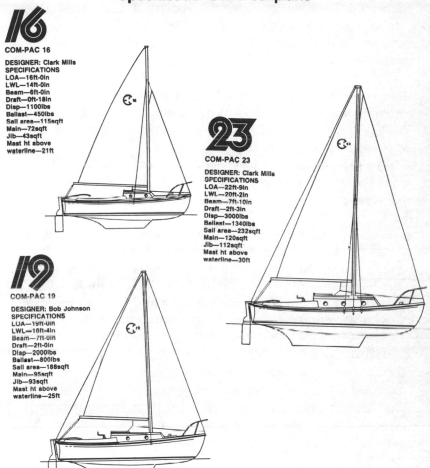

16

COM-PAC 16

DESIGNER: Clark Mills
SPECIFICATIONS
LOA—16ft-0in
LWL—14ft-0in
Beam—6ft-0in
Draft—0ft-18in
Disp—1100lbs
Ballast—450lbs
Sail area—115sqft
Main—72sqft
Jib—43sqft
Mast ht above
waterline—21ft

23

COM-PAC 23

DESIGNER: Clark Mills
SPECIFICATIONS
LOA—22ft-9in
LWL—20ft-2in
Beam—7ft-10in
Draft—2ft-3in
Disp—3000lbs
Ballast—1340lbs
Sail area—232sqft
Main—120sqft
Jib—112sqft
Mast ht above
waterline—30ft

19

COM-PAC 19

DESIGNER: Bob Johnson
SPECIFICATIONS
LOA—19ft-0in
LWL—16ft-4in
Beam—7ft-0in
Draft—2ft-0in
Disp—2000lbs
Ballast—800lbs
Sail area—188sqft
Main—95sqft
Jib—93sqft
Mast ht above
waterline—25ft

age, shelves, and ice chest. The sink drains into the bilge where the waste water can then be pumped out with the bilge pump that is operated from the cockpit. If not in use, the entire galley unit can be taken out by removing five screws and two hose clamps. A filler cushion fits into this space and increases the size of the V-berth.

There is ample room for a portable head behind the step in the companionway. The step board hinges so that it may be lifted up and secured across the companionway with a length of shock cord. The head must be slid forward into the cabin to be used.

At the Hutchins Company plant I talked with Vice-President Gerry Hutchins about some of the differences between the Com-Pac 16 and the Com-Pac 19. Here is what he had to say:

"The two basic differences, I think," said Gerry, "is that on the Com-Pac 19 the bow is quite a bit finer. It has a finer entry, which is the way Bob Johnson designs his boats. It carries the beam farther aft in order to have more buoyancy there so that it can better carry the load of the cockpit. Now these are my perceptions as to why he does this. He may have a whole other list of reasons. But this is my feeling.

"It also has a flatter bottom and a harder chine. The 16 and the 23 are very round at the chine. The 19 is round but it is more abrupt there. It comes down almost straight sided and then curves under and goes flat. That flatness of the bottom gives you more interior room and it provides the boat with more initial stability. The kind of stability that is derived from the hull shape.

"The broadness of this boat and the flatness of the bottom cause it not to sail well at larger angles of heel, whereas the 16 and 23 can be sailed with their rails virtually in the water. The 19 does not sail as well on that large an angle of heel. However, it compensates for this by its stability. The same amount of wind that might put the rail in the water for a 16, would not put a 19's rail in the water. It doesn't limit a boat because you can't put its rail in the water—you can sail the 19 to its rail—but it loses efficiency there.

"All three of our boats have long waterlines relative to their lengths. We don't have overhangs. The 16 and the 23 both have nearly plumb bows—the bows have a nice graceful curve but they go almost plumb up at the top, which causes very little overhang on the bow. The 19 is more of a slope, so percentagewise there is probably a little more overhang but certainly nothing excessive. It's not a real pointy sleek bow.

"In all three of our boats, when there are people in the cockpits, the transoms touch the water so there is no overhang there at all. We have long waterlines for the length of the boats.

"The Com-Pac 19 is not just three feet longer than the 16, it is twice as big. In boats, nothing is in direct proportion. A boat that is twice as long is not twice as big; it's probably four times as big. There is no direct relation there.

"The three boats are made identically. The hulls and decks are all joined the same way and they are all ballasted with concrete. Conceptually they are the same boats," said Hutchins. When I pressed for details as to what these differences meant in the 19 as opposed to the 16, he said:

"Proportionately, the 19 is a whole lot deeper. The 19 draws two feet and the 16 draws eighteen inches, and there is probably also a little more refined shape to the 19's keel. Proportionately, the 19 goes to weather much better and being a masthead rig you get more drive out of your sail plan. The 16 is about a seven-eighths rig. You'll find that you can set the mast of the 19 plumb with the waterline and there will not be a weather helm problem. The 16 and 23 tend to be heavy on the helm. They are sensitive to rig tuning—the helm can be tuned out but they are sensitive to weather helm—and that is partly because they are so fat forward. Clark's boats are very full in the bow, whereas the 19 is finer in the bow and you consequently have a different handling characteristic."

Though only three feet longer than the Com-Pac 16, the Com-Pac 19 has almost twice the displacement and is a masthead rig. Here she is shown under cruising spinnaker and her Sun-Brella Bimini.

The larger Com-Pac 19 will surely have a strong appeal to the family sailors—those with youngsters who might normally find the Com-Pac 16 somewhat confining. Most women will enjoy the spaciousness of the 19's interior. This large a boat, however, takes it out of the compact car category and puts it in with the family car. Prices of these big little boats, as of this writing, are as follows:

Base prices range from under $5,000 for the Com-Pac 16 to under $13,000 for the Com-Pac 23/II. All prices FOB Clearwater, Florida. For further information about these boats contact: The Hutchins Company, Inc., 1195 Kapp Drive, Clearwater, FL 33515. Tel: (813) 443-4408.

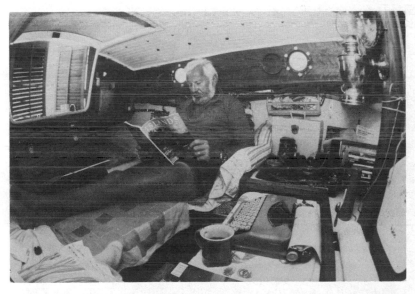

Flanked by books, cameras, and typewriter, the author's "office" aboard his Com-Pac 19, *WindShadow*, provides some idea of the spaciousness of this nineteen foot sailboat.

5

Flicka: A Deluxe Big
Little Boat

The economical Com-Pacs with their wine-glass hulls, traditional lines, snub-nosed bows, and gentle catboat looks, have
a counterpart in another unique boat that bears striking
design similarities, but enjoys another price category. It is the
twenty-three-foot seven-inch Flicka designed by Bruce
Bingham. This traditionally designed small cruising boat,
with 5,500 pounds displacement, bears a standard production
model price of $25,000. A deluxe model is available for
$35,000. Steep though these prices may seem for such a little
boat, what designer Bruce Bingham has managed to include
in this tiny package would put many bigger, far more expensive boats to shame. When all is considered, Flicka is not only
in a class apart and the only one of her kind being built, but
she is indisputably the Cadillac of big little boats. In 1983,
over 200 production boats of the Flicka (which in Swedish
means cute or vivacious) were built by Pacific Seacraft of
Santa Ana, California. Before that an unknown number were
built from kits by amateurs throughout the world.

Again we have a sailboat with both traditional and contemporary lines, and interestingly, with the exception of the
deeper, fuller keel, some are quite similar to those of the
Com-Pacs. The Flicka is actually twenty feet long not count-

ing her perky bowsprit. She is eighteen feet two inches on the waterline with an eight-foot beam and a three-foot three-inch draft. Her displacement of 5,500 pounds includes 1,750 pounds of lead ballast. On the standard sloop-rigged boat her sail area is 250 square feet; on the optional gaff-rigged boat she carries 288 square feet.

In her hull lines we see the wine-glass configuration and the compound curves that Clark Mills used in his designs of the Com-Pacs. But the idea for the Flicka goes back to the late 1950s when Bruce Bingham, stationed at Rhode Island on naval duty, saw something that started him thinking. On weekends he would explore the backwaters of Narragansett Bay in an eight-foot sailing dinghy he had built. On one of these trips he came upon two beached derelict wooden sailboats.

He liked what he saw. Their traditional lines appealed to him. He learned later that they were called Newport boats and that most were between twenty-two feet and twenty-eight feet long. He found out that these were old-time commercial fishing boats in use at the turn of the century by lobstermen in the area. They had large working cockpits with small forward cutty cabins. There was enough left of them to show that once they had a single forward bunk and a small galley with only crouching headroom. As far as Bingham could determine they seemed to have been rigged as cat ketches or cat schooners.

The designs of both this Newport lobster boat and the Cape Cod Cat seem to have evolved for the kind of year-round weather and sailing conditions in that area—everything ranging from flat calms to raging gales, the transition sometimes so swift that there is often not much in between.

Bingham drew some sketches of the boats and filed them away while he completed his naval duty. They stayed filed for another decade before they finally came to his attention again in 1971, shortly after he had opened a San Francisco design office.

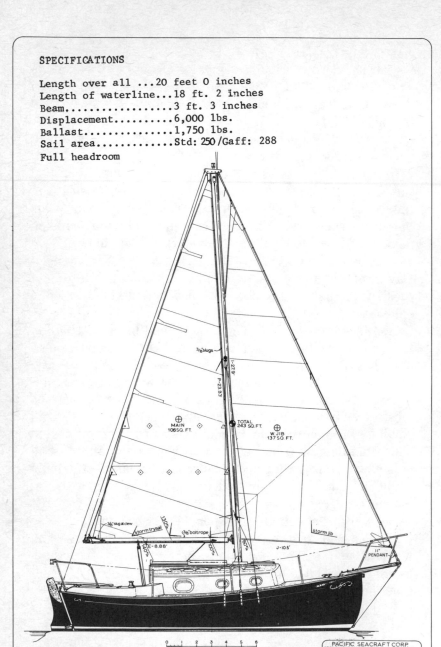

SPECIFICATIONS

Length over all ...20 feet 0 inches
Length of waterline...18 ft. 2 inches
Beam...................3 ft. 3 inches
Displacement..........6,000 lbs.
Ballast...............1,750 lbs.
Sail area.............Std: 250/Gaff: 288
Full headroom

MAIN
106 SQ. FT.

TOTAL
243 SQ. FT.

W. JIB
137 SQ. FT.

storm trysail

storm jib

11"
PENDANT

0 1 2 3 4 5 6
INCHES   SCALE IN FEET

C. ADDED PULPITS & STANCHIONS 5-16-83 *W.B.L.*
B. Shorten main foot from 9'-3" to 8'-10½", changed mast rake from 3½" to 1¾"
   Added 140% genoa, changed drifter from 130% to 140%
   Added S.F. Working Jib, added clew slug, 11-2-79 *W.B.L.*
REV. A. Shorten main foot from 9'-6" to 9'-3", 7-20-79 *W.B.L.*

PACIFIC SEACRAFT CORP.
3301 So SUSAN ST., SANTA ANA, CA. 92704
DWN. W.B.L. | DATE 1-16-78 | DO NOT SCALE | SCALE ¾"=1'0"
SAIL PLAN-MARCONI, FLICKA

Again, he became enthusiastic about the Newport hull design and began thinking of it in terms of a small cruising sailboat. But he wanted to keep the boat within the budget of amateur builders. So he began sketching ideas around a vessel that was twenty feet long.

In working with the sketches, Bingham felt that he could figure out a way to give this little boat full headroom inside. No small feat when you hope to maintain a relatively shallow draft. But he managed to work some really remarkable things by designing the cabin sole so that it would be flush with the internal ballast and by giving both deck and cabin high crowns. By doing this he was able to keep the cabin side height from looking too large and out of proportion with the length of the boat. A perky bowsprit and bow pulpit helped to add to the illusion of lengthened lines so that the design was aesthetically pleasing.

In 1971 Bingham submitted preliminary designs of the boat to boating magazines and soon, over the next five years, more than four hundred plan packages were sold to amateur builders around the world who began constructing Flickas of wood or fiberglass in their backyards.

In time, Bingham began hearing from satisfied Flicka sailors who were sailing the minicruiser on ocean voyages all over the globe. Four owners even attempted around-the-world cruises in their Flickas. Though Bingham never heard if any of them made it, he assumed that some of them did.

Bingham was so sure he had designed a boat that had long-term live-aboard capabilities that he closed his California office and decided to build a Flicka of his own in 1974.

He and his fellow naval architect, Kate Burke, constructed the hull of fiberglass, taking their time to incorporate all the fine details, the carving of the bow, and the quarter scroll work. Even planking seams were scribed in the original plug. But business pressures eventually kept them from finishing the job.

Pacific Seacraft Corporation bought the only existing mold

Inspired by the traditional lines of Newport, Rhode Island's old commercial fishing boats, designer Bruce Bingham created a remarkably big little cruising sailboat. For a boat that is only eighteen feet two inches on her waterline, he somehow managed to give her a full six feet of headroom.

Despite their size, Flickas have carried their owners many thousands of miles across the sea. Though it is trailerable, it is not the kind one would be apt to trail out to a lake for a Sunday afternoon's sail.

and, in 1978, Flicka hull number 25 became Bingham's long-awaited dream boat, the *Sabrina.*

To prove his theories about the boat, Bingham and his friend Kate Burke promptly moved onto their new boat to live aboard and cruise her for some 6,000 miles in the next two years. No greater faith could a designer have than to take on that kind of challenge in a compact living area much smaller than most people's bathroom.

Not only was their experiment completely successful but what they learned in the process about how to customize a boat for maximum comfort is in itself a study in ingenuity.

"The Flicka was never intended to be a high performance boat," says Bingham. "The prime criteria were seaworthiness and a comfortable, liveable interior for long-distance and offshore cruising."

Although he had heard other Flicka owners praise the better than five-knot averages they said the boat could make, it was not until Bingham owned his own boat that he had a chance to see for himself how well she sailed.

Four days after her delivery, with an untried crew and an untried boat, he entered the 200-mile Round Long Island Race where the *Sabrina,* after 125 miles of racing, was still sailing bow to bow with such well-known boats as a Tanzer 22, a Cal 25, a Seafarer 33, and others. Bingham's *Sabrina* was the smallest boat in the race, yet she managed to take an astonishing fourth place in the cruising class.

Bingham found her light air performance not only satisfactory but phenomenal. *Sabrina* seemed able to ease past boats up to fifteen feet longer than she was. But it was in the heavier winds where she seemed to really come into her own and get down to business. Bingham's tests indicated that she was capable of 5.68 knots and that 5.25-knot passages were quite common.

When one sees the Flicka at close range for the first time, two words seem to pop into mind almost simultaneously: quality and stability.

While never intended to be a high performance boat, the Flicka was designed for seaworthiness and a comfortable, livable interior for long distance and offshore cruising.

The builders have spared nothing to accomplish these ends. The boat is sturdily made of hand-laminated fiberglass over mat and roving. The hull lamination sequences are: mat, cloth, two units of mat and roving plus two more units of mat and roving down the centerline; one thirty-six inches wide and one sixty inches wide. This results in a hull that is ³⁄₈ inch thick at the sheer, ⁵⁄₈ inch thick at the waterline, and ³⁄₄ inch thick at the keel. Core material for the deck is plywood while the deckhouse crown, because of its extreme arch, is cored with end grain balsa.

The hull to deck flange is bedded in polyurethane and bolted with quarter-inch stainless steel machine screws through the aluminum toe rail.

The inner hull has a liner to help cut down on condensation.

All deck fittings, stays, and chain plates are backed up by heavy stainless steel plates to help distribute pressures over a larger area.

When one steps inside the Flicka and glances into the cabin one is amazed to see so little space with so much in it. There is not a bit of wasted space; every inch has been used

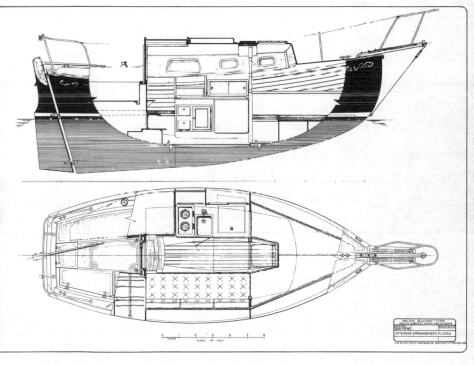

This shows the interior arrangement of the Flicka. Another that is available features an enclosed head.

wisely and functionally. The first surprising feature is the Flicka's incredible full six-foot headroom in the main cabin. Where you most need the headroom—in the galley with its compact stove, sink, icebox, and table compressed into a six-foot two-inch unit along the port side of the boat—you have it. In addition, you have sleeping accommodations for four—a six-foot seven-inch V-berth forward with room for a portable head between the V, a six-foot six-inch quarter berth on the port side, and a six-foot three-inch settee on the starboard side with a large storage bin underneath.

Shelves extend along both bulkheads over all berths. The cabin has four opening ports and a forward hatch for ventilation.

Bingham has eliminated the need to break up the interior with a vertical pressure post to support the mast that is stepped on the cabin roof. He has done this by reinforcing that area with a broad beam and layers of mat and roving laminations that are glassed over so that the load is transferred to the cabin side and bulkhead. So far there have been no reported problems with this arrangement.

The builders wisely built in stowage areas at every opportunity. Living aboard what began as a stock production boat, Bingham and Burke undertook a masterful customizing job that not only lightened their boat considerably, but vastly increased stowage areas and *Sabrina*'s comfort capabilities. Since some of these ideas are worthy of being used on boats other than the Flicka, I believe it might be worthwhile to detail some of them.

To lighten the boat, to provide ventilation to areas, and to make more room for stowage, Bingham started in on *Sabrina* with a saber saw. First, he sawed holes in all the lift-out locker and berth lids, eliminating weight and providing these stowage areas with much needed ventilation. Then he went to work under the cockpit sole. In the standard Flicka, this area is reinforced with a liner against the hull that has molded-in engine beds in case an owner wishes to install a small inboard engine there. But since Bingham and Burke's *Sabrina* was powered by an outboard, the removal of this liner opened up a space large enough for them to add a flexible auxiliary tank for their outboard fuel.

Next, he did the same with the liners on the bottom of all the storage bins. None of these areas were structural bulkheads or bonded to the hull. To be sure that he cut only to the depth of the liner thickness, he broke his saber saw blade to that thickness.

In this cutting away of unnecessary material, Bingham eliminated four hundred pounds of weight. This was then replaced with more usable weight such as stores for two and a half months that the *Sabrina* could carry in addition to a flexible tank under the V-berth that would hold the boat's forty-gallon freshwater supply.

In their unceasing search for more space, a hanging locker at the aft end of the settee was reworked. The rod was lifted several inches so that clothes no longer bunched up at the bottom, hooks were added, and this provided room for all their foul weather gear. Spare batteries, flares, and emergency gear were stored in a large plastic box to join shoes and books in lockers behind the settee.

Adhering to the idea of removing something before adding something else, Bingham's gradual modifications to *Sabrina* became a carefully thought-out process of taking and giving. For example, the top of the hull liner which became a shelf over a hanging locker was too narrow even to support the width of a paperback book. So Bingham sawed out this flange that had been glassed to the hull, cutting out the center portion of the shelf. This left enough to still serve as a hull stiffener and on it he epoxied a new shelf of quarter-inch plywood that was at least four inches wider so that it extended over the top of the settee cushion. This immediately opened up a wide area for books and a variety of other quite large items.

The storage bin under the settee contains canned goods,

dry stores, two tool boxes, and a portable typewriter. The storage bin under the V-berth contains the water tank and two more bins for canned goods.

As on most stock production boats, *Sabrina* came from the factory with a shelf on each side over the quarter berth and extending to the chain locker. At first they tried hanging stowage hammocks there, but when these proved inconvenient Bingham built small shelves to hold personal items. They also had the factory install a hanging locker which would hold clothing at the forward end of the V-berth just aft of the forepeak bulkhead. This unit was high enough to amply clear the feet of anyone sleeping on that berth.

Other small shelves were added wherever there was room. Such space was found in often overlooked areas such as the backs of doors. On the *Sabrina* the clothing locker doors have racks for forty-two cassette tapes, while the outside of the galley door supports an acrylic magazine rack large enough to hold several folded charts. On its inside, two small shelves hold toothbrushes, toothpaste, comb, and other items.

Sabrina's electrical supply consists of two 105-amp batteries which power a radio/tape recorder, a portable black and white TV, three fluorescent lights, and two incandescent lights. With kerosene costing 90 cents a gallon, Bingham and Burke chose to use electricity whenever possible. The battery-powered fluorescent lights proved less of a drain than the incandescents. With the exception of running lights and a masthead trilight, the fluorescent lights became their main source of illumination at night. Electricity also powers their autopilot on long cruises and when dockside electricity is available, they prefer heating *Sabrina* with a small electrical heater. In one northern winter, when they lived aboard at a marina, their electrical costs came to $30. Had they been heating with kerosene in the heater they had which consumed about two gallons every twenty-four hours, the cost for that same period would have been $270.

To cope with the condensation in the boat that winter, one-and-a-half-inch-thick planks of polyurethane were sandwiched between the wooden ceiling and the cabin roof. The decks were insulated in the same manner with three-quarter-inch foam. It stopped the dripping.

Over the *Sabrina*'s five-foot-long cockpit, Bingham installed a sun awning/rain catcher top to provide shade and a means of restocking their freshwater supply.

Proceeding with their plan to provide more ventilation and a lightening of their boat, Bingham saber-sawed panels in the front of their galley, the berths, and sections under the settee. These large holes were then replaced by panels of woven pine trimmed with teak. Similarly, the bottom was cut out of the clothing locker which was originally heavy teak-veneered plywood and it was replaced with quarter-inch-thick perforated masonite, which provided through-ventilation while cutting down on the weight.

To brighten areas, Bingham added an opening port in the cockpit side over the quarterberth and some self-contained battery lights in locker areas that needed them.

In the galley, additional work space was added by constructing a drop-leaf table that extended over the seldom used quarterberth. When not in use it was folded up against the hull.

Topside, Bingham constructed small box bins of quarter-inch plywood and glassed them inside the coaming. Then he cut openings through the coaming so that these became handy little niches to store a variety of odds and ends ranging from coffee cups and sunglasses to sail stops and lip balm.

Sabrina's cockpit sea lockers contain mainly bags of sails, a spare outboard propeller, and several collapsible water jugs. Other sails—the spinnaker and reacher—are cleverly concealed underneath the cockpit sole where they are securely held by supporting lengths of shockcord. The storm sails are rolled tightly and secured in a similar manner with shockcord underneath the clothing locker. All sails are reachable in a hurry, but are stowed out of the way when not needed.

One-and-a-half-inch PVC tubing—two in the cockpit and one on the mast—holds winch handles so they are not misplaced or lost overboard.

There are port and starboard compass mounts on either side of the companionway so that the compass can be switched depending upon the tack they are on. A third bracket in the cabin secures the compass when not in use.

A cockpit table was fashioned simply by using one of the berth bin covers and placing its bracket through one of the holes in the tiller normally used for the autopilot.

The size of the boat makes it easy for both Bingham and Burke to handle sails, anchors, or any other problem that might arise. For example, when *Sabrina* ran aground on one of their cruises, it was a simple matter to jump overboard and push her off—something that just cannot be done with a bigger boat.

With these modifications, Bingham and Burke have managed to keep low maintenance on a boat that is easy to handle while still providing the comforts one would want while living aboard for a long time. Granted, these are not the comforts of a large yacht, but it is quite amazing how easy it is to adapt to compact comforts when one decides to do so.

"We found that being small does not have to mean being deprived of creature comforts," wrote Kate Burke. "It is true we have made a lot of changes and improvements on *Sabrina,* but we didn't do them all at once and none of them cost an inordinate amount of money. We just keep working away at little projects, increasing the comfort and livability of the boat all the time."

What was done on the *Sabrina* to make her more comfortable is an example of what can be done on other stock production boats. Maybe not on such a grand scale, but every little bit pays off with big dividends.

In all respects, Flicka is a big little boat, a pocket cruiser deluxe. She may not be the kind of boat to whisk out to the lake for an afternoon's sail, then trail back home again a few hours later. But she is trailerable and that fact automatically opens up unlimited cruising possibilities for this vivacious little lady. Whether she voyages by land or by sea, one thing is certain: no matter where she goes, her wake will be strewn with admirers.

6

The New Boat: Outfitting and Setting Up

At last you have brought home your new boat on its new trailer. Well, maybe it's really just a used boat on a used trailer. Either way it's new to you and nothing can change the nice feeling that comes over you when nobody is looking and you let your eyes slide over her sleek curves, her gentle sheer, her well-proportioned hull with a bow line so sweet it's enough to make you catch your breath every time you see it.

If the boat has had a former owner who loved her as much as you know you will, then certain things will already have been attended to. Stays and mast may already be in place and require merely setting up to be ready for launching and a sail. On the other hand, if the boat has come from the factory or from a dealer, it will require some preliminary preparation. Chances are the dealer will have already briefed you on how to go about this, or perhaps all you will have to go by is the instruction booklet that came with the boat. If you are really unlucky, you've received no dealer prep and no booklet of instruction. But not to worry. Monohull boats are not that complicated. But anything over more than one hull might be. Catamarans, for instance. The kind that might come completely disassembled for shipping with all their various parts in long cardboard cartons and large plastic bags full of strange-looking stainless steel hardware.

With these you definitely need an instruction book. Don't proceed until you have one. Such kits are far worse than any child's toy you've had to assemble on the night before Christmas with all its nuts and bolts and complexities. Even with instructions, proceed carefully. They can be tricky.

Chances are, however, your boat will come fully assembled and all that will concern you will be attaching the rigging. Often, the spars—mast and boom—will be wrapped, padded, and taped or tied to the frame of your boat trailer. All the essential rigging will be coiled in the boat's cabin, usually tagged as to what it is—whether a backstay, forestay, or whatever. Keep those tags on these cables until ready to attach the stays to the boat.

Boats as simple as the Com-Pac 16 will have only three cables, or stays: one to be attached to the front of the mast near the top which will be the forestay; and one on either side of the mast which will help support it. Your instruction booklet will explain the fittings at these junctures and how they are attached. If a former owner has removed them from the mast and failed to tell you how they should go, contact him and find out exactly how it is done.

Any time you handle these stainless steel stays, do so with infinite care. Usually they are coiled. When you uncoil them be absolutely sure that you do it without crimping or causing a sudden springy loop to be kinked. Any bending of these stays—even stepping on one may cause a kink—can be disastrous later. A catamaran stay that inadvertently kinked slightly on my Hobie 16 later broke one strand of the multiple-stranded stay. I soldered it together, then tightly wrapped the area with wire and flowed solder through all the coils, hoping to reinforce it. But a few trips later, with the stays all cinched down taut and the boat taking a beating as we sailed at top speed through large breakers, the stay snapped. Sails, mast, and the whole rig went overboard. The failure came at the

Glossary

1. Boom
2. Mast
3. Headstay
4. Backstay
5. Fwd. Lower Shroud
6. Upper Shroud
7. Aft Lower Shroud
8. Masthead
9. Mainsail Leech
10. Mainsail Foot
11. Mainsail Luff
12. Jib Leech
13. Jib Foot
14. Jlf Luff
15. Batten Pocket
16. Spreader
17. Clew
18. Tack
19. Head
20. Clew
21. Tack
22. Head
23. Jibsheet
24. Mainsheet
25. Bow
26. Transom
27. Rudder Head
28. Rudder Blade
29. Keel
30. Chainplates
31. Cockpit Coaming
32. Tiller

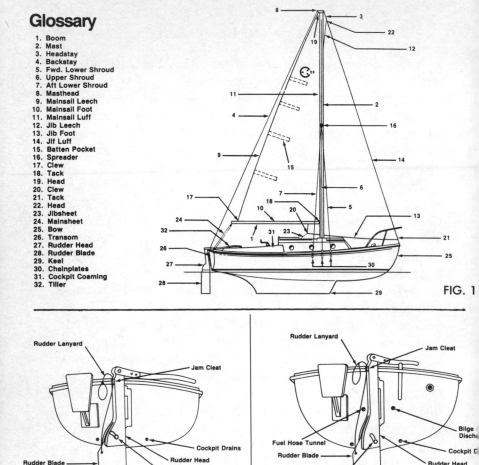

FIG. 1

Rudder Lanyard

Jam Cleat

Rudder Blade

Cockpit Drains

Rudder Head

Tension Nut

FIG. 2

Rudder Lanyard

Jam Cleat

Fuel Hose Tunnel

Rudder Blade

Bilge
Disch

Cockpit D

Rudder Head

Tension Nut

FIG. 3

(Fig. 1) No matter what make sailboat you decide on, all owner's manuals will describe the various parts of the sailboat with their proper names. The glossary will help familiarize you with those parts and their proper names. The transom of the Com-Pac 16 (Fig. 2) provides a means to change the position of the movable rudder blade whenever desired. To raise it, tension is removed by loosening the tension nut handle, then lifting the rudder blade by the rudder lanyard. The blade can be positioned at any angle by snugging the lanyard in its jam cleat. When the blade is down, tighten the tension nut (Fig. 3). Similar features are found on the transom of the Com-Pac 19 along with a bilge pump discharge opening and a convenient tunnel for the fuel hose to the outboard on its mount.

point that had been weakened earlier by the kink. Fortunately, in this instance we were rescued by boaters from shore almost before we got wet.

"The instructions don't tell you what to do in this case, do they?" one of our benefactors said with a grin as he and his comrades helped haul in our rigging and towed us ashore.

He was right. But you learn fast to handle those coiled cables with utmost care and not to put them under so much pressure the next time.

The fittings on each end of all the stays (or shrouds) are swagged (pressed) onto the stainless wire. All of them should be closely inspected at least once a season. Some owners go over them with a magnifying glass looking for any hairline cracks or excessive corrosion that may cause trouble when you least need it. Some of these fittings may develop slight rust stains that are usually only on the surface. A periodic shot of WD 40 lubricating oil will keep these areas trouble free for many years. But any hint of serious corrosion or cracking calls for instant replacement of that part.

Smaller boat masts will have the simplest standing rigging arrangement. The bigger the boat the more complex the rigging. Small boats will lack spreaders on the mast, as does the Com-Pac 16. But the Com-Pac 19 and 23, like most other cruising sailboats their size and larger, will have spreaders on the mast. Once the spreader tube is fastened to the spreader base, the upper stay for that respective side is usually screw-clamped into a slot at one end of each spreader. If there is no set screw, an eight-inch length of stainless steel single strand wire can be used to wrap it snugly to the hole in the end of the spreader. After that, the juncture may be covered with an appropriately sized spreader boot obtainable at marine supply stores. The spreader and shroud illustration shows this in detail.

When attaching the stays to the mast, be sure all fittings are locked with rigging pins and cotter keys. Then attach all halyards (the running lines) and bend on a shackle to the

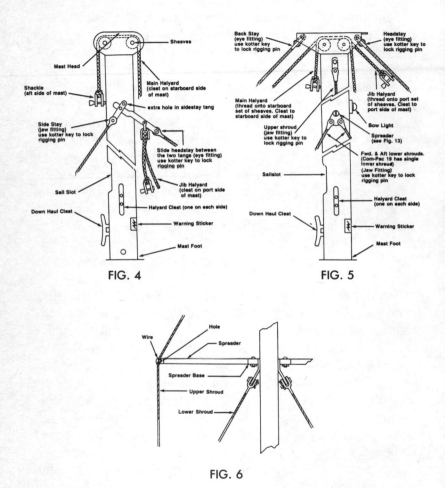

FIG. 4   FIG. 5

FIG. 6

Courtesy of Hutchins Co., Inc.

Fig. 4 typifies the rigging found on many smaller sailboats that are not masthead rigs. Fig. 5 shows the masthead-rigged sailboat with its slightly more complex fittings. Fig. 6 shows the arrangement of upper and lower shrouds. The point where the upper shroud joins the spreader may be protected with a rubber spreader boot obtainable at marine supply stores.

running end of each, and cleat their bitter ends to the mast. See the illustrations for rigging the simple and the more complex masthead arrangements.

Halyards are the lines that raise and lower the sails. One fits the mainsail and another the jib sail. These lines, usually made of low-stretch Dacron, probably come with shackles spliced on. These shackles attach to the head grommet of their respective sails by withdrawing the shackle pin, sliding in the sail, and replacing the pin so that it passes through the grommet. Some pins screw in and out, others are shaped to fit a special slot. Just be sure they are locked or screwed together snugly before hoisting sails.

Setting Up the Mast

Make sure that all stays are attached to the mast and locked with cotter keys and rigging pins in their proper places before starting this procedure. Also, be sure that all halyards are installed and running freely in their sheaves.

Before you set up the mast, always remember: *Aluminum masts and all components conduct electricity. If they touch or come near an electrical power line, it can result in serious injury or death. Stay away from overhead electrical power lines when sailing and/or when launching your boat.* Be especially careful if you step your mast in one area and then decide to pull your boat to another. Contact with telephone or electrical wires en route can cause damage and possible injury.

Again, this latter point had to be learned the hard way. I had stepped the mast on my Com-Pac 16 and prepared to launch at a lakeside ramp. But by then the wind had risen and heavy waves were breaking on the ramp. An alternate ramp was a short way down the road in a protected canal. So, with no wires over the road, I headed there. Just as I turned off the road to go to the ramp I realized how tall my boat's mast was on the trailer. Too late, the upper two feet of the spar caught on an electric wire and, by the time I stopped, my mast was bent backward at a 45° angle three feet from the top.

I was sick. My sailing buddy and I sagged down in the grass beside the boat and tried to think what to do. Across the canal stood a row of pine trees about eight inches in diameter. On a hunch, I removed the mast from the boat, we carried it around into the pine trees, braced the spar between tree trunks, and began bending it back into proper alignment.

Fortunately, the tubular aluminum had not distorted too badly at the bend. Before we were through with it we had not only straightened the spar so well that except for the scrape on its leading edge it was unnoticeable, but even in sighting down the spar lengthways, it proved to be perfectly true. We restepped her and went sailing, feeling incredibly lucky and a whole lot wiser.

Small Boat 3-Stay Mast-Stepping

The procedure for stepping the mast on a small, simply rigged boat such as the Com-Pac 16 is as follows:

With the mast lying aft resting on the companionway hatch, bolt the mast foot to the mast step snugly enough so that the mast will pivot easily in the plate. Attach the port and starboard side stays to the chain plates with pins and cotter keys. Loosen all three turnbuckles by unscrewing them to their maximum length. Lift the mast until it is standing upright. Attach the headstay (forestay) to the outboard bow chain plate with pin and cotter key. Screw the headstay turnbuckle almost closed so that there is forward rake in the mast. Take up the slack equally in the two sidestays until they are snug. Lock the turnbuckles so that they will not unscrew by attaching cotter pins to the holes in the ends of the threaded shafts in the turnbuckles.

When this is done, slide the boom gooseneck into the sail slot on the mast (Fig. 7) and tie the topping lift to the butterfly

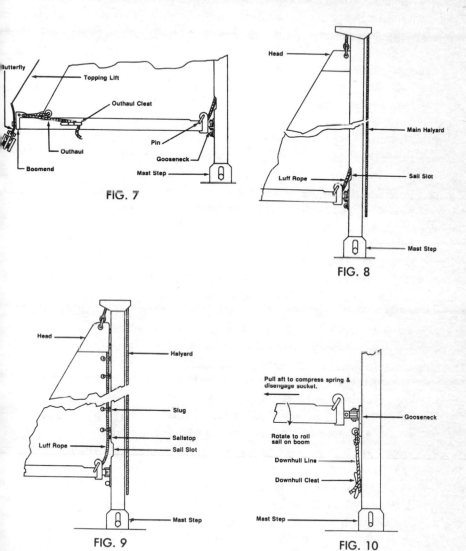

FIG. 7

Butterfly
Topping Lift
Outhaul Cleat
Pin
Gooseneck
Outhaul
Boomend
Mast Step

FIG. 8

Head
Main Halyard
Sail Slot
Luff Rope
Mast Step

FIG. 9

Head
Halyard
Slug
Sailstop
Sail Slot
Luff Rope
Mast Step

FIG. 10

Pull aft to compress spring &
disengage socket.
Gooseneck
Rotate to roll
sail on boom
Downhull Line
Downhull Cleat
Mast Step

on the boom end as shown. The topping lift is a light line that runs from the top of the mast to the end of the boom where it supports the end of that spar when the sail is lowered.

When lowering the mast, always remove the boom first. Then loosen the headstay turnbuckle and detach the headstay only while the mast is being supported so it does not fall. Lower the mast. The sidestays need not be detached or adjusted every time you rig your boat. Unbolt the foot and slide the mast forward so it can be tied securely to the boat for trailering.

This is the basic procedure, but one might wonder how it is possible to support the mast and attach or detach the headstay at the same time. Having a companion to assist will help, but most small boats with this kind of bolted mast foot can be easily set up single-handedly. One method of doing this is to push the mast into its upright position and, while holding it there, grasp the topping lift before it has been secured to the end of the boom and, while maintaining tension on this line, walk it forward and secure it to something such as the bow pulpit rail. I usually lay two coils around the rail, haul down to flex the masthead forward, then secure the bitter end of the topping lift with a couple of half hitches. Then I am free to attach the slackened headstay to the bow chain plate. To do this quickly I use a properly sized quick release pin—the kind on which you push an end button that releases two tiny metal stoppers on the other end of the pin—allowing me to insert it through the chain plate and the headstay turnbuckle eye. Releasing pressure on the button prevents the pin from being removed. Undoing the topping life line takes slack from the headstay. Then I walk aft and, placing the gooseneck on the boom into its mast slot, I lift the boom to its proper level and secure the topping lift line to its butterfly with an easily untied half hitch in case I want to release it and readjust the height of the after end of the boom.

Once I establish the correct tension on the headstay, I leave it that way. There is no need to readjust the turnbuckle.

In lowering the mast, a reverse procedure is followed.

If the mast is especially long and heavy or one feels safer by remaining at the mast when lifting and securing, one can jury rig a line from the end of the headstay that passes through a block mounted somewhere forward, such as on the bow pulpit, and back to the mast again. By hauling on this line as the mast is lifted, even a small person can step a fairly heavy, unwieldy mast. Once the mast is upright, the line may be secured to the mast to maintain tension while the individual goes forward and attaches the headstay to the bow chain plate.

After lowering the mast, unbolt the foot and slide the spar forward so that it can be secured in its regular trailering position.

Larger Boat 6- and 8-Stay Mast-Stepping

In rigging a larger boat such as the Com-Pac 19 with six stays, a similar procedure is followed: Bolt the mast foot to the mast step with the mast lying aft resting on the companionway hatch or stern pulpit if one is present. Run the upper stays outboard of the lifelines if they are there and attach them to the outboard chain plates with pins and cotter keys. Run the lower stays inboard of any lifelines and attach them to the inboard chain plates with pins and cotter keys. Run the backstay inboard and under any stern pulpit rail and attach it to the stern chain plate with pin and cotter key. Make sure all the turnbuckles are screwed out to their maximum length. Lift the mast to its upright position, using whichever method is easiest for you. On the Com-Pac 19 and 23/II, you would stand atop the companionway hatch to do this. Maintaining tension on the upright mast, go forward and attach the headstay to the bow chain plate with pin and cotter key or quick release pin.

After it is secured, release tension on the mast and screw the headstay and backstay turnbuckles closed until the stays are taut and the mast stands perpendicular to the waterline. The final tightening of the forestay and backstay turnbuckles should be done with a screwdriver in the turnbuckle's slot while the pressed cable fitting is being held with pliers to prevent it from turning. Usually four or five turns should be adequate. Only the forestay and backstay are tightened until they are quite taut.

Next, take up slack equally on the two uppers until they are snug. Then take up the slack in the two lowers but do not snug them. If the lowers are too tight they will cause the mast to bow aft. Sight up the mast to make sure it is not crooked or bowed. If it is, make adjustments accordingly. Lock all the turnbuckles so that they will not unscrew by attaching cotter pins to the holes in the ends of the threaded shafts in the turnbuckles. Slide the boom gooseneck into the sail slot and tie the topping lift to the butterfly on the end of the boom.

When lowering the mast, always remove the boom first. Then loosen the forestay turnbuckle with screwdriver and pliers, and while maintaining tension on the mast, detach the headstay only and lower the mast until it rests on the aft pulpit or companionway hatch. The uppers, lowers, and backstay need not be detached or readjusted each time you rig your boat. Unbolt the mast foot, move it forward so that it can be secured for trailering. An easy mount for this is atop the bow pulpit and stern pulpit, using scrap carpet to cushion the contact surfaces, then lash the spar securely in place. Loose stays are coiled and secured with shockcord or line to the mast. To prevent the spar from flexing while trailering, another shockcord may be looped around the mast and secured to the mast foot plate.

For boats such as the Com-Pac 23/II with eight stays, a similar procedure with slightly different variations would be followed: Bolt the mast foot to the mast step with the mast lying aft, resting on the companionway hatch or stern pulpit. Run the upper stays outboard of any lifelines and attach them to the center chain plates with pins and cotter keys.

Run the lowers inboard of the lifelines and attach them to the aft chain plates with pins and cotter keys. Run the backstay inboard of any stern pulpit rail and attach it to the stern chain plate with pin and cotter key. Raise the mast. Attach the headstay to the outboard bow chain plate with pin and cotter key. Run the forward lowers inboard of the lifelines and attach them to the forward chain plates with pins and cotter keys. Screw the headstay turnbuckle almost closed so that there is forward rake in the mast. Screw the backstay turnbuckle closed until the headstay and backstay are tight. Next, take up the slack equally with the two uppers until they are snug. Take up the slack equally with the respective sets of lowers until they are snug. Sight up the mast to make sure it is not crooked or bowed. If it is, make adjustments accordingly. Lock all of the turnbuckles so that they will not unscrew by attaching cotter pins to the holes in the end of the threaded shafts of the turnbuckles. Slide the boom gooseneck into the sail slot and snug the backstay pigtail (on the 23/II) into the aft hole on the boom end (Fig. 7).

When lowering the mast always remove the boom first. Then loosen and detach the forward lower turnbuckles. Loosen and detach the headstay turnbuckle, taking precautions to maintain tension so that the mast does not fall. The uppers, aft lowers, and backstay need not be detached or readjusted every time you rig your boat. Lower the mast, unbolt the foot, and slide the mast forward so it can be secured to the boat for trailering.

Rigging the Sheets

Sheets are lines that control the sails on a boat. Today most of them are made of easy-on-your-hands, easy-to-handle braided nonstretch Dacron. Most sailboats have a mainsheet and a jib sheet, the lines that adjust these respective sails. Wherever sheets rub against a hard surface, they will eventually chafe. Whenever excessive chafing occurs, the sheet

MAINSHEETS

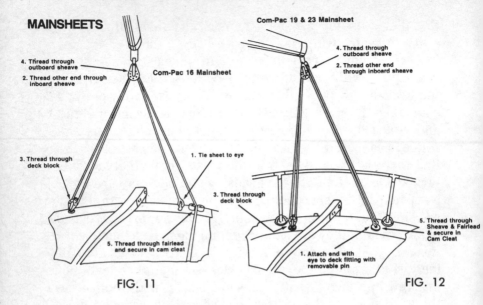

Com-Pac 19 & 23 Mainsheet

4. Thread through
   outboard sheave
2. Thread other end through
   inboard sheave

Com-Pac 16 Mainsheet

4. Thread through
   outboard sheave
2. Thread other end
   through inboard sheave

3. Thread through
   deck block

1. Tie sheet to eye

3. Thread through
   deck block

5. Thread through fairlead
   and secure in cam cleat

FIG. 11

1. Attach end with
   eye to deck fitting with
   removable pin

5. Thread through
   Sheave & Fairlead
   & secure in
   Cam Cleat

FIG. 12

JIBSHEETS

The jibsheets should be folded in half then threaded through
the clews of the jibs as shown (Fig.13).

Clew of jib
Sheet folded in half

FIG. 13

Run sheet outboard
of shroud

Thread through Fairlead

Com-Pac 16 Jibsheet

FIG. 14

Courtesy of Hutchins Co., Inc.

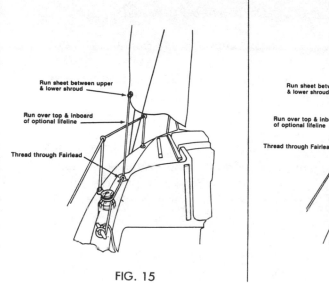

FIG. 15

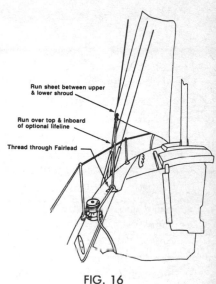

FIG. 16

Courtesy of Hutchins Co., Inc.

should be replaced before it fails when you may need it the most.

The rigging of jib sheets on most sailboats is generally similar, but there are several ways of rigging the mainsheets. On catamarans, for example, where a lot of sail powers a small amount of boat, a more complex line-to-sheaves combination with handy jam cleats makes managing the pull of the big mainsail less difficult for the helmsman to handle. Some boats employ traveler systems that enable the sheeting arrangement to shift from one side to the other during different angles of sail to better position the boom and mainsail for optimum performance.

Rather than try to discuss all these various arrangements, those shown Figs. 11-16 will explain the basic installation of the sheets on standard sloops such as the Com-Pac yachts.

Bending On (Putting On) the Sails

Modern sails are made of Dacron, a marvelous synthetic material ideally suited for the kind of job sails are expected to do. It is relatively lightweight, hard-surfaced, practically impervious to air passing through its pores, mildew resistant, fast drying, and extremely durable. Truly a miracle material. About the only things that may eventually bother Dacron sails are the prolonged exposure of the sails to the ultraviolet of sunlight which causes deterioration, and repeated chafing. Dacron sails are so tough that any sewing leaves the thread in an exposed position on its surface. If a section of sail is repeatedly rubbing against something such as a sidestay, these threads are the first to go. For that reason, sidestays, where this may occur, are often enclosed in such antichafing materials as plastic tubing or lengths of PVC that sometimes act as roller guides to cut down on sail wear and tear.

New boat sails will be stowed inside the boat in heavy-duty Dacron sailbags, each usually tagged with the sail it contains. The first thing you will want to do is to remove the mainsail from its bag and insert the sail battens.

These are thin wood or plastic pieces one to three feet long in some cases. They are extremely important in shaping the mainsail properly so that it and your boat will perform at their best. If these battens are made of flexible plastic or fiberglass, they can be inserted directly into the batten pockets located along the leech of the sail (see Figs. 1 & 18). In some boats, such as the racing catamarans, these pieces, of two or three different lengths, are made to fit individual correspondingly sized pockets. Select the correct pocket, insert the batten, and secure it with the light line provided by passing the line through the grommets in the batten pocket and the hole in the end of the batten, if one exists. These battens are intended to protrude a couple of inches from the batten pocket.

On other boats such as the Com-Pac yachts, the battens are

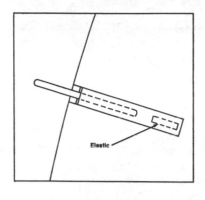

FIG. 17

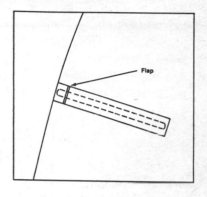

FIG. 18

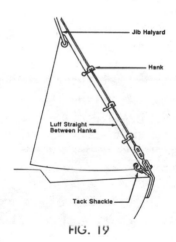

FIG. 19

Courtesy of Hutchins Co., Inc.

of wood and will be inserted completely into their individual pockets. Failing to install them properly can lead to their being lost under sail. Before you insert them, however, it is advisable that you give them two coats of new wood sealer such as polyurethane. This precaution prevents the battens from remaining damp in their pockets and attracting mildew.

Once the battens are properly sealed, insert them in the batten pockets of the correct length. When it is inside, press the batten further into the pocket against the elastic at the inside end of the pocket so that it stretches. Then pull the flap or leech seam at the outer edge of the sail over the end of the batten and release the batten so that the elastic pushes it into the outer end of the pocket (Fig. 8).

Bending On the Mainsail

On most boats the mainsail is held to the mast and boom by one of two ways: slides in a track, or by a rope sewed into the luff and foot of a sail (called a bolt rope) that slides into a groove on the mast and boom. The mainsail on the Com-Pac 16 has this kind of bolt rope.

With the boom in place, and supported by its topping lift, insert the mainsail's clew bolt rope into the groove along the top of the boom and slide the sail out to the boom end. Next, attach the tack of the mainsail to the gooseneck by sliding the pin on the gooseneck through the grommet in the tack of the sail (Fig. 8).

To tension the foot of the mainsail, attach the outhaul line to the grommet in the clew of the sail, run it through the hole in the boom end and tie it off at the outhaul cleat as shown in the illustration.

Now, start the mainsail head into the slot on the aft side of the mast. Attach the main halyard to the head of the sail by the shackle and pin through the grommet that is provided for it, and pull the sail up with this halyard while feeding the luff rope into the slot (Fig. 8).

Hoist it until it is all the way to the top; then tie off the main halyard on the starboard cleat provided for that purpose.

If your mainsail has plastic slugs shackled to the luff rope, then these slugs go into the slot on the mast as you hoist the mainsail and once they are all in, the provided sail stop will hold them in place (Fig. 9).

No matter how your mainsail attaches to the mast, the luff of the sail must be tensioned additionally to pull out the wrinkles and shape the sail. This is done by pushing down on the boom, allowing the gooseneck to slide in the mast groove. A downhaul line secured to the bottom of the gooseneck will help do this. When is is snugged down to the desired tension, tie off the line on the downhaul cleat (Fig. 10).

Boats with topping lifts that hold the boom end up when the mainsail is down should now be loosened sufficiently so that the weight of the boom is supported by the sail. Com-Pac 23/IIs have a pigtail on the backstay to hold the boom. It should be disconnected from the remaining boom end hole while the mainsail is being raised.

Reefing the Mainsail

There are two methods of shortening the size of the mainsail so that the boat will sail with less heeling in high winds. On sails that are traditionally reefed, a line or two of grommets run parallel to the foot of the mainsail at two or more levels up the sail. These are called reefing points. They may or may not have short lengths of light line called reefing ties sewn in beside them.

When shortening sail and putting in a first reef, uncleat the main halyard and, while holding it in your right hand allowing the line to slip through, pull down the sail with your left hand until the closest line of reefing grommets is just above the boom. Cleat off the halyard. Roll up the loose sail and secure it atop the boom with either the light reefing ties, or by using a separate line to thread through the grommets and around the boom and sail, securing it at the forward and after end of the boom at the clew or leech ring cringle and at the luff or tack ring cringle (Fig. 20). Harden (take up) any slack in the downhaul.

The other method for shortening the mainsail is called roller reefing. Lower and cleat off the mainsail with the main halyard as before. Grasp the boom in each hand, pull aft to disengage it from the spring-loaded gooseneck socket, then roll up the loose sail on the boom by rotating the boom until the excess sail has been taken up. Be sure that the sail rolls smoothly and that the topping lift does not get tangled in it (Fig. 10).

Roller reefing will allow you to shorten sail to almost any amount. If you wish to reef beyond a batten, it will have to be removed from its pocket. When you finish rolling, allow the boom to snap back into position at the gooseneck. Then take up any slack in the downhaul. Since the leech of the sail is longer than the luff, the end of the boom will have dropped lower than before, giving less clearance in the cockpit. This is normal. When sailing it this way, however, you will have to duck your head when the boom crosses the cockpit while coming about from one tack to another.

Bending On Jibs

The jib or foresail is attached to the boat by snapping the tack to the tack shackle and the jib hanks to the headstay (Fig. 19). With the jib halyard attached, the jib is ready to be raised. The jib luff should be tensioned so that it will be straight between the hanks when the wind has filled the sail. Haul the jib halyard taut and cleat it off to its cleat on the port side of the mast.

Preparing the Boat for Trailering

Masts and booms that came taped to the frame of your new boat trailer will now be carried atop the boat. How, is a matter of choice, depending upon the kind of boat and the optional equipment you have. Bow pulpits and stern pulpits make excellent supports, if you have them. The Com-Pac 16, however, may have only a bow pulpit. And since I want to be

REEFING PROCEDURE

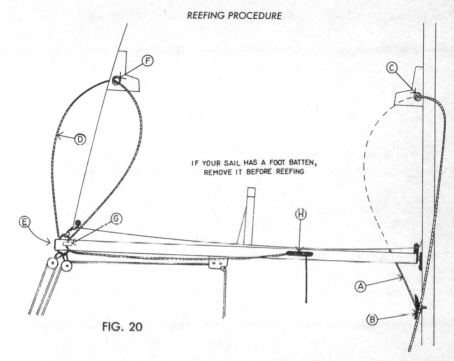

IF YOUR SAIL HAS A FOOT BATTEN,
REMOVE IT BEFORE REEFING

FIG. 20

Courtesy of Capital Yachts, Inc.

Run a knotted ¼" line (A) through the center of the downhaul cleat (B), up through the "tack" reefing cringle (C), and back down to the downhaul cleat. Tie or run a knotted ¼" line (D) through an eye-strap (E) on the end of the port side of the boom and run it up through the "clew" reefing cringle (F), down through a bullseye (G) on the end of the starboard side of the boom and forward to a cleat (H) on the starboard side of the boom. These two lines may be installed permanently or rigged only when excessive wind threatens.

Release the main halyard and lower the sail enough so that the reefing cringles come down to the top of the boom. Release the downhaul and pull line A down so as to bring cringle C snug against the boom and secure the line on the downhaul cleat. Pull forward on line D so as to bring cringle F down to the boom to the desired tension and secure it to the boom cleat H. If your sail has reef points, tie these securely under the boom with reef knots (square knots). Raise the sail to the desired tension (usually firm for strong wind conditions) and your mainsail is reefed.

able to get inside the cabin of my boat while it is on its trailer, I do not want the mast interfering in this area. The best way I have found to avoid it is by fashioning a boom and mast crutch. If your boat lacks a bow pulpit, two such crutches will do the job. They simply support the mast with boom lashed beside it atop a V-post fore and aft. The forward one fits the mast foot plate and is through-bolted snugly in place as if it were the foot of the mast. The aft crutch was built to fit a two-by-four-inch cross bar on which are mounted the rear trailer lights. The first thing one should do to any boat trailer is to remove the taillights and get them up high somewhere where they will be out of the water during launching. Once water enters these lights they may corrode and fail to work.

On my Com-Pac 16, the light bar is secured in place by a boat strap obtainable in most boat supply stores. Standard lengths are eight and twelve feet, and they easily tighten under a boat's hull to (in this instance) cinch the light-bar/boom-mast crutch in place. The best type of tie-downs I have found for quickly securing the mast and boom together, then this unit to the crutches, are those that have padded metal loop hooks on each end and can be bought in a variety of lengths from many different outlets. They are bungee shock-cords and those used at the crutches have four, rather than two ends and are linked together in the middle. In attaching these tie-downs, be extremely careful. If one of the hooked ends accidentally slips out of your grasp while under tension, it is likely to do more than just bruise you. So when fastening them, give them plenty of leeway in case they come loose.

As mentioned earlier, all but the forestay on most boats can remain attached to the boat. Coil the slack and secure them to the mast and boom with short shockcord tie-downs. Be sure that the coils are not where they can bounce against the gel-coat while the boat is trailered or they leave unsightly dark marks. Use pieces of foam rubber or carpet squares wherever chafing might occur, for example between the boom and mast. These spars have a special anodized finish and if they

The homemade light-bar/boom-mast crutch on my Com-Pac 16 does two things: it supports the mast and boom when trailering and gets the trailer's taillights up where they will be out of water during launching. The unit is strapped to the boat's stern; the electric wires unplug from it.

rub against one another, that finish will be finished for good. The aluminum in time will begin to turn chalky and will weather there.

On boats that have bow and stern pulpits, these are quite strong enough and high enough to support the mast with buffer pads between the metal surfaces. The spar is secured with shockcords. On my Com-Pac 19, I prefer to leave the mainsail rolled loosely atop the boom protected by its sail cover and the whole thing stowed in the cabin on the starboard berth with the cockpit cushions. Although there are a couple of stays to climb over, the companionway hatch is clear enough for easy entry. There are various ways to rig taillights so they are high enough to be out of water. Some run electrical wires up two-inch-by-four-foot lengths of PVC

On my Com-Pac 19, the mast is supported by the bow and stern pulpits. These are packed with strips of carpeting, and the mast is secured with shock cords. The coiled stays are secured to the mast similarly.

pipes and mount the lights atop them. These pipes are then jam-fitted over the short hull guides on the after end of the trailer. Another way that I used on *WindShadow,* my Com-Pac 19, was to make wing-nut clamps for each light and clamp them to the vertical supports of the stern pulpit. Plugs near the trailer frame enable me to remove each of the taillights before the boat is launched.

7

Trailers and Trailering

If you buy a used sailboat be sure that the trailer it is on is fully capable of transporting it. Few things are more disastrous than to spend a large amount of money for a trailerable cruising sailboat and then lose it in a highway accident caused by something preventable like a broken-down trailer.

Before taking it out on the highway, examine the trailer from one end to the other. It will take no expert to tell where the stress points are. Does the carpeting over the bolster boards hide rotten wood? How bad is the rust on the trailer? What conditions are the leaf springs and axle in? Are the tires about worn out? Are the wheels equipped with Bearing Buddies—easily regreased wheel bearings that can stand being submerged—or do they have standard bearings that might be dry and on the verge of burning out?

All these matters are vital to the well-being of the cruising sailboat you will be transporting on it. Your boat will represent not only a considerable investment, but a considerable payload. Be absolutely certain that your used trailer can handle it without question. If there is any doubt in your mind, correct the problem before you try hauling the boat. Your trailer is like an insurance policy. Far more accidents are likely to happen to your boat while it is being trailered on the highway than when it is being sailed on the water. Rather than chance a doubtful trailer, either junk it or trade it in for a new one. If nothing else, it will give you peace of mind.

Whether it is new or used, your trailer must be registered. Federal law requires compilation of trailer and tire registration information. Forms are provided for you to complete and send in to comply with this requirement.

The purpose of these forms is to make it possible for the manufacturer of the trailer to contact first purchasers of his product if it becomes necessary to issue a defect notification concerning the tires and/or trailer. Be sure to complete these registration forms and mail them in according to the instructions. It is your guarantee that you will be notified in the unlikely event that a recall of your trailer becomes necessary.

Trailer laws covering such things as brakes, lights, safety chains, licenses, etc., will vary from state to state. Be sure your trailer is in full compliance with your state laws. Your trailer dealer can usually help you in this regard. If not, contact your nearest state motor vehicle department for full information.

A Proper Match

The key to carefree boat trailering is proper matching of boat and trailer. A proper match is one in which the trailer is designed and built to carry the full weight of your boat, engine, and gear, and which provides proper support for the boat hull. Most sailboat companies that sell custom-made trailers as optional items for their sailboats will have already made sure that their trailer is more than adequate for carrying their company's product. The boat trailers used for the different sized Com-Pac yachts, for example—boats with full keels—must have the supports positioned to adequately fit the special shapes of the company's boat hulls and keels.

(top) Because of the different hull designs, some boat companies sell custom-made trailers with their boats. For example, the Stiletto catamaran shown has a trailer that is expandable for proper hull positioning prior to launching and retractable to meet highway trailering laws. Moreover, the trailer winch and special arm (bottom) facilitates stepping the mast on this twenty-seven-footer.

Your boat will probably spend more time on its trailer than in the water. Therefore, it is vitally important that the hull is evenly and uniformly supported at all times, and that it is held securely in place when underway. An improperly supported hull can lead to poor, even unsafe, boat performance, if the hull surfaces become warped.

A professionally built trailer that comes from the factory with your boat will have its bolsters and sets of rollers already properly positioned beneath key structural members of the hull and keel. Still, minor adjustments in the location and/or angle of bolsters, winch, or rollers may be necessary if problems develop in the trailering or launching of the boat. For example, your boat may be properly balanced on its trailer with adequate tongue weight when it comes from the factory empty. But by the time you load the boat, add a heavy outboard motor to the motor mount along with other heavy additions aft, such as a pair of scuba tanks and diving gear stowed temporarily in the boat's cockpit, that balance will change. Now the trailer may have so little weight on its tongue that as it is being towed at higher speeds it begins to fishtail (sway from side to side) as it moves down the highway. This puts excessive strain on the trailer, the towing equipment, and sometimes causes an accident. To correct it, you will have to change the balance by shifting the load farther forward.

Experts on such matters tell us that 5 to 10 percent of the total weight of your *loaded trailer* should be felt at the trailer coupling ball when the trailer tongue is parallel to the ground. A bathroom scale supported at the proper level can be used to weigh the tongue. Check the information supplied by the trailer manufacturer to see if there is a specific percentage for your trailer model. For example, if the gross weight of the trailer and gear is 2,000 pounds, the weight on the tongue should not be more than 200 pounds, nor less than 100 pounds. (Most auto manufacturers recommend that the

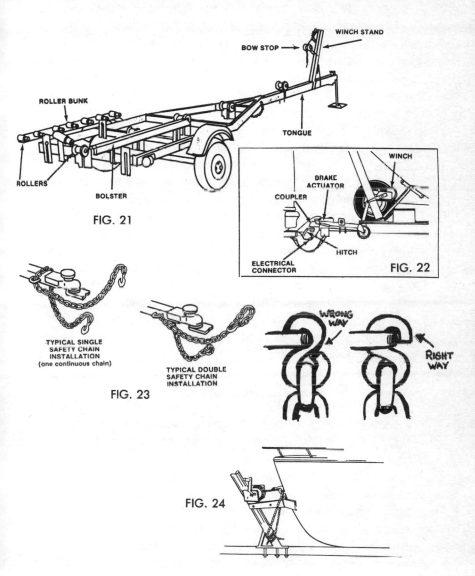

WINCH STAND

BOW STOP

ROLLER BUNK

TONGUE

ROLLERS

BOLSTER

FIG. 21

WINCH

BRAKE
ACTUATOR

COUPLER

ELECTRICAL
CONNECTOR

HITCH

FIG. 22

TYPICAL SINGLE
SAFETY CHAIN
INSTALLATION
(one continuous chain)

TYPICAL DOUBLE
SAFETY CHAIN
INSTALLATION

FIG. 23

WRONG
WAY

RIGHT
WAY

FIG. 24

Courtesy of the National Marine Manufacturers Association

weight on the tongue should not exceed 200 pounds when using a weight-carrying hitch with their full-sized cars.)

If the tongue weight on the coupling ball does not fall within the proper range, you should take steps to achieve it. Only a small adjustment may be required. Possibly you can solve the problem by simply shifting some of your gear in the boat—gas tank, anchor, motor, diving equipment—from the cockpit or transom area, more toward the bow of the boat, or vice versa. If you feel there are trailer alterations needed that are more than you care to cope with, ask your dealer about making the adjustments for you. Sometimes, just shifting the winch and boat toward the hitch a few inches will provide the needed tongue weight. But the importance of having the proper weight on the hitch ball cannot be overemphasized.

Once your loaded trailer is properly balanced, you may find the tongue weight more than you care to lift when hitching up. Remember, that's 200 pounds worth on a 2,000-pound boat. You can save yourself a lot of backache by investing in a heavy-duty trailer tongue jack. An electric power winch to assist in loading the boat might be considered for the same reason. Both are available from trailer dealers and marine supply houses.

Trailer Hitches

A trailer hitch is the ball and associate coupler that attaches to your towing vehicle so that you may pull a trailer. Bumper hitches—a ball that attaches only to the towing vehicle's bumper—are *not* recommended with boat trailers.

Trailer hitches are rated according to the gross weight they carry. Gross weight means the weight of the trailer plus the weight of the boat plus the weight of everything being carried in the boat. These hitches are categorized in classes or types numbered one to four. Class one hitches will handle gross weights up to 2,000 pounds; class two hitches from 2,000 to

3,500 pounds; class three from 3,500 to 5,000 pounds; class four from 5,000 to 10,000 pounds.

These hitches bolt directly onto the towing vehicle's frame. Thus the weight is distributed evenly. Be sure that the total weight of your trailer, boat, and load does not exceed the hitch's load capacity. The maximum weight a hitch can carry is stamped on it. Also, be sure the hitch ball is the right size to match the coupler on your trailer. The correct ball diameter is marked on the trailer coupler, too. The hitch also should provide a place for attaching the trailer's safety chains—two rings or holes on either side of the hitch ball. Not every vehicle will take just any kind of trailer hitch. Each make of car and each type of towing vehicle will take a certain kind of hitch that is made especially for that kind of vehicle. Your trailer dealers and such places as Sears, Roebuck and Co. will have listings of the make, year, and model of vehicles and the type of trailer hitch that will fit that particular vehicle.

Once you have selected the proper trailer hitch and ball to fit your trailer, unless you are a professional, do not try to install the hitch yourself but have it done by a professional who has the correct tools and knows how to do the job properly. Your dealer can advise you.

Fig. 21 shows a basic boat trailer and its parts. Fig. 23 shows the arrangement of safety chains on the trailer tongue. Whether your trailer has a single safety chain or a double chain, almost all state laws require that these chains be crisscrossed under the trailer tongue and properly hooked to the holes or rings on each side of the hitch ball. The reason for crisscrossing the chains is to prevent the tongue from dropping to the road if the trailer coupler separates from the hitch ball. The chains should be rigged with just enough slack to permit tight turns. Special care should be taken in how the "S" hooks are hooked onto the rings. Hook them in such a way that a bumpy road will not jump the hooks out of their rings. Fig. 23 shows a proper hookup. If a chain requires replacing, select a replacement that has the same minimum breaking strength as the original. Never replace it with a lighter weight chain. Minimum breaking strength of the safety chain should equal the gross weight of your boat, load, and trailer.

If you are towing quite a heavy rig, look into the heavy-duty hitches employing spring bars. These bars help take up the stress of a heavy load on the rear end and redistribute it over the entire vehicle; thus the hitch becomes a device for pulling the load rather than supporting it.

Trailer Winches

All but the smallest trailers are normally equipped with a winch assembly to assist in loading your boat on its trailer. These are hand-cranked affairs with special gear-locking devices to prevent the load backing up on you. Supposedly adequate winch rope or cable to handle your size boat will be coiled on the winch drum. Again, if this is a used trailer, or a universal trailer that has been used for other boats, make sure the winch and its rope or cable are in good shape throughout and can take the enormous stresses that will be expected of them. If the rope or cable shows signs of excessive wear, replace it. On all new boat trailers, the industry standards require that the minimum breaking strength of the winch rope or cable must be at least 150 percent of the minimum breaking strength of the winch rope, or 125 percent of the breaking strength of a steel cable. Fig. 25 shows the minimum breaking strengths of trailer winch ropes and cables presently in use on trailers.

Ideally, your winch assembly should be located so that it will pull the boat in a straight line onto the trailer and draw the bow firmly against the bow stop on the winch stand. Boat trailer winches are designed to load and unload boats, not to hold boats in place on the trailer. A severe bump in the road

FIG. 25

MINIMUM BREAKING STRENGTH (Pounds) FOR TRAILER WINCH ROPE* AND CABLE

DIA. OF ROPE	POLYETHYLENE		POLYPROPYLENE		NYLON		DACRON	Dia. of Cable	7x19 AIRCRAFT CABLE	
	Twisted	Solid or Diamond Braid	Twisted	Solid or Diamond Braid	Twisted	Solid or Diamond Braid			GALVANIZED OR TINNED PREformed	STAINLESS STEEL PREformed
1/4″	1200	1100	1275	1100	1650	1200	1450	1/8″	2000	1760
5/16″	1750	1700	1900	1750	2500	2000	2200	5/32″	2800	2400
3/8″	2500	2500	2600	2450	3200	2750	3100	3/16″	4200	3700
7/16″	3400	3400	3250	3000	4650	4400	4200	7/32″	5600	5000
1/2″	4100	4000	4200	4000	6000	5000	5300	1/4″	7000	6400

*Rope should withstand a sustained load at 2/3 of the tabled values for at least 5 minutes. Rope that does not meet this minimum requirement is not suitable for trailer winch rope.

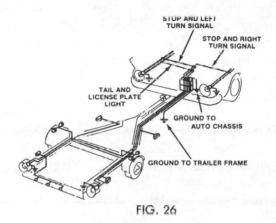

FIG. 26

might cause the winch to release. Use a separate bow tie-down that will pass through your boat's towing eye and tie low on the winch pedestal while trailering, as shown in Fig. 24.

Your trailer/boat dealer should see to it that your winch assembly is properly positioned. It is a good idea to check frequently to see that nothing has shifted and that the bow of your boat is being held properly in place while the stern or transom is resting squarely over the transom supports of the trailer.

Even on new boats with new trailers and winches that have not caused any problems, be careful in loading the boat. I've known of at least one instance where for some reason a heavy new boat was not rolling up properly on the bed of its trailer when being loaded at a launching ramp. The whole rig was so new that the boat owner did not yet have a feel for the difficulty he could expect in this procedure. So, when the boat seemed more reluctant than usual in coming aboard, rather than pushing it back and starting over, the owner continued to winch it in. He winched until he bent his winch pedestal severely enough that it was then impossible to bring the boat all the way onto the trailer. What he did was unload, leave the boat tied to a dock, and tow the trailer off in search of a welder who could straighten and reinforce the winch. On top of his difficulties, it was Sunday, the most popular day in the week for these troubles to occur.

The lesson learned: If the boat doesn't feel right when it is coming onto the trailer, stop winching and find out what is wrong. Far better to start over again than to do it wrong. This advice is especially important when using an electric winch. With one of them you may not be able to feel an obstacle that may be holding back your boat. But with any change in the sound of the winch as if it is laboring, be ready to stop winching at once.

Lights

Probably one of the biggest bugaboos to afflict the trailer boater is getting his trailer lights properly wired so that they perform in the same way as his towing vehicle lights. When you switch on your right turn signal, you surely don't want your left turn trailer signal to go on. Since state and federal regulations require all types of trailers to be equipped with tail, stop, turn, and side marker lights, you want them all working properly. Once they do so, take time to check them often so that you can maintain them in good operating condition. Fig. 26 shows a standard wiring diagram for car and trailer.

A special wiring harness, often called a pigtail, for connecting trailer lights to the lighting system of the tow vehicle will either come with the trailer or may be purchased separately at most auto supply houses. Be sure that the white ground wire from the connector is attached to the frame so that the hitch ball does not have to act as an electrical connection. Note: Some late model cars have yellow turn signals and separate (red) stop lights. In this case, a special wiring adapter will have to be installed in the car, unless you have a similar system on your trailer. If you run into insurmountable problems in hooking up your car-to-trailer lighting system, take it to an auto mechanic who knows what he is doing and let him connect it properly for you. All trailer dealers are also capable of helping you do this.

Beware of any jiffy connectors that pinch down over wires to make contact through the insulation. Some of these contacts may vibrate loose or the connectors may be so inferior that the next bumpy trip you make may douse some of your trailer lights. For more permanence, take the time to solder and tape all connections.

Here are a few things you can do to keep your trailer lighting system in good working order:

(1) At lease once or twice a year, trace the wiring system from the tow vehicle to the trailer lights and back. Look for bare wires, cracked or chafed insulation, and corroded or rusted terminals. Notice if any wire may have rubbed off its insulation and shorted against the trailer frame. Look for and replace any corroded or rusted terminals. Be sure the white ground wire is still connected to the trailer frame. Repair or replace any questionable wiring.

(2) A dab of waterproof grease on plug contacts and light bulb bases will help prevent rust and corrosion. A shot of WD 40 lubricant into the pigtail connectors will eliminate corrosion and keep them working.

(3) Before every trip check for burned-out or broken bulbs, cracked or broken light lenses, etc.

(4) Carry spare bulbs and at least one extra pigtail connector. Both have been known to get broken or damaged before a boating trip is over.

Wheels, Tires, and Hubs

Because they are often exposed to water, trailer wheels and tires require more attention than the wheels and tires on your family car. The three major items to check are lug nuts, lubrication, and tire pressures.

Loose lug nuts can cause more than just annoying wheel wobble. You could lose a wheel! Before each trip, check for loose or missing lug nuts. When tightening lug nuts use a wrench of the right size and, if you lose a nut, replace it promptly. Take special care to assure that the replacement is the right type. While the threads of a lug nut may match, the nut may be a size that does not hold the wheel securely against the hub, even when fully tightened. Be sure a replacement nut is an exact match for the original.

Unless your trailer is equipped with water-protected hubs ("Bearing Buddy Protectors") try not to submerge them when launching or retrieving your boat. Water has a special talent for finding and seeping through the smallest opening. When a warm hub is submerged in cold water, any air inside the hub will contract and suck water into the best of seals. Since it is virtually impossible to avoid getting your wheels not only wet but, on full-keel boats, deeply submerged during the launching and boat retrieval, your best protection against wheel bearing damage from water is to always keep your wheel assembly fully lubricated.

If your trailer uses conventional wheel bearing grease, remove all old grease and water from the hubs, then repack the bearings with a water resistant wheel bearing grease and fill the hub cavity with this lubricant to allow as little room as possible for air or water. Saltwater submersion of your wheel bearings can be double trouble. Avoid the hassle: remove the caps of your hubs and replace them with a set of Bearing Buddy Protectors. These relatively inexpensive items provide permanent bearing protection and lubrication for your bearings. Water and dirt are kept out of the hub because the internal pressure of the Bearing Buddy is always automatically maintained at 3 psi. Once the protector is in place, all you have to do is keep it filled with grease from a grease gun made for this purpose. Bearing Buddy Protectors have an automatic relief feature that prevents overfilling or overpressurizing. The lubricant level can be quickly and easily checked by pressing on the spring-loaded protector's piston. These protectors have stainless steel interior parts, and triple chrome-plated barrels. Each unit is inspected to ensure tight hub fit. They will not crack or pop out and are built to outlast the trailer. They cost less than a set of replacement bearings and end the mess of repacking. I have repeatedly dunked my boat trailer in salt or brackish water for the last eight years without any problem due to leaking hubs and it still has its original set of Bearing Buddy Protectors in its wheels. They are available from most auto supply houses and marine supply outlets.

Tires

The most common cause of trailer tire trouble is underinflation. Trailer tires gradually lose a few pounds of pressure between trips. Since you seldom see a small loss, you may think they are properly inflated. Anxious to get off on your trip and go sailing, you'll have a natural tendency to overlook this seemingly small matter. But with today's high pressure, small diameter trailer tires, this slight loss may cause big problems.

Boat trailer tires often bear up under extreme loads. Being small they work harder than would larger size tires. Low inflation can cause overheating at high speeds and on a hot summer's pavement, hour after hour, the tire rubber can almost reach its melting point. If this is repeated long enough or if the tire's walls already are showing signs of stress and old age, you are courting high speed tire failure, the kind that may be serious enough to lead to a serious accident.

Always check your trailer tire pressures *cold* before starting on a trip. Keep them inflated to the maximum pressure for their load range which is printed on the wall of each tire.

Boat trailer tire treads seldom wear out before the side walls do. One reason for this kind of deterioration is habitual underinflation. Another is that your boat and trailer spend a lot of time sitting still in one place constantly being stressed in one direction. Couple that with weathering—wind, rain, hot and cold temperatures—and soon tiny cracks of deterioration and breakdown begin to appear over the sidewalls. Here's how to double the life of your trailer tires:

If your boat trailer is merely stored and not used through the winter, get its wheels off the ground. Jack the wheels off the ground and block your trailer securely. Then wrap the wheels in plastic garbage bags to help protect them from the elements. This, a tire expert assured me, will make boat trailer tires last twice as long as they would without this care. Considering the cost of those tires today, it's well worth the trouble. Indeed, it would pay to do it any time of the year that your boat will be sitting unused on its trailer for a prolonged length of time.

The one problem I have had with trailer tires had to do with the fact that they were rated right on the borderline of the boat and trailer's combined load capacity. When I loaded an additional few hundred pounds of boating gear and cruising supplies into the boat, I was that many hundreds of pounds over their load limit.

That indiscretion cost me a new set of tires, a set that jumped up into a much better load range so that the tires were more than adequate to carry the excess.

To learn how much your trailered load weighs, pull into a highway truck weighing station, leave just the loaded boat and trailer on the scales, and find out. It may come as a surprise—as it did to me when I trailed in my 1,100-pound Com-Pac 16 fully supplied for a two-week cruise in the Florida keys. The trailer, boat, and load of gear weighed 1,900 pounds! Fortunately, my tires were rated for Load Range D of 1,075 pounds each, capable of carrying a total 2,150 pounds.

Tire failure on the highway can make you more than ever appreciate the Good Fairy who suggested you carry a spare. That third wheel coupled to your trailer tongue may never be used, but if you ever need it, nothing ever looked so good. In that regard, be sure that your towing vehicle carries a jack that will properly and safely jack up your boat and trailer. Modern bumper jacks and some of those special types made just for hoisting low-slung compact cars won't cut it. You need a good basic hydraulic jack or scissor jack adequate for your boat trailer's frame height. Better also carry a few pieces of two-by-fours to block it if necessary. And to be on the safe side, you had better try everything out before you leave home, just to be sure that the jack will do the job. Fig. 27 will give you an idea of available tire sizes and their load

TIRE LOAD CAPACITY AT VARIOUS INFLATIONS

Tire Size	Ply Rating	30	35	40	45	50	55	60	65	70	75	80	85	90	95	100
4.80/4.00 x 8	2	380														
4.80/4.00 x 8	4	380	420	450	485	515	545	575	600							
5.70/5.00 x 8	4		575	625	665	710										
5.70/5.00 x 8	6		575	625	665	710	750	790	830	865	900					
5.70/5.00 x 8	8		575	625	665	710	750	790	830	865	900	930	965	1000	1030	
6.90/6.00 x 9	4		785	850												
6.90/6.00 x 9	6		785	850	915	970	1030	1080								
6.90/6.00 x 9	8		785	850	915	970	1030	1080	1125	1175	1225	1270				
6.90/6.00 x 9	10		785	850	915	970	1030	1080	1125	1175	1225	1270	1320	1365	1410	1450
20 x 8.00-10	4	825	900													
20 x 8.00-10	6	825	900	965	1030	1100										
20 x 8.00-10	8	825	900	965	1030	1100	1155	1210	1270	1325						
20 x 8.00-10	10	825	900	965	1030	1100	1155	1210	1270	1325	1370	1420	1475			
4.80/4.00 x 12	4	545	550	595	635	680	715	755	790							
5.30/4.50 x 12	4	640	700	760	810	865	915									
5.30/4.50 x 12	6	640	700	760	810	865	915	960	1005	1045	1090	1135				
6.00 x 12	4	855	935	1010												
6.00 x 12	6	855	935	1010	1090	1160	1230	1290								
6.50 x 13	6	895	980	1060	1130	1200	1275									

FIG. 27

limit per tire. On a two-wheeled boat trailer their total load limit ratings should be in excess of the gross weight of your fully loaded trailer.

Trailer Brakes

In most states, trailers with a gross weight rating of 1,500 pounds or more are required by law to have brakes on all wheels. (Auto manufacturers generally recommend brakes with even lighter trailers.)

Most trailer brakes are designed to operate automatically when the tow vehicle's brakes are applied. These are known as "surge brakes." When the tow vehicle slows down or stops, the forward momentum (surge) of the trailer against the hitch ball applies pressure to a master cylinder in the trailer coupler. This pressure activates the trailer brakes through a hydraulic system much as the brakes on your automobile are activated.

Surge brakes usually do not have an automatic brake lining adjustment system; therefore, they should be adjusted regularly to compensate for wear, depending upon how often you use your trailer. The effectiveness of surge brakes decreases significantly if they are not properly adjusted. If the tow vehicle has power brakes, this is not always noticeable.

Try out your brakes before each trip and after each time your trailer wheels are pulled for lubrication. On a regular basis, have your brake linings inspected, necessary adjustments made, and any damaged or worn parts replaced.

If your trailer has surge brakes, do not shift to a lower gear and use your engine as a brake when going downhill. This would activate the trailer's brakes continuously for the duration of the downhill run, causing them to overheat and "fade" to the point where you may lose the trailer brakes entirely.

A better method is to slow down as you approach the crest of a hill, then maintain slow, controlled downhill speed with repeated applications of your tow vehicle's brakes, allowing enough time before brakings for the brakes to cool off.

Warning: Wet brakes usually don't hold very well. If your wheels have been in water, several brake applications at slow speeds will dry them out.

Tie-Downs

Ensuring that your boat is held securely in place on the trailer's hull supports, especially when underway, is extremely important. If it is not firmly and properly secured, your boat can be damaged as it bounces against the hull supports, or it may slide or fall off the trailer while being towed. Most large cruising type sailboats—those weighing 2,000 pounds and more—may not do as much bouncing as a lighter boat might. However, a safety strap that hooks to the trailer, passes over the after end of the boat, and can be cinched down snugly is always a good idea.

Depending upon your boat model and keel style, all the necessary tie-downs for holding boats on trailers may not be provided by the trailer manufacturer. Regardless of your trailer's make and model, there are two key areas to consider:

(1) Bow Tie-downs. A bow stop to hold the front of your boat in place is located on the winch pedestal. It should be positioned so that the winch line pulls the boat bow forward against the bow stop. A separate tie-down should then be attached to hold the boat *downward and forward.* This may be accomplished by a line from the bow eye on the boat to an attachment point on the trailer frame or winch pedestal. Be sure the line does not pass over a rough edge that may chafe it, or that it is not rigged so that it will slide back on the tongue and fail to hold the boat against the bow stop (see Fig. 24).

(2) Rear Tie-downs: As noted previously, it is important to

be sure that the transom of your boat is resting fully and securely on the supports provided at the rear end of the trailer, and that it remains in place when parked or underway. Special rear tie-downs are available for this purpose. Check often to be sure that these tie-downs are securely locked in place and that they are tight enough to prevent any movement of the boat. Check by rocking the boat on the trailer. If it does not remain firmly in place on the supports, tie-downs should be tightened or rerigged.

Hitching Up

Hitching your boat trailer to your tow vehicle usually is a one-man job, but it is easier if you have a second person to help you. Here are the basic steps:

(1) Back your tow vehicle as close as possible to the trailer; it is easier and safer than pulling the trailer to your car or truck.

(2) Check to be sure that the coupler locking device is released.

(3) Raise the front end of the trailer and boat, position the coupler directly over the hitch ball, and lower it until it is all the way down over the ball.

(4) Check under the coupling to be sure that the ball clamp is *below the ball* and not riding on top of the ball.

(5) Lock the coupler to the hitch ball. To be sure that it is in the locked position and securely in place, raise up on the trailer tongue. If it comes loose from the ball, unlock it and go back to step #3.

(6) Be certain the jack is in the fully raised position.

(7) If you have a weight-distributing hitch with spring bars, follow the above procedures, then attach the spring bar chain or cable to the trailer and tighten until the trailer and car are in a normal level position.

(8) If your trailer has a surge brake breakaway cable or

chain, attach it to the tow vehicle, making sure there is enough slack for tight turns.

(9) Attach the safety chains as shown in Fig. 23.

(10) Connect the trailer wiring harness to the lighting system of the tow vehicle and check its operation.

Trailering Tactics

With a boat trailer in tow you are operating a vehicle combination that is longer, heavier, and sometimes wider and taller than your car or truck. This means that you will have to make a few adjustments in normal driving practices to compensate for the difference. Here are some tips that will help:

Take a "Shakedown" Cruise: Before you make your first trip with your trailer, take at least one short trial run to familiarize yourself with its handling characteristics and to be sure everything is working properly—lights, brakes, hitch, etc.

Slow Down: There is less strain on your car, trailer, and boat at moderate to slow speeds. Also, many states have lower speed limits for vehicles towing trailers.

Allow Extra Time and Space: You will need more of both when passing and stopping, especially if your trailer is not equipped with brakes. Watch not only the vehicle ahead of you, but those ahead of it to anticipate possible sudden stops.

Check Rearview Mirrors: Outside rearview mirrors on both sides of the tow vehicle are recommended and required in some states. The addition of small wide-angle mirrors helps cover blind spots but remember that they distort reality: vehicles will appear farther away than they actually are. Make it a habit to check the mirrors frequently to see that your trailer and boat are riding properly.

Swing Wider: Trailer wheels are closer to the inside of turns than the wheel on your car or truck. This means you should swing wider at curves and corners.

Pass With Extra Care: With a trailer in tow you need more time and distance to accelerate, get around a slower vehicle, and return to the right lane.

Watch the Wind: Be prepared for sudden changes in air pressure and/or wind buffeting when larger vehicles pass you from either direction. Slow down a little and keep a firm hold on the steering wheel.

Conserve Fuel: Wind resistance against the boat and trailer will reduce your gas mileage significantly, especially at higher speeds. Make sure all hatches and ports are closed, and any ventilators are turned to the rear so they will not scoop in rain or bugs.

Avoid Sudden Stops and Starts: Even if your trailer has surge brakes, a sudden stop could cause it to skid, slide, or even jackknife. (Be especially careful to avoid the necessity for quick stops while turning.) Smooth, gradual starts and stops will improve your gas mileage and put less strain on your tie-downs, etc.

Signal Your Intentions: Well before you stop, turn, change lanes, or pass, use your light signals to let following and approaching vehicles know what you intend to do.

Shift to Lower Gear: If your tow vehicle has a manual transmission, traveling in lower gear when going up steep hills or over sand, gravel, or dirt roads will ease the load on your engine and transmission. If your tow vehicle has an overdrive gear (manual or automatic) you may get better gas mileage in a lower gear.

Always Be Courteous: Make it as easy as possible for faster moving vehicles to pass you. Keep to the right side of the road and be prepared to slow down if they need extra time to return to their proper lane.

Don't Tailgate: Allow at least one car and trailer length

between you and the car ahead for each 10 mph on your speedometer.

If a Problem Occurs: The general rule is to stay cool, don't panic, and don't do anything more suddenly or violently than you have to. A sudden bumping or fish-tailing (trailer swaying) may mean a flat tire. Don't jam on the brakes or mash the accelerator to drive out of it. Stop slowly and in as straight a line as possible. If conditions permit, allow your rig to coast to a very slow speed and try to avoid braking, except when your wheels are straight ahead and the trailer and your tow vehicle are in line.

If your trailer begins to fish-tail as you accelerate to highway speed, back off a little and it should cease. If it begins again as you accelerate, stop and check your load. Your load probably is not evenly distributed side to side or the load is too far back resulting in insufficient load on the hitch ball. Redistribute your load before continuing.

Launching

Every trailer sailor develops his own favorite launching technique. Until you do, here are a few helpful tips:

Check the Ramp First: Whether you are launching from an unimproved or a surfaced ramp, check it out before starting your launching procedure. How steep is it? Is the surface firm enough to support the weight of trailer and tow vehicle? Is it wide enough? How deep is the water at the end of the ramp? Some surfaced ramps become slippery when wet—is there enough traction? Is there debris such as seaweed or driftwood that needs clearing away first? Do you have wheel chocks to prevent your rig from sliding down the ramp?

Rig the Boat: Drive as close to the ramp as possible, select an out-of-the-way place, and set up your boat for launching. Take off the tie-downs. Ready (fuel if necessary) your outboard motor. Lift your rudder blade if necessary. Step your mast and bend on the sails. Do not hoist them but secure them with shockcord preparatory to hoisting. Be sure everything you want is loaded aboard your boat, ready for leaving the ramp.

Back Trailer to the Ramp: Have someone stand to one side of the ramp to direct you. Backing up a trailer can be tricky. A good way to simplify the procedure is to grasp the steering wheel with one hand at its lowest point (at 6 o'clock). When you want the trailer to go *right,* move your hand on the wheel to the *right;* to make the trailer go *left,* move your hand to the *left.* If the trailer goes too far in one direction or the other, you may have to straighten it out by driving forward again before backing up.

Stop when the rear of the trailer is a few feet from the water's edge (with most shallow draft sailboats). Otherwise, back down and stop before your *vehicle* wheels are in the water. (Again, this depends upon your keel and hull design.) Put your gear shift in Park, set the parking brake, and place chocks under either the front or rear wheels of the towing vehicle, since the lower ends of ramps are often wet and slippery. Trailer sailors with full-keel boats may have to back their trailers into the water until their trailer wheels are partially or entirely submerged. I use one large chock for the rear wheel. A line from it to the tow vehicle's bumper brings the chock with it when I leave the ramp.

Prepare for Launching: Attach a long bow line to your boat and be sure it is not tangled. Release the trailer tilting mechanism, if you have one. Release the tension on the trailer's winch cable and unhook it from the bow eye. Now push the boat off its trailer bed while letting the bow line slip through your hands. As it rolls off, give it plenty of slack until the boat clears the trailer and can be led either to one side of the ramp or to a nearby docking facility for securing and boarding.

Final Launching Step: Wind up and secure the winch

Before backing the boat and trailer into the water, be sure the mast and rigging is up, the boat trailer straps and tie-downs off, and that someone is watching out as the boat is backed into the water.

cable. Remove the wheel chocks and park your car and trailer where they will not obstruct access to the ramp. If you have had to submerge your trailer in brackish or salt water during the launch, drive to a nearby water faucet and wash off the trailer with the length of garden hose you always keep in the towing vehicle for this purpose.

Retrieving

Depending upon whether you have a full-keel sailboat or not, you may have to back your trailer farther down the ramp and into the water to retrieve the boat than when launching it. Essentially, however, it is the same process in reverse. To facilitate heavy boats sliding more easily over their carpeted trailer bolsters, some owners lubricate these with liquid detergent before loading the boat. Once the trailer is in position in the water, be sure the rear wheel chocks are in place, the towing vehicle is in Park, and the foot brake is on. Now release the dog on the winch and pull enough slack in the winch cable to be able to clip on the winch hook to the bow eye when the boat is within reach at the end of the trailer. With the bow line, lead the boat to the rear of the trailer. Release the trailer tilt mechanism and, while holding the boat in position with the bow line, attach the winch cable to the bow eye.

Winch up the slack and continue winching in the boat until it is on the trailer and its bow is up against the bow support. Secure your trailer tilt mechanism with the chain provided. Remove the wheel chocks. While maintaining pressure on your vehicle's foot brake, release the hand brake, then gradually give the vehicle gas as you remove pressure from your foot brake, and drive the trailer up out of the ramp to an out-of-the-way area nearby and park it. Unstep the mast and secure the boat with tie-downs, etc., for trailering home.

Final Retrieving Step: Drive the boat and trailer to a water faucet, hook up your hose, and give the entire rig a good rinsing off, remembering that if you used your outboard in salt water, it should be flushed out with fresh water.

Warning: To avoid injury if the winch line or hook gives way, always stand to one side while winching the boat onto your trailer.

Be sure all tie-downs are properly fastened and the outboard motor properly braced or removed from its motor mount and secured inside the boat before departing from the launching ramp area. Remember, wet brakes often will not hold. A few brakings at slow speed will help to dry them out.

As a final precaution before leaving the area and entering highway traffic, check to make sure that all your trailer lights and signals are working properly.

8

The ABCs of Sailing

Before you set sail, the Coast Guard requires that your boat carry certain safety items. Requirements vary according to the size of your boat. Check Coast Guard regulations to learn the specific requirements for your boat. Generally speaking, however, all boats should carry the following:

(1) At least one (two for larger boats) fire extinguisher capable of extinguishing gasoline, oil, grease, and electrical fires. These are usually dry chemical extinguishers and must be Coast Guard approved.

(2) A flame arrester for inboard gasoline engines. This unit is a metal screen set in a frame which is installed over the air intake over a carburetor.

(3) At least one wearable life jacket for each person in the boat.

(4) One hand, power, or mouth-operated horn or whistle audible for at least half a mile. (May be used as fog horn, emergency or bridge signal.)

(5) Ventilation ducts and cowls required to vent any fuel tank or engine compartment in which gasoline or other fuel is used. One duct should vent the bilge and another duct the

PERSONAL FLOTATION DEVICES (P.F.D.)

You are required to carry a type I, II, or III for each person on board and at least one type IV (Fig. 28). For maximum safety your P.F.D.s should be worn or at the very least stored in the open so that they are quickly accessible.

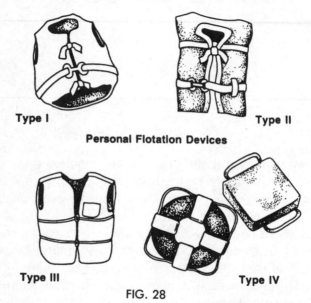

Type I

Type II

Personal Flotation Devices

Type III

Type IV

FIG. 28

Courtesy of Hutchins Co., Inc.

midsection of the gasoline compartment. A mechanical blower to vent fumes from the compartment should be installed. Diesel-powered engines require none of these.

(6) Visual distress signals will be required on all boats other than rowboats or open sailboats. For daylight use an orange flag or orange smoke signal is required. For night use a flare or signal light is required.

(7) Vessels are to be numbered (registered) in the state in which the vessel is principally used. If a vessel is equipped with propulsion machinery of any type and is used principally on the waters subject to the jurisdiction of the United

States and its territories, the certificate of number will be issued by the U. S. Coast Guard. A vessel used principally on the high seas is required to be numbered by the state in which it is principally used when not on the high seas.

Navigation Lights

If you operate your sailboat between sunset and sunrise, you are required to display appropriate navigation lights, or when anchored in or near a channel. *Running lights* required consist of a green starboard light, a red port light, and a white stern light. *Under power:* A forward white light is added to the running lights. It is usually located part way up the mast. *At anchor:* A 360° white anchor light, visible for two miles, is required.

For dinghies or sailboats under sixteen feet, only a flashlight is required. When needed to make other boats aware of your presence, it is suggested that the light be directed up onto the mainsail for maximum visual effect.

Once all these regulations are observed, you can take your boat sailing. But here is some recommended equipment you should have aboard in case it is needed: an anchor and anchor line; extra lines for mooring or towing; boat fenders to avoid hull scrapes at dockside; a portable light; a paddle; a compass; sunburn lotion; charts of the area; spare flashlight batteries; rainwear; a basic tool kit; spare bulbs; spare fuses; a shear pin; and spare plugs if you have an outboard motor.

Many books are written about sailing and many courses offered in safe boating procedures and sailing instructions. Gain your experience slowly. Read whatever books you can on the subject and try to take whatever lessons are available in your area. Sometimes in just one afternoon a friend can teach you a great deal about the basics of sailing. In any event, your first outings in your new boat should be in ideal conditions. Pick a day with clear skies, light breezes, and calm water conditions. In this way you will be able to familiarize yourself with your boat and the sensations of sailing under the best of conditions. Once you become more proficient at handling your sailboat, you can work progressively toward gaining experience in more varied conditions when the winds and seas are higher. It is important that you know your limitations and use prudence and common sense in all boating situations that you encounter. This discussion on sailing basics is intended only to give you an idea of how to begin so that you will understand some of the procedures that must be followed in order to sail.

I am not going to burden you here with the theories and principles of sailing. Other books do it better and far more thoroughly than I can in this short discussion. To better understand these things, however, I suggest that you study those books. They will help you be a better sailor.

For the purpose of this discussion, I will assume that you have a sloop-rigged cabin cruiser anywhere from sixteen to twenty-eight feet long. Assume too that we have a beautiful day for sailing with a breeze blowing about five or six knots.

When you get aboard your boat you will probably be in a somewhat enclosed area, a boat basin perhaps with other boats and docks nearby. The trick will be to get from this point out into the body of water where you will actually do your sailing.

I hope you will not have to rely on such things as a paddle or oars to move you and your boat out into the sailing breezes. Most people in this class sailboat will have some kind of power—an outboard or a small inboard engine. That is not to say that one cannot sail without these conveniences, or inconveniences as some purists might consider them. Some modern-day live-aboards have successfully cruised the waters of the world for decades without engine power. And while it may eventually become a point of pride with you to be fully able to sail anywhere you wish without such assistance, your boat will most likely also be equipped with some kind of auxiliary power. For now, this is what will get you from your boat dock, through other traffic, and onto the waterway.

Assuming you have an outboard on your motor mount, lower it into the water, make sure the fuel is on, the air intake valve open, and gear shift and throttle in their proper position before firing off. Make sure too that your docking lines are all in when you are ready to shove off.

Outboards that lack gear shifts may be turned 360° to provide such things as reverse when needed. Just be careful when turning the motor that its propeller does not strike the sailboat's rudder blade which may shear a pin. One quickly learns to manipulate both the tiller and rudder angle parallel to the angle of the outboard. In other words, to turn your boat acutely you must turn both the rudder and outboard motor simultaneously rather than allowing simply the outboard to power straight ahead while you try to turn the boat with its tiller.

Some of these marina boat basins are fairly tight so, whatever you do, do it at a slow rate of speed. Once you set in motion this heavy boat of yours it will tend to stay in motion. You had better be able to control where it goes, realizing of course that if you power along *too slowly,* you may not have any directional control at all. Only experience will teach you how slowly to go while maintaining adequate control.

Take your time and work your boat out onto the open water. Assuming you have cleared all obstacles without a problem, you now move out to where breezes can be utilized for sailing.

If possible, always try to begin a sail in which you intend to return to the same place, by sailing upwind: the direction from which the wind is coming. You do this so that, in the event the weather changes and conditions become more violent, it will be easier for you to turn tail and run before the weather, sailing downwind back to your boat dock or marina, rather than to get caught somewhere downwind and have to beat your way back upwind against possibly stormy conditions.

You can sail your boat in any direction except straight into the wind. You can sail to windward all right but you must do so by sailing a zigzag course that gradually takes you upwind, as shown in Fig. 29. Theoretically, sailboats can sail no closer than a 45° angle into the wind. This is called beating into the wind, or sailors say they are sailing a beat.

Any time the sailboat changes course and switches from taking the wind on one side of the sails until the boat is taking it from the other side, this turning from one course to the other, while *moving upwind,* is called tacking. The bow of your boat is said to pass through the eye of the wind.

When the boat is *moving downwind* and changes course so that the wind is shifted from one side of the sails to the other, this is called jibing as shown in Fig. 29A. So, with that bit of information, let's hoist the sails and beat upwind awhile.

With your outboard motor running slowly, turn your boat's bow into the wind. You can tell which direction the wind is blowing from by looking at the riffles on the water, or at the telltale—a wind pennant—you have wisely mounted atop your mast for telling you such things. This pennant will stream downwind telling you that the apparent wind is coming from the opposite direction.

Point your boat so that your pennant lies straight back over the center line of your sailboat. Now, while one of your crew members helps the boat maintain this heading, go forward to your mast, undo whatever binders are holding your furled mainsail on the boom and see that it is loose and ready for hoisting. Ask your helmsman to loosen the mainsheet sufficiently for the boom to swing freely.

Note: Always hoist sails with your boat bow pointing *into* the wind. If you try hoisting them in any other way, the wind will blow them aside and put such strain on the luff rope or sail slides that they will be difficult to hoist properly.

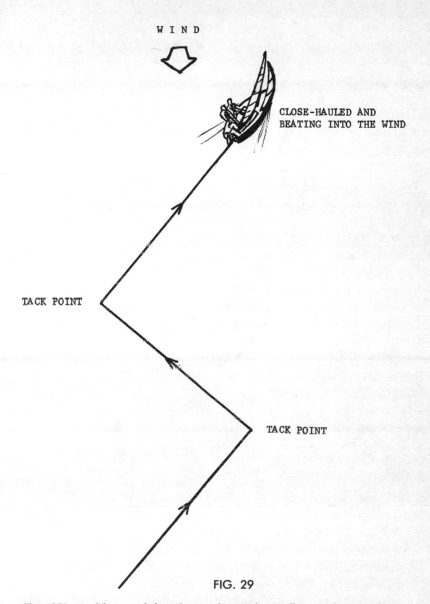

W I N D

CLOSE-HAULED AND
BEATING INTO THE WIND

TACK POINT

TACK POINT

FIG. 29

(Fig. 29). Unable to sail directly into the wind, a sailboat sails upwind on a right-angle zigzag course. Each time it changes course so the bow passes through the wind and the wind strikes the opposite side of the sails. This is called tacking.

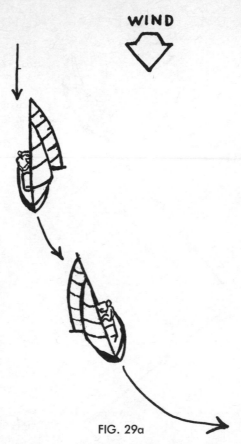

WIND

FIG. 29a

(Fig. 29a). The opposite of tacking into the wind is jibing downwind, as shown here. As the boat changes course while running downwind, shafting the wind from one side of the sails to the other, the helmsman should help the boom and sail swing across. Avoid jibing on a strong wind.

Uncleating the mainsail halyard, hoist the sail while guiding the sail slides or luff rope into the sail groove on the mast as you haul away.

With the sail up and fluttering, cleat off the halyard on the starboard side in the manner shown in Fig. 30. Next, undo the jib halyard, and hoist the sail to the top of the head stay, cleating off the line on the port side. Coil both the main and

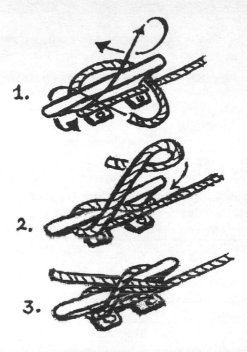

FIG. 30

jib halyards and hang them out of the way on their respective cleats. They are done this way so that you will be able to shake loose the coils and drop the sails quickly without the halyards becoming entangled.

Finally, pull down on the downhaul, pushing the boom lower in the mast groove so that the sail luff will be taut. Cleat off the downhaul.

Now the outboard can be shut off. Remember to screw shut the air vent, then lift the motor mount and tilt the motor forward to avoid drag. Steer the boat slightly off the wind and trim the sails by drawing in first the mainsheet and then the jib sheet until the sails stop fluttering and fill with air as the boat moves forward under sail.

The helmsman will want to sit on the windward side where he can handle the sails and rudder more easily. Once you have established the direction in which you want to sail, trim

135

(adjust) your sails so that they are getting the most drive out of the wind at that particular angle. To do this, let your sail out until it starts to luff (a fullness or fluttering of a sail as it is backwinded), then draw it in with its respective sheet until the luff stops. At this point the sails' angles and the boat's angle are just right for the angle of wind striking the sail. The boat will then move forward at its best rate of speed under these conditions.

All of these factors are variable. The wind angle can change suddenly and require either a change in the angle of the sails or a change in the angle of direction in which you are sailing. Or, you may change the direction of sail with the wind maintaining its same angle and then need to alter the angle of the sails. Each time these changes are made you can tell exactly what position the sails must have by finding the point where the sails luff, then sheeting them in to where they no longer luff.

You can do the same thing without touching the position of your sails. Simply steer the boat more into the wind or off the wind while you watch to see at which point your sails luff. Then steer a course just off enough to avoid the luff. When both your jib and mainsail are angled so that the luff has just gone, the sails are said to be in perfect trim.

Sailing then is almost a constantly changing experience if you wish to get the best performance possible from your boat under the existing conditions. That is not to say that one cannot sail badly. Unfortunately this is often done when sails are incorrectly adjusted to the available winds. The boat will still continue sailing but sails may be fluttering along their luff lines or they may be hauled in so tightly that certain sail configurations cause the boat to almost stall out. There is no need to go into these problems here; you will learn more about them as you become a more knowledgeable sailor. Concentrate instead upon watching sail luffs and trimming main and jib to obtain the best performance possible.

If you prefer to leave the sails where they are and the wind shifts slightly enough to cause the sails to luff, you can then change your boat's course to correct this.

Sailors have termed the direction in which a boat sails as her point of sail. There are five such directions or points of sail with their nautical terms which you will hear most about. If you think of a huge imaginary clock's face with the wind coming from the 12 o'clock position, when your boat is *beating* into that wind it will be traveling on an angle between 1 and 2 o'clock, or between 10 and 11 o'clock (Fig. 31).

If you sail the boat so that it is taking the wind on its side or beam, the boat is said to be on a *beam reach* and will be going in the direction of 3 o'clock or 9 o'clock.

If you turn the boat so that it is sailing with the wind, it will be heading toward 6 o'clock and the boat is said to be *running* before the wind.

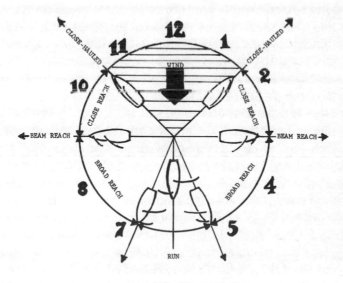

FIG. 31

The directions of sail between these cardinal points are termed sailing on a *close reach* or a *broad reach* as shown on the clock face. Also indicated are the changes in sail positions required for these different points of sail.

As you sail your boat more off the wind or downwind, you must let out your sails more. Note that on a beam reach, as the boat sails toward 3 o'clock or 9 o'clock, the sails are now almost halfway out. Again, as you sail this angle with the wind striking the side of the boat, the exact position or angle of your sails can be determined by watching for the flutter of the sail luff as you let out the sail, then trim it back to the point where the flutter stops. As you continue sailing more off the wind into the broad reaching areas, you will continue to let out both your sails until you reach a downwind point in which the wind is coming directly from astern, behind you; then your sails should be let all the way out so that they are able to catch as much wind as possible. In actually doing this, your mainsail will blanket or cover your jib, blocking it from the wind astern. At this point, with your mainsail perhaps on the port side, pull on your starboard jib sheet and bring the jib sail across to the opposite side so that it is now exposed to the wind on the starboard side and both sails are in a configuration termed "wing and wing"—the main full out on one side, the jib full out on the other.

In the illustration of the clock (Fig. 31), note that the sailboat sailing toward 6 o'clock and the one sailing toward 7 o'clock have their sails at quite different positions. This is exactly what would occur if you were sailing this course from a dead run with your sails as shown, the main to starboard, the jib to port. If you were to change course now into a broad reach toward 7 o'clock, a problem would occur in which your mainsail would begin to backwind: the wind would begin to strike it from the back side and it would have to be shifted over to the other side. This is called jibing. It is when the boat's stern passes through the eye of the wind. To do this you would sheet in on the main and help it around manually.

This changeover can be sudden if winds are high and can be a strain on rigging. Jibing is not something you would do on an excessively windy day. But in light airs it can be carried off quite easily. Failure to anticipate this can cause accidental jibes.

Similarly, the jib would need to be changed over to its opposite side. And if the sailboat continued angling back into the wind, then the sails would gradually be trimmed into their proper position, past the beam reach point eventually to the close-hauled configuration of the boat beating as closely as it can into the wind. In making this circuitous route, you have boxed the compass, sailing on all points of sail, and adjusted your sails accordingly.

If, on our imaginary clock face, 12 o'clock happens to be your destination, your marina or boat launching ramp, then to get there you must tack or turn the boat when it figuratively reaches the point between numbers 10 and 11 or 1 and 2 where the boat can be tacked across the eye of the wind on a 90° course directly to your docking destination.

Generally speaking, when you are on a beat, close hauled and sailing as tight as you can to the wind, when you face forward and extend your arm straight out at right angles, it will point directly at your next angle of sail when you tack, assuming that your boat is capable of sailing this closely to the wind and making good this 90° course. Many boats will not do this and are not that capable of achieving a right-angle approach. More often than not they can get no closer than an angle off their stern quarter.

How well your boat will handle this situation, only experience will tell. The important thing is that you learn where this angle is for your boat so you will know how far to sail on a tack before changing over to another. The ability of a boat to sail well close to the wind and to be able to maintain those 90° angles on her tacks is called "pointing." When you hear someone say that a sailboat really points well, this is what they mean. They know that when their final destination is directly off their beam, they can change course to a 90° angle and beat their way back directly to their mark.

There you have it, the bare bones basics of sailing. Some of the more important finer points, such as how to lay an anchor or how to sail in stormy weather, will be discussed in a later chapter.

9

The XYZ of It

What do you do when you are out sailing on a nice day with fair winds and suddenly the weather turns bad: both winds and waves begin to mount?

For those who know how to handle their boats, stronger winds and higher waves need not be something to fear. The classes of sailboats we are discussing are designed to handle these conditions and much worse. Stronger winds can provide some of the finest thrills in sailing. When conditions go beyond this and the weather actually threatens, that is the moment to be prepared to take precautionary actions.

Ideally, you want strong winds that are steady and not gusty. Gusty winds blow in short, powerful puffs, often from several different directions, making sailing more difficult. No longer are things moving smoothly and easily. The winds buffet your sails, your boat may lurch repeatedly under their onslaught, heeling more quickly and more often than you want it to. These conditions can sometimes grow more dangerous with the appearance of squalls—usually brief but possibly very violent combinations of high winds and rain. These should be avoided, if possible. Wind gusts in such sporadic storms may be as high as sixty miles an hour.

If you are caught offshore where you cannot avoid this disturbance, you can do one of several things: Drop your jib sail, secure it, and sail on the reefed mainsail as described earlier; or haul down and secure all sails and ride out the short storm under bare poles (with nothing standing but your mast). Naturally, the latter tactic should never be undertaken if your boat is anywhere near a lee shore. Another option is to lower and secure your sail, then head bow on into the turbulence with your iron wind (outboard or inboard engine).

If the weather deteriorates to the point where it looks as if you will be in for a long siege, the best bet is to reduce sail by reefing and try to ride it out. If in water shallow enough to anchor you might want to simply drop and secure sails, deploy your anchor, and duck below to wait it out.

In storm seas a sailboat is generally safer remaining away from land, rather than trying to claw back to harbor through possibly chaotic narrow channels between rock jetties or other narrow seaways that might under these conditions cause a calamity.

As you sail, learn to preview weather conditions so that you will have a general idea of what might come along. If your vessel is not equipped with a marine radio, a few dollars will buy you an inexpensive weather radio from your local Radio Shack. These miniature radios powered by inexpensive batteries will bring in any weather station broadcasting within fifty miles. Their continuous reports will give you a good idea of the kind of weather conditions that will develop over the next few hours. Similarly, before you go sailing on a weekend trip, take time to listen carefully to your television weather report, noticing from the satellite pictures what kind of weather fronts are due from the prevailing direction of your weather.

While sailing, keep a weather eye out at all times, watching for the buildup of clouds and possibly threatening local weather conditions. Learn to read the skies. Here is an invaluable tip for forecasting the weather by watching the winds:

When in the Northern Hemisphere—
- Face the prevailing wind.
- Look upward to the highest clouds. If they are moving *from left to right*, fair weather will follow.
- If the upper and lowermost clouds are moving *in the same direction*, or *in opposite directions*, the weather will not change.
- If the upper clouds are moving *from right to left*, the weather will deteriorate.

When in the Southern Hemisphere—
- If the highest clouds are moving from *right to left*, fair weather will follow.
- If the upper and lowermost clouds are moving *in the same or opposite directions*, the weather will not change.
- If the upper clouds are moving from *left to right*, the weather will deteriorate.

When winds become gusty, you can see them creating their characteristic "cat's paw" flurries of rough water around you. Such signs will give you a moment's warning that your boat is about to be pushed more intensely by a puff of wind. Under such conditions you might want to ease your sails and head up into such puffs so that your sails actually begin luffing and spill some of the powerful thrusts that might cause the boat to heel more steeply. A good rule of thumb if you are new to sailing is to start heading in when whitecaps begin covering the water. These foaming wave crests indicate intensifying wind conditions and if there is any doubt as to what may come afterward or in your ability to cope with rowdier conditions, it is far better to sail back to more sheltered waters to see what develops.

At all times when you go sailing be sure to be prepared for

any adverse weather: stow aboard sufficient rain gear to take care of everyone aboard. Ponchos are a quick and easy lightweight spring-shower type of rainwear but if you want more comfort and a drier seat, I would advise heavier duty rain gear that would include a waterproof jacket, hood, waterproof pants, and low-cut rubber boots. Be sure when buying such rainwear that you get a size large enough to allow you to wear heavy sweaters and shirts underneath for warmth.

When sailing in light airs, your sail will be shaped more in a full-pocket configuration. This is done by loosening the downhaul and outhaul so that the fuller the mainsail is the better it will catch and make use of the lighter breezes.

As the wind freshens, however, the sail should be flatter. Now you will want to reduce its curve or belly so that it no longer pockets the wind but is flat and less likely to luff. To do this the sail should be downhauled tightly and tensioned up on the outhaul so the sail has no wrinkles.

Some sails have a thin line sewn into the leech with a plastic fitting that will enable you to tighten or loosen this line which controls a cupping of the mainsail leech. As the winds increase and you flatten your sails, this leech line should also be untensioned so that the leech will uncup and hang straight.

Ever since the early days of sail, mariners have used a technique called "heaving to" to maintain their boat's position in good weather or to survive a storm in bad weather. What it amounts to is balancing the rudder with the sails in such a way that the boat stalls and remains in the same general area. Sometimes when you are sailing in fair weather you might like to park your boat in this manner while you have lunch. The easiest way to do it is as follows:

(1) Begin to tack, bringing the bow through the eye of the wind.

(2) Do NOT change your jib. Leave it where it is so that it *backwinds*.

(3) Instead of steering the boat all the way around, when the jib backwinds, bring the tiller smartly over to the opposite side from where it would be in a normal tacking position and lash it there with a line to the stern cleat.

(4) Slack the mainsheet so that the mainsail lies downwind like a pennant. Secure it there with a preventer line from the bow to the boom end.

The balanced boat is now stalled, and will do no more than slowly drift to the leeward.

Boats with deep full keels will probably heave to in this manner more easily than shallower draft centerboard boats which may be tossed around more by the wave action. Still, this is a neat maneuver for marking time in high or low winds with all sails standing. Deep water cruisers often heave to in this manner for overnighting at sea, losing comparatively little leeway in the process.

Another tactic worth knowing is how to jibe your boat while running downwind in a wind that is actually too strong to make jibing safe the regular way. Assume for example that you are on a port tack. This means that you are in a wing-and-wing configuration with your mainsail full out to starboard and your jib whisker-poled out to port. A whisker pole is a spar used to hold out the clew of the jib while you are running. On my Com-Pac 16, a five-foot-long pole spear serves this purpose quite nicely, the rubber for propelling it looped around the mast foot while the other end slips into a valve from a rubber innertube (details on this later).

To jibe the boat in such a way with these strong winds coming from astern, simply sail a loop to port, which will cause you to come back up into the wind, at which time the sails will be changed over as the boat tacks bow first through the eye of the wind. Naturally, in rounding up into the wind you sheet in your jib and main on the starboard side and after executing a normal tack you end up on a starboard tack with the main out to port and jib to starboard.

Incidentally, whenever sailors speak of a boat being on a

starboard or port tack, it always means that the wind is *coming across* the port or starboard side while the sails will always be deployed on the opposite side. Thus when a boat is on a starboard tack, its mainsail and jib will be on the port side.

Sometimes, especially with catamarans in the sixteen- to twenty-foot size, in high winds and seas, and in sloops—especially the heavy displacement hulls—in light winds, it is easy for these boats to begin a tack and find themselves suddenly "in irons." This means that although you begin to make a tack, your boat lacks sufficient forward movement or momentum to carry itself around the eye of the wind. A sloop may stall out simply because of insufficient wind. The catamaran in high winds sometimes stalls because the twin hulls and trampoline create a kind of wind tunnel effect that tends to "lock" it head on into the wind. Sails flutter, the boat stalls, and the uninitiated sailor suddenly feels totally frustrated.

No need for it, because sailboats can sail backward almost as easily as they sail forward. Should you find yourself in irons, simply push your tiller over to the same side your mainsail was on. This will cause your stern to move to windward, the bow will fall off the wind, and your sails will once again fill. Pull back on your tiller and your boat will sail off on another beat. With sufficient speedup, you can try tacking again. On one of the lightweight catamarans, with high winds and waves, carry out this maneuver keeping your weight as far forward on the trampoline as possible to prevent the wind from lifting the bows and trying to make the boat go airborne. If you still have difficulty getting the bows around, unsheet the main and push the boom upwind. The bows should then fall off downwind.

No matter what size sailboat you have, a sailmaker can make you a cruising spinnaker. These huge, ultralight, colorful sails are absolutely phenomenal. Some manufacturers may call them "Drifters," or "Flashers," but no matter what they are called, these big colorful balloon sails, that stow so compactly and deploy so quickly, can make your boat seem to fly under average sailing conditions. They are ideal light-air sails shaped and rigged to enable your boat to sail on every point up to a broad beat, and are well worth the investment if you are interested in adding quite a bit more sail power.

As author and editor Tony Gibbs said while writing on the subject of spinnakers and other sails in his book *Advanced Sailing,* "My own feelings about owning a chute have already been aired—it is one of the things that make a sailboat fun, and if your boat can set one and your bank account handle one, you ought to own a spinnaker."

The cruising spinnaker requires no spinnaker pole. You will find it far easier to handle than the conventional spinnaker. The sail is symmetrical. The point at which you will attach the jib halyard is called the head. The other two corners are called the tack and the clew. To the tack is attached a short line that passes through a bow ring or bow block and is then secured to the bow cleat. The clew takes a double line or sheet that reaches back to the cockpit, passing one on each side of the mast and outside all shrouds. If the boat has lifelines (safety lines running around the outboard edges of a deck), the sheets should go *over*, not through, them.

The tail end of these lines will pass through port and starboard track blocks and have a figure 8 knot tied in their bitter ends (see Fig. 32). All this can be rigged in advance with the spinnaker still in its bag and a short line through the loop in the bag bottom secured to some convenient point forward such as the bow pulpit. From the top of the open bag will protrude the three sail points: the head, the tack, and the clew. The rest of the sail will either be stuffed into the bag or it will be neatly folded in a serpentine manner for swift deployment.

The easiest way to hoist the spinnaker is on a downwind run in which the mainsail is well out, blanketing air to the foredeck. Haul down and remove the jib sail. Bend on the

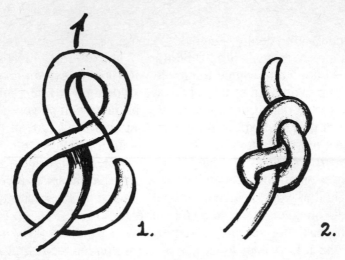

FIG. 32

(Fig. 32). This simple variation of the overhand knot, which forms the figure 8 knot, is often used to prevent a line from running out through a block or other piece of tackle. The advantage of the figure 8 over other knots is that it can be untied quickly.

head of the spinnaker to the jib halyard and hoist away. The sail will run out quickly from its bag at the bow pulpit. If it is adequately blanketed by the mainsail, it will not fill out yet. But if your helmsman turns onto a port tack, let the port sheet run free, sheet in on the starboard, and run the tail three times around the starboard winch, preparatory to taking up the slack and trimming the sail as the boat falls off to starboard. The spinnaker will balloon out and you will adjust its clew either in or out for maximum efficiency. The closer you sail to the wind, the shorter your tack line will be and the tighter you will sheet in on the clew to flatten the sail.

As you sail more off the wind, however, you will be letting out more on both the tack and the clew (as well as your mainsail). This will create a more full-bodied, billowing sail until you reach a downwind run. Now you will want to set up a wing-and-wing arrangement with the mainsail jibed to port and the spinnaker ballooned out to the end of its sheet to starboard. Trimming this big sail is a little like flying a giant kite. You adjust it so that it is pulling nicely throughout with no backwinding, cupping, or hint of a luff along its tack. One thing to watch out for: flying the spinnaker is great fun in reasonable winds; just don't fly it too long in strengthening winds.

The sail can be doused just as easily as it was set by collapsing it with such harnesses as are designed for this purpose, i.e., a "Spinnaker Sally," or you again blanket it with the mainsail on a downwind run. Then haul down the collapsed sail and feed it back into its bag. If you stuff it in, start in the middle of the sail and end up with the three corners again at the top ready for rigging.

Since sailboats have no brakes, be prepared to use the mainsail for this purpose. Whenever you approach a dock or a mooring buoy, or simply the point where you wish the boat to stop, you will sail so that when approaching that point you can turn the boat into the wind so that the sails immediately lose their drive. Free both the jib sheets and mainsheet, making sure there is plenty of slack in the latter. After a short coasting the boat will stall out and start drifting stern first downwind. If you have calculated exactly when to turn the boat into the wind and how long it will coast before stopping, you will learn from experience just how much leeway to allow. It will vary according to the size and displacement of your boat. If you find the boat is moving forward against the wind, coasting under its own momentum too quickly so that you will pass or collide with your intended target, then use the mainsail as a brake. Grasp the boom and push the sail out into the wind so that the backwinded sail creates a braking effect.

If you are under power, your sails are down, and you are coasting in to a dock, and realize you are traveling too fast to stop, then either steer away and make a more gentle approach, or do one of two things: jump off the stern and drag the boat to a stop; or throw your body between the boat and the dock to fend it off.

If you survive, you will be better informed about how far your boat will coast without any power, and be a better judge of when to cut your engine before you pile up on the waterfront.

10

Anchors and Anchoring

Anchoring is an art that takes a little practice to perfect. Never assume that just anyone can anchor your boat for you. How easy it is to come into an anchorage at dusk with the sails furled, you handling the helm with the boat under power while your companion is up on the bow conning you in. Then, as you cut the motor and coast to a stop, how perfectly natural to ask your friend on the bow to put out the hook, let the boat drop back an appropriate distance, and then cleat off the anchor rode.

This happened to a friend and me, just as it was becoming dark, in a snug little lagoon behind a long rock jetty. It was a narrow waterway with steep sand dunes on one side, the jetty on the other, protected except from the north side. Since my friend was a retired navy man I assumed more than I should have; I thought he knew how to set an anchor. He didn't.

Half an hour later when we were hit by a sudden line squall, the first gust sent us dragging anchor toward the rock jetty just a few yards away. As I dived for the outboard and fired it up, I shouted for my friend to get forward and haul in on the anchor rode while I powered us into the squall.

Moments later we were in safer, deeper water where I could go forward and set the hook properly, and we rode out the rapidly diminishing winds without any more problems.

But that experience taught me a never-to-be-forgotten lesson: not only your boat but possibly your life depends upon how well your boat is anchored. Whenever there is any question about how it is done, do it yourself. Never, *ever* assume that someone else knows how it should be done. If it is easier for them, rather than you, to do it, tell them exactly how you want it done; then later check to make sure it was done properly.

Certain steps must be taken to ensure that a boat will be securely anchored. Never sail into an anchorage, toss your anchor overboard, secure the rode to the bow cleat, and think that your boat will stay put. A certain proper procedure must be followed. First, pick a good place to anchor. The site should offer as much shelter from the wind and waves as possible. Try to select a spot that will be out of the way of other boats' wakes. Know where your prevailing winds and weather will be coming from to avoid anchoring near a lee shore. Pick a place where you have plenty of swinging room. If others are nearby, stay well away from them. If a number of boats are crowded in and there is nowhere else to go, plan to anchor both bow and stern to prevent your boat from swinging into others.

Know the depth of water you will have and the kind of bottom there. Local charts will give you an idea whether you have sand, mud, rock, or coral to contend with and a lead weight on a light line will tell you the depth. Get your anchor and rode all ready for deploying. Sail or motor up to the area where you intend to anchor. When the boat stops its forward motion and begins falling back, *ease* the anchor into the water, lowering it to the bottom. If you throw or toss it, it may foul. If you let it down gently, chances are it will land flat, ready to dig in. Be sure, if you have a bow pulpit, that you pass the anchor between the pulpit and the boat; otherwise your anchor rode will be over, rather than under, the bow pulpit.

As the boat drifts sternward, pay out slack. Generally, you will let out a total length of rode equal to seven times the water's depth. For example, if the water is ten feet deep, you will let out a minimum of seventy feet. More, if conditions are stormy.

Before you reach your full scope, however—when about a third of it is out—grasp the rode and give it a series of short, sharp tugs to set the anchor, to force the flukes into the bottom. Do not jerk so hard that you actually pull the anchor out. "Feel" it in, then let more scope slip through your hands and again give it the series of sharp little tugs. You will sense the point where the anchor is actually snugly set and at that time you can let the boat drift back to its full scope, then secure the rode to the bow cleat. As an extra precaution you might secure its bitter end around the mast foot.

The rode should pass through a bow chock and/or be wrapped with chafing gear to prevent any wear on it at that point. It is important in deploying this rode that it does not become snarled. For that reason some boaters flake it down (lay it in parallel rows) on deck ahead of time so that it deploys freely. Another way to avoid tangling is in retrieving the rode: just drop the coils into a plastic bucket with no thought to any order. Let the rode pile atop itself in a natural way and when you hand it out again, it will go in the same untangled way. This method has always worked well for me. So has a "figure-8" coiling I do. Catch the rode between your thumb and index finger and proceed to coil it in a figure 8 between your elbow and thumb. If you coil it on your right arm, the line should go first around the outside of your elbow, then across the front of your forearm and over your thumb from the *right side,* then back down to the right outside of your elbow again.

The crossing of the coils in this manner will prevent them from fouling each other even if you lay the coil on deck and

Shorter rodes can be coiled in the figure 8 fashion between thumb and little finger to prevent them tangling when uncoiled.

feed rode off the top of the stack of coiled 8s. On half-inch anchor rode I do the same figure-8 coiling between my right thumb and little finger. It is quick, tangle free, and makes a neat bundle for stowing. On longer lines with the elbow-to-thumb figure 8, finish off by wrapping several coils around the middle of the 8, then pass the rode through the top of the 8 and secure it with a lower part of its own length to make a loop.

If desired, chafing gear (protective wrappings) can be used around the nylon rode where it rubs, to prevent unnecessary wear. Short pieces of old canvas or a split length of old hose might be used for this purpose. Twine or tape can be used to secure it in place.

A more secure set to the anchor may be achieved by backing down on it under power. Again, be careful not to pull the anchor out but merely set it securely.

Coiling any long line in this manner will prevent it tangling. This figure 8 coil is especially good with anchor rodes of a manageable diameter.

Once your boat has settled back on its anchor, take a sight on nearby landmarks to make sure that everything is secure and the anchor is not dragging.

If you plan to be swimming in the area and the anchor is not too deep, check it. Dive down and make sure that it is well set with its flukes driven into the mud or sand bottom. If coral or rocks comprise most of the bottom, wedge in the flukes or maybe even add a rock or two atop the anchor. In any event, be sure it is secure. In the sound at Key Largo in the Florida Keys, the bottom of this large lagoon, with its average six-foot depths, is deceptively bad holding ground. It is largely weeds over a few inches of mud covering a hard limestone bottom. Here, it is wise to always dive down and set your anchor. Feeling around through the silt will reveal small nooks and crannies where an anchor's flukes can be securely wedged. This is especially important in this area where line squalls in August may occur every three or four hours, day or night, with exceptionally strong, blustery winds accompanying them.

After anchoring your boat it is always a good idea to periodically check how it is holding. Take a look at the rode and make sure nothing has fouled it, that there is no chafing where it passes through the bow chock, and that all is secure. Glance at a fixed spot on the landscape—a tree, the loom of a sand dune, for instance. If your anchor is dragging, these points will appear to be moving. If you are anchored in a coastal area where the tide may go out swiftly, watching the fast-moving water go past your hull will create the illusion that it is the boat, rather than the water, that is moving. The quickest way to dispel this is to look at something you know is stable, such as the distant landscape. If it is too dark to see, turn your spotlight on it. Especially in a tidal race, terra firma sitting there nice and solid is a reassuring sight to see.

Sometimes the question arises about when and where to use a bow and stern anchor. The only criterion I suggest is: When you positively don't want to swing.

Now there are different degrees of this. For example, the first time I left my boat moored to a dock at a state park marina, I came back later that night to find that every square inch of deck was covered by a raccoon's muddy footprints.

The solution was to anchor bow to shore and toss out a stern anchor so that the critters found my boat less accessible. Also, in this marina, I did not want the early morning wakes of the fishermen's powerboats washing my stern onto the beach. Similarly, in a crowded mooring area, a bow and stern hook may be the only way to keep boats from swinging together.

The bow and stern method can cause a problem, however, as I learned one night on a Florida reef. A friend and I had sailed my Com-Pac 16 six miles out to Molasses Reef off Key Largo just before dusk one summer evening. Since the seas had been relatively calm, we planned to spend the night anchored over the reef to do some night diving.

To make sure that we did no anchor damage to living coral, I dived down and set both bow and stern anchors in rocks so that the boat was over a reef-ringed patch of sand in about twenty feet of water. We were right at the edge of the Gulf Stream and underwater visibility was about 150 feet.

As night moved in, so did some windier weather. Soon, our little boat was doing some fancy dancing in the growing swells. My companion, despite the fact that he lived aboard a forty-foot power cruiser on Lake Superior, became extremely seasick. About all he could do was clutch onto the starboard cockpit cushion and try to keep from rolling off. Trying to make it back to the security of the sound was out of the question because of the dangerous reefs between us and shore. We decided to stay where we were.

At midnight, the wind changed and the seas began slopping aboard. We were anchored bow and stern in a position that now put the seas broad on our port bow. Hauling in the stern anchor would let the boat fall off more downwind so that she would take the seas more on her bow.

The only trouble with that was my inability to haul in the stern anchor. I had set her too well. When things really began getting sloppy, I did the only thing left to do: I released the anchor rode aft and tossed it overboard with a small boat cushion tied to its bitter end.

The boat lay back into the wind, the seas were now easier to take, and by dawn, when things moderated, we collected our stern anchor and made our dive. From that time on I have been more cautious about when and where I used a bow and stern anchor; moreover, it taught me to carry a third anchor and rode in the event of such emergencies. If really severe weather came and we absolutely *had* to sail our way out of there, chances are *both* anchors would have been impossible to hoist. Freeing both on cushions would have made their retrieval easier later, and the third anchor would have then been worth its weight in gold for mooring the boat later that night in a safer harbor.

Over the years, I've made a habit of double anchoring. It is a modification of the Bahamian moor which is the way Bahamian fishing boats in the islands deploy two anchors to prevent their sloops from swinging dangerously in the narrow confines of a waterway when tidal currents might overcome a boat's tendency to lay to the wind.

Essentially, here is how they do it: The boat sails up to the mooring site, turns into the wind, and drops a bow anchor, which is then set. The boat is allowed to drift downwind as the rode is payed out to twice its normal scope. At this point, a stern anchor is dropped over and set. The boat is then pulled back to half the scope of the bow anchor rode while the stern rode is payed out. Both anchor rodes are then drawn taut and secured at the boat's bow cleat. In this way, no matter which direction the wind or currents go, the boat will pivot at its bow. The only drawback to this method is if the boat is left for any length of time with many wind or tidal changes; then the two rodes will become entwined.

My variation of this is to lay my main anchor, drop back to its normal scope, set it, and cleat it off. Then I cast out a second lightweight anchor at an obtuse angle from the first. My main anchor is an eight-pound Danforth and my casting anchor is a two-and-a-half-pound Danforth. It may take a couple of throws to get the small anchor to set properly but once it does, it holds tenaciously to the bottom. I then draw in on both the main and secondary rodes through the port and

WIND DIRECTION

THE BAHAMIAN MOOR

A

1. Sail into the wind
   Drop Bow anchor here. SET IT.

2. Let out twice the scope
   to drift back to point "B"

C

4. Cleat off Both Anchor rodes
   at the bow. The boat may
   pivot but will hold this
   general position.

3. Drop Anchor #2 here. Set it.
   Pay out scope while
   drawing boat back to point "C"
   by taking up primary anchor rode.

B

Modification of the above
uses a main large anchor #1
and a smaller anchor
deployed as shown.
Tighten rodes equally.

FIG. 33

starboard bow chocks until the boat is snubbed tautly between the two. Then I cleat off the rodes.

With this method the boat never rides around her anchor, and is doubly secured for anything that might come up in the night. In Largo Sound, I swim out the second anchor so that it lies in a direct line with the primary anchor rode. This in effect is the Bahamian moor with the anchors and rodes on a 180° angle.

Recovering these two anchors preparatory to leaving the anchorage is a bit more difficult than if only one anchor were involved. With one anchor you would pull your boat forward by its rode or by powering ahead until over the anchor, recovering the rode as you went. The anchor would then be raised to the waterline, sloshed up and down to rinse off any mud, and brought aboard. The rode should be stowed in a bucket as it comes in or coiled in the figure-8 manner so that it will be ready for quick and easy deployment the next time.

You may find both anchors of a Bahamian moor so deeply dug in that you are unable to haul in either one. In this case, I would tie off a boat cushion on the lightest anchor rode and toss it overboard. Then pull the boat up to the primary anchor and hoist it. After that it is a simple matter to circle back and recover the buoyed rode and second anchor.

An alternate method is to use a dinghy to row out and pick up the smaller of the two anchors and recover it in this manner.

All anchors can be pre-rigged with a tripping line. The line should be tied at one end to the anchor crown and be slightly longer than the water's depth. The surface end is tied to a float such as a small plastic bottle. By tugging on the line the anchor will be freed and can be easily lifted. Tripping lines and floats are good ways to get anchors out of rocks or corals where they may be snagged so securely that only a vertical pull will free them.

Whenever a new boat is outfitted, the owner is always confronted with the question of what kind of anchor to use and what kind and how much rode will be needed to secure it under the conditions in which it will be used.

Several types of anchors are available, ranging from the old kedge type often called the fisherman's anchor to one resembling a plowshare and one that folds up for easy stowage. Often, the kind of bottom you most often anchor in will suggest a certain type of anchor. The fisherman or kedge anchor is a good rock or coral anchor that will bury its fluke nicely in mud. However, wherever this type of anchor is used, there is always the danger that if the boat undergoes a wind or current shift, swinging around the anchor, the rode may loop about the exposed fluke and drag out the anchor.

An anchor that uses much the same idea but in a more modern design is the Northill type which is also good for rocks or coral and buries itself well in sand or mud. But, like the fisherman's anchor, an exposed fluke can foul on the anchor rode.

The Navy anchor or stockless type that commonly is seen on large ships, especially naval vessels, has its stock lying in the same plane as the anchor's flukes so that, in use, as the flukes bury so does much of the stock. This type is generally unsuited for anything but large ships because its efficiency depends mainly on its excessive weight.

A Mushroom anchor is also designed to be highly efficient when buried deep so that its dish-shaped base exerts enormous holding power. However, this anchor is not easily set and is unsuitable for anything but long-term permanent moorings where it can be deeply embedded in the bottom to provide an anchor for a surface mooring buoy.

The Grapnel anchor, with its many flukes, is at its best when used on a rock, coral, or grassy bottom. It is easily set and can be thrown without difficulty; however its holding power is not great. Its many arms make it susceptible to rode fouling and it is a difficult anchor to retrieve unless used with a trip line.

The Wishbone is a single fluke anchor mounted in a V-ed

TABLE OF SUGGESTED ANCHOR SIZES (Anchor Weight in Pounds, Normal Conditions)

Boat Length	Danforth	Plow	Northill	Yachtsman
under 17'	4-8	5	6	10
17-20'	8	10-15	6-12	12-25
20-25'	8	15	12	25-35
25-30'	8-13	15-25	12-27	35-45

(The above is for working anchors. For storm anchors,
  take one size larger in each instance.)

KEDGE TYPE
(Fisherman,
Yachtsman)

ANCHOR RODE SIZES, NYLON LINE

Boat Length	Rode Diameter	Rode Circumference	Strength
to 14'	5/16"	1"	2,850
14-20'	3/8"	1 1/8"	4,000
21-25'	7/16"	1¼"	5,500
26-30'	½"	1½"	8,350

NORTHILL TYPE
(Danforth,
Utility)

NAVY TYPE
(stockless,
patent,
Sea Claw)

MUSHROOM

TYPICAL HORIZONTAL LOADS (pounds)

Boat Length	Lunch hook	Working anchor	Storm anchor
10'	40	160	320
15'	60	250	500
20'	90	360	720
25'	125	490	980
30'	175	700	1,400

GRAPNEL

WISHBONE

HORIZONTAL HOLDING POWER OF DANFORTH ANCHORS (pounds)
S = Standard   H= High Tensile

Anchor Type	Soft Mud	Hard Sand
2½-S	140	800
4-S	230	1,600
8-S	480	3,200
13-S	720	4,900
22-S	1,200	8,000
5-H	400	2,700
12-H	900	6,000
20-H	1,250	8,750
35-H	1,600	11,000

LIGHTWEIGHT TYPE
(Danforth, LTW,
Viking)

BRUCE

PLOW (plowright,
plough, CQR)

Note: 1 pound = 0.4536 kg

FOLDING TYPE

FIG. 34

arrangement so that once the single fluke is driven in there is no likelihood of anything fouling the rode. But laying to a single fluke may not be everyone's idea of security.

The Danforth is a popular anchor which, for its size and weight, provides excellent holding capabilities. Its unique design enables it to bury its twin flukes and leave nothing showing that may foul a rode. Top of the line for this kind of anchor style is the registered, trademarked Danforth. Its imitators are legion, and closely resemble the original anchor at less expensive prices as well as lower quality design, workmanship, and materials.

The Bruce anchor is a modification of a popular design and has no moving parts. Its one-piece construction provides a single plow-like fluke with curved arms that make it an anchor capable of holding in a variety of bottoms.

The Plow anchor is another of the more popular styles that lack flukes for fouling and has a pivoting shank that allows the anchor to remain in place when winds or tides change the position of the boat. This anchor can be broken free of the bottom fairly easily and stows well on bow rollers.

The Folding type anchors are modern versions of the Grapnel with four flukes that ingeniously can be folded up alongside the stock for easy stowing. This lightweight anchor is best used as a lunch hook for rock or coral. It makes an ideal dinghy anchor but should not be considered for any long-term anchoring of a larger boat.

The information in Fig. 34 will give you an idea of the various sizes of anchors recommended for boat size and similarly recommended rodes.

All trailer sailors should be sure that, no matter what anchor or rode size they select, the two are joined by at least six feet of chain. This chain not only helps hold the stock of your anchor to the bottom but it also prevents the rode from being chafed in a vulnerable area close to the bottom where it might encounter sharp rocks or coral. Anchors and rodes are usually shackled together with an appropriate size shackle.

Bottom tackle will last a long time if you check it periodically for wear and tear. Replace any questionable things. Shackles should be greased from time to time and the short wire that prevents the pin from unscrewing may be replaced when necessary. Galvanized chain will be well worth the extra cost if you anchor in salt water where nongalvanized chain will eventually rust and cause rust stain problems.

Take good care of your anchor and it will always take good care of you.

11

Customizing for Comfort: Topside

Anything you do to your boat to make it more comfortable or easier to handle can be called customizing. Most trailerable sailboats have an enormous capacity to be customized in this manner. Being able to do this yourself is part of the pride and the pleasure you will have in owning a stock sailboat that is normally devoid of these refinements.

Some of the things you may consider adding will be items you yourself may not be able to make. With these items, you will need experts proficient in doing the job for you. Cockpit cushions are a good example. They may well be your *only* large expense for the entire boat. But to me the value of cockpit cushions far outweighs their cost. Compared to deep-water ocean-going sailboats, those designed especially as day sailers, overnighters, or weekenders usually feature larger cockpits. The reason for this is obvious. Trailer sailors spend more time in their cockpits than in their cabins. Nor do they worry, as deep-water sailors might, about the dangers of overly large cockpits taking heavy seas from astern. They are more concerned about whether there is enough room in their cockpit to accommodate family and friends. When a family sails together aboard a trailer sailer, no one wants to be relegated to sitting in the cabin or clutching on to a tilted foredeck because there is no room in the cockpit for everyone to sit.

Fiberglass cockpits are notoriously hard and small boat cushions are not particularly comfortable for one day or a week of cockpit sitting. The addition of cockpit cushions shaped and fitted to your individual boat not only guarantees comfort in this area but in full-length cockpits they furnish space that may now be usable for two more sleeping berths.

The important thing in selecting someone to make your cockpit cushions is that you pick an upholsterer who is entirely familiar with boaters' specialized requirements. The recent experience of choosing someone to make custom cushions for my Com-Pac 19 *WindShadow* was an education in itself. I detail it here in the hope that it will save you some of my problems. Here is how it all began:

Since I live inland and not in a coastal community where upholsterers might be more familiar with boaters' nautical needs, I telephoned several upholsterers and told them what I needed. I knew I wanted top quality marine grade material throughout. The vinyl material had to be marine quality; nylon sewed to avoid rotting. The polyurethane foam was to be top grade high density foam about two and a half inches thick. Better yet, could they furnish closed cell foam, the kind that would not soak up water? Each cushion would be about six feet long and zipperless because on an earlier set of cushions the one place that finally broke down was the material between the zipper and the vinyl cover. I cut out the zipper, resewed the seam with heavy nylon cord, and got two more years of use out of them. I figured this time I would avoid the zipper entirely.

I finally located an upholstery shop that had made cockpit cushions for several sailboaters in the area. The woman said she could get the marine grade material, had high density but not closed cell foam, and would sew it all together without a zipper for $140 a pair. So she got the job.

I obtained a large piece of wide wrapping paper, placed it on the cockpit seat and, with a Magic Marker, drew the outline of the pattern that was to be the *finished* size of the cushion, a fact that was written in alongside so that there would be no mistake about this. After cutting out the pattern I placed it on the seat and double-checked it for accuracy. Then I took it to the upholsterer.

She showed me a sample book of marine grade vinyl. I wanted something light-colored that would not be too hot. Even slightly off-white will absorb heat. But since my boat was an off-white buff color, I tried to find a matching vinyl. All the samples she showed me had a slight texture to the surface, a molded-in texture that supposedly made it look like fine leather.

Knowing how mildew likes to hide in fine crevices like that, I held out for a vinyl that was completely texture free. Unfortunately there was nothing in her book that was like this. Finally, I found a top grade commercial vinyl that was just what I wanted. The only trouble was that it was not considered marine grade. Still, it was twice as expensive as marine grade.

"What in the world would make the difference?" I asked.

The upholsterer did not know, but said she would find out. She telephoned the manufacturer but came back with no satisfactory answers. The top grade commercial material I was interested in had, they assured her, been used to make boat cockpit cushions before. But whether it would be as waterproof as marine grade vinyl, no one could say. The one difference they said we might notice was that the vinyl I had selected tends to become soft and pliable in the heat of the sun.

Pliable was acceptable, but if they turned soft as marshmallows in the sun, this would not do. Again, nobody could say for sure what would happen. However, I was assured that many satisfied customers had used this vinyl for boat cushions. So I went with that and told the upholsterer to go ahead and make the cushions, requesting again only high density foam, which she assured me the cushions would have.

In due time the cushions were completed and they looked fine. I put them in the cockpit of the boat and went sailing. Everything was all right except their size. They extended beyond the seat about two and a half inches in some areas. How could this happen? I wondered. Supposedly they were made exactly like my pattern.

Back to the upholsterer I went. I asked to see my pattern so we could compare the finished cushion with it. They had thrown out the pattern. The head upholsterer was called into the discussion. The foam was removed from its cover. "It's the same size as the pattern," said the lady who had done the cutting.

When I saw that she had written the word "Frunt" along the edge with a Magic Marker, I had some doubts. Finally, she admitted that the foam had been cut a bit larger to "plump out the cushion" a bit. They had plumped it out all right. About two and a half inches worth.

The head upholsterer apologized and said if I would return with another pattern they would see that the cushion was made to fit it exactly.

Several days later it was done. Both cushions fitted the cockpit as they should. The only difference now was that the upholsterer had taken it upon herself to add a zipper along the backside of each. From all appearances it was a brass zipper. Rather than cause any more fuss, I accepted the unwanted zipper.

A week of cruising on the coast with the cushions revealed that not all of the zipper was brass. The slide was something else that left a large rust stain on the vinyl. The upholsterer then told me this was impossible. It was an all-brass zipper, she said, and brass does not rust.

In exasperation I began casting around for another upholsterer, one that could replace the "brass" zipper with a heavy duty nylon zipper.

My search led me to a shop specializing in automobile upholstery. But at least it had the long heavy duty nylon zipper that was required for this kind of cushion. By the time they were installed, the two cushions, which were originally to cost me a total of $140, had now cost me $252. But at last I had my top quality cockpit cushions.

I trailed the new boat to the Florida Keys for two weeks of cruising, diving, and hurricane season squalls. By the time I got home, both cushions were so waterlogged I could hardly carry them out of the cockpit and get them unzipped. I removed their covers.

The top quality high density foam was completely saturated. No sponge could have done a better job. I tried to wring out the cushions. I rolled on them. I hung them over the bow, hoping that gravity would make them drip dry.

A week later when I compressed the foam I still got water. I started the process all over again, putting them in the bathtub and rinsing all of the salt water out of them that I could. Again I wrung them out and let them drip dry. At the end of another week they still retained moisture. No way was I going to be able to give my cushions this kind of tender loving care each time they got wet.

Back to the telephone I went to phone the last upholsterer who had put in the zipper. If he knew enough about cockpit cushions to know what kind of zippers they required, maybe he would know how to solve my wet foam dilemma.

"This is not an uncommon problem," he told me. "To get all the water out of them, we put the foam in an oven and do it that way. To begin with," he added, "they should have been wrapped in plastic."

I had had a similar idea earlier. I promptly went to my local hardware store, bought enough 4-mil plastic sheeting to do the job and with a roll of duct tape completely encased the foam so that if water got past the cover it would be a lot easier to dry out than was the waterlogged foam.

This worked up to a point. Ultimately, I did what I should have done in the beginning. I contacted North American Nautical Industries, Inc. They advertised in *Cruising World* magazine that they made cockpit cushions of closed cell. Back came a letter from the company's president, Bill Hefner, saying that their closed cellular flotation foam would do what I was looking for and since they had the Com-Pac's cockpit pattern on file, all I had to do was select a color from the vinyl swatches he enclosed and the cushions would be sent to me in two or three weeks.

Few things make sailboats more comfortable than cockpit cushions. The proper kind is important. These closed-cell foam cushions made by North American Nautical Industries, Inc. can also double as life preservers.

The results were everything I had visualized in the beginning, and more. The closed cell material need not be as thick as standard foam cushions, affording the same amount of cushioning but because of their thinness they expose more coaming for back support. Moreover, both cushions could be considered life preservers because they float high and dry in the water. Best of all, they cost far less than those I had had done with inferior material by the inexperienced upholsterer.

Other companies may supply the closed foam for this purpose but most of the upholsterers I contacted were unaware of them. So in the hope of saving someone else the troubles I have had, here is the full address of the source that supplied me with exactly what I needed. I was to learn later that they were equally well known throughout the nautical community worldwide for their famous yacht canvas, cushions, and sails. They are: North American Nautical Industries, Inc., 255 10th Street North, St. Petersburg, FL 33705. Tel: (813) 821-0189.

Once the cushions are in, the next step in customizing a cockpit is to consider converting the cockpit to a full berth—actually, a queen-sized berth.

You can do this quite simply with the addition of a floorboard for the cockpit well. I made mine of half-inch marine plywood, contact cement, and outdoor carpeting. Here's how:

(1) Measure and saw the plywood slightly smaller than the floor of your cockpit well. Also, saw three three-inch-wide strips the same length.

(2) Give them four heavy coats of sealant such as polyurethane.

(3) Measure and cut the carpet to fit the floorboard with two-inch overlap on the sides.

(4) Brush contact cement on the underside of the carpet and on one side of the floorboard and three inches around the opposite side.

(5) When ready, bond the two materials together and let dry.

(top) When lifted and supported over *Nomad*'s cockpit footwell as shown, her carpeted floorboard turns the cockpit into a queen-sized berth.

(bottom) The addition of an inflatable cushion or foam mattress over the floorboard provides a large sleeping area in the Com-Pac 16's cockpit. In this manner, we have overnighted four adults on this sixteen-foot sailboat quite comfortably.

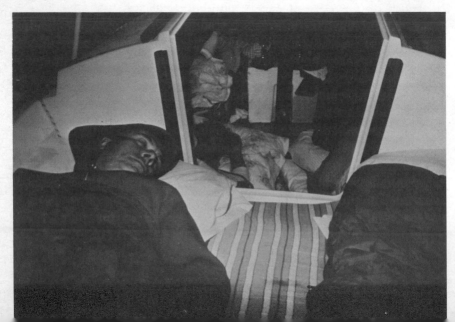

(6) Paint the three strips with several coats of white paint.

(7) When dry, place the strips (one on each side and one in the middle) on the cockpit floor and lay the floorboard on them with the carpet up. Your feet will delight in its feel and any water taken into the cockpit will run off underneath through the scuppers.

(8) To complete the cockpit berth, lift the floorboard and support it at the head, middle, and foot with the strips now laid across the footwell with their ends supported on the cockpit seats *under* the cockpit cushions. Add an inflatable cushion to the floorboard in the middle and you now have a berth wide enough to sleep at least two or three more persons.

The next logical step in comfortizing a cockpit is the addition of a sunshade. The first one I made for my Com-Pac 16 was nothing more complex than two one-inch-thick and seven-feet-long bamboo poles with a cockpit length of thin material stitched so the poles slipped into wide seams at the forward and after ends. This shade was easily rolled up and stowed below while sailing. I modified it with three-quarter-inch PVC poles capped with crutch tips, and liked that so well that I decided to design a Bimini top that could remain up and be used under sail.

While the dimensions I worked with were suitable for the large cockpit of the Com-Pac 16, with only slight modifications such a top will work just as well for any other sailboat. The nice thing about it is that everything rolls up into a compact bundle that slips well out of the way alongside the boat's starboard berth. Here's how to make it:

(1) With the boat on its trailer, step the mast and attach the boom with its after end supported by its topping lift. Sheet in the boom with the mainsail sheet and start taking measurements for the height of the supporting struts and the size of the top that will cover your cockpit at least a few inches over your head, with a couple more inches clearance for the boom.

(top) A length of cloth and two spreaders of bamboo or thin-walled aluminum conduit pipe can be combined to make a boom shade, guyed off to cleats and side stays. Few things are more welcome on a hot summer's day in the sun than a patch of cool cockpit shade.

(bottom) Breakfast for four in the cockpit of a sixteen-foot long Com-Pac sailboat can be more comfortable than one might suspect with the addition of a cushioned floorboard over the footwell.

(2) Measure the distance between the starboard stay and a point about twelve to sixteen inches forward of the transom. If your mainsheet and block are *inside* this measurement, shorten it to amply clear them.

(3) Measure the widest part of your cockpit, add six inches, and consider this the width of your Bimini, while Step 2 will give you its length.

(4) Obtain this size vinyl top material plus ten inches for five-inch seams on forward and after edges and you will have the basic shape of the Bimini to fit your boat. Two six-foot lengths of thin-walled aluminum conduit pipe slip into the forward and after seam sleeves and two-foot ties girth hitched to the forward spar tie directly to your side stays so that the spar just clears your boom.

(5) Have a companion hold the after spar with the top on it just under the boom but parallel to it and your cockpit.

(6) Measure from the after spar on a 45° angle to the outboard edge of your deck and pencil a marking. This is where your deck fitting will go for the one-inch diameter thin-walled aluminum conduit pipe strut—one for each side. The length of this strut can be determined by measuring between the aft spreader spar and that point on your deck. The above is for all general sailboats.

Specifically for the Com-Pac 16 and any with similar sized cockpits and mainsail sheeting arrangements, here are the exact specifications:

Materials needed

(1) Two thin-walled aluminum conduit pipes 1″ × 72″ long (spreaders).

(2) Two thin-walled aluminum conduit pipes 1″ × 36″ long (struts).

(3) Thin white untearable top vinyl 82″ long × 62″ wide (unfinished size).

(4) Two sets chromed deck and top fittings from marine supply shops.

(5) Two lines 70″ long for the after ties.

(6) Two lines 24″ long for the forward ties.

Fold over four inches of the material on each end and double sew a seam that will enclose the spreader spars (the 1″ × 72″ pipe). In line with the boat's side stays, punch a hole in the material and girth hitch the twenty-four-inch lines at these points so the lines pass around the spar. These tie the forward spar to the stays. The two aluminum struts attach to the after spar as shown in Fig. 35. The deck fitting on the Com-Pac 16 goes exactly 46½ inches from the corner of the rub rail to the deck edge outboard of the coaming where it is screwed and bedded in place. One goes on each of the port and starboard sides and mates with the fittings in the folding struts. Quick release pins will simplify putting up and taking down the Bimini. Be sure to tie the pins to the fittings with monofilament to prevent their loss.

Once the forward spar is tied off to the side stays and the struts pinned to their deck fittings, tie on the after ties as shown and secure them to the stern deck cleats tightly to set. For releasing the Bimini, free these tie-downs, fold the struts alongside the after spar, and roll forward tightly. Untie the port and starboard stay ties, use them to secure the roll, and lay the rolled Bimini alongside or on brackets over the starboard berth.

This Bimini top is extremely stable because there is nothing about it that can come apart. It has served me well aboard my Com-Pac 16 through the days and nights leading up to a tropical depression that produced winds in excess of forty knots and deposited five inches of rain on our anchorage.

On wintery nights when winds over the water were agonizingly cold, we devised a simple but totally effective solution. On *Nomad,* with the Bimini up, it provided a perfect frame for a plastic dodger. We just used a length of four-foot-wide 4-mil polyethylene plastic and wrapped up the cockpit,

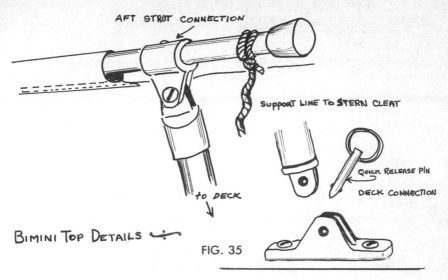

AFT STRUT CONNECTION

SUPPORT LINE TO STERN CLEAT

QUICK RELEASE PIN

DECK CONNECTION

to DECK

BIMINI TOP DETAILS

FIG. 35

(Fig. 35). *(top)* These chrome-plated fittings for the Bimini top are available at most marine hardware stores. Size selected depends on the diameter of the aluminum pipe used.

(bottom). Here is how the Bimini top fits over the cabin and cockpit of my Com-Pac 16, *Nomad*. The forward spar attaches to the side stays; the after spar guys to stern cleats. Tension on these guys determines the tautness of the top.

securing it at the four spreader corners with cord and clothespinning the upper edges to the sides of the top. We could not have created a cozier cockpit that New Year's Eve but, admittedly, the brandy helped.

One of the simplest, most inexpensive additions to any sloop's foredeck can be purchased in any hardware store in the country. It could be a lifesaver; it surely is a trouble saver. It is a quarter-inch-diameter nylon line that must be as long as the luff of your jib sail and reach beyond that from your bow to the foot of your mast. Tie it there. Run the line through your bow jib shackle and clip or tie it to the head of your jib. Now, rather than have to go up on your foredeck to haul down the jib, just free the jib halyard and let it slip through your hand as you pull the line at the base of the mast. Down will come the jib, and cleating off both halyard and line keeps it secure. The line that enabled you to avoid going forward on that slanting and slippery wave-washed foredeck to bring in the jib is called a jib downhaul, a pretty handy little line, especially in bad weather.

Aboard my nineteen-foot *WindShadow,* necessity prompted us to rig another invaluable line, another length of quarter-inch nylon. These were the conditions that brought it on: We were anchored at night in the Florida Keys during a period of tropical weather that brought heavy rainfall about every two hours. Humidity was dripping off the overhead and temperatures at night were in the high nineties. We needed every hatch open just to breathe. But to reach our foredeck hatch meant scrambling over two large bags full of diving gear secured there. If we didn't get to the hatch in time, everything in the forepeak would be soaked, and so much gear was packed in there, the hatch was also almost unreachable from inside the cabin.

We ran the nylon line from a vent on the deck hatch back through the main hatch and companionway; then back to the vent again from inside the cabin. Now, as soon as we heard the rain on the overhead, a tug on the line in the cabin closed the forward hatch. With the rain over, pulling the companionway line across the deck opened it again, and we never left the comfort of our berths in the process. We dubbed that one the Hatch Haul.

Tiller extenders are nice additions. But when I look at a beautifully laminated ash and mahogany tiller to which I have already added an additional seven coats of high gloss urethane and hand rubbed and waxed it to a smoothness guaranteed to send shivers down the back of anyone who lays a hand on it, I am not about to drill that tiller to make way for a commercial tiller extension. However, on certain days it is so nice to be sitting with your back against the after cabin bulkhead quaffing a cool beverage while steering your ship from a bearing off her stern. So the tiller extension I made consists of eight inches of two-and-a-half-inch-diameter foam insulation used to slide over water pipes. The diameter was selected because it just fit the end of my tiller snugly. A stainless steel clamp secured the other end to a tip-padded fir dowel half an inch in diameter and three feet long. The dowel was wrapped with a length of half-inch-wide leather stripping and two inches from its opposite end a 2″ × ¼″ dowel was driven through a drilled hole to serve as a crossbar for two-fingers-and-a-thumb steering. The flexibility of the sleeve provided the universal joint I needed to operate the tiller from anywhere in the cockpit.

The tiller of a sailboat gets as much attention as the steering wheel of an automobile. Like automobiles, the standard stock boat comes with the basic steering mechanism. No frills. If you want cruise control, you pay for the option. Similarly, if you want cruise control on a boat, it can cost several hundreds of dollars. Either that, or you devise a cruise control of your own making. There are several ways to do this, some of them involving lines and blocks from foresail to tiller, etc., but those I will describe here are simple, yet quite effective, provided your boat has sufficient weather helm on a beat. Here, then, are the three different kinds:

The Block and Line

Materials consist of a three-foot length of braided clothesline (any other kind may not work) and a block of wood measuring 5″ × 1¾″ × ⅝″. One inch in from each end, bore a ⅜-inch hole and wallow it out a bit with the drill. Sand the block with the exception of the holes. Thread the rope through it as shown in Fig. 36.

The loop in the block goes over your tiller and the loop in the other end slips over a port or starboard cleat. By cinching the block as you would a similar device used for tightening tent ropes to their stakes, you can position the tiller anywhere you like. The cleat-to-tiller line will always be used to *counter* the pull of the weather helm when beating to windward. I have used this tiller tender to sail many miles without a hand on the tiller. The boat will steer a reasonably

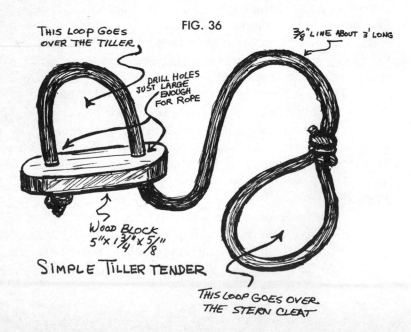

FIG. 36

THIS LOOP GOES OVER THE TILLER

DRILL HOLES JUST LARGE ENOUGH FOR ROPE

⅜″ LINE ABOUT 3′ LONG

WOOD BLOCK 5″ × 1¾″ × ⅝″

SIMPLE TILLER TENDER

THIS LOOP GOES OVER THE STERN CLEAT

straight course, eventually heading up into the wind a few degrees until the jib starts to luff, and then she will fall off and steady again.

Line and Loop

This is essentially the same idea except, in place of the block, a loop of half-inch surgical rubber fifteen inches long is tied to a line running to port or starboard cleat. Another line looped at one end runs from the tiller to the opposite cleat. By tensioning and cleating this line, you can adjust the position of the tiller. The rubber loop acts as a shock absorber for the tiller. The preceding two methods work only on windward beats with weather helm. The next method will work on any point of sail.

Jiffy Tender

This one tends the tiller on or off with the flick of a finger. It works well for holding the boat on course under power into the wind while you hoist the sails, or for momentary minding while you duck below to pour a cup of coffee. The secret is a wooden jam cleat screwed to the underside of the tiller. Carved to resemble one leg of an old-fashioned clothespin, the 6″ × ³⁄₄″ wood tooth, shaped as shown in Fig. 37, is sanded smooth, sealed with a couple of coats of urethane, and brass screwed in two points to the underside of the tiller forward of midlength. The other part of the jiffy tender is a shockcord with plastic covered hooks that attach to the port and starboard stern cleats. Since you want the shockcord to stretch up and engage the tooth fairly tautly, the length of cord used and the positioning of the tooth on your boat may vary from mine. But the important thing is that the elastic cord be snug enough to position the tiller, but not so snug you cannot easily disengage it. If you find too much weather helm

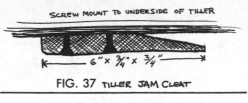

SCREW MOUNT TO UNDERSIDE OF TILLER

← 6" X ¾" X ¾" →

FIG. 37 TILLER JAM CLEAT

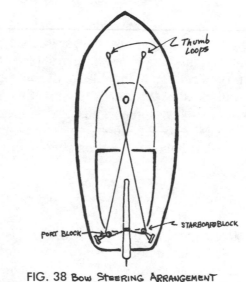

Thumb Loops

PORT BLOCK

STARBOARD BLOCK

FIG. 38 BOW STEERING ARRANGEMENT

offsets it on a beat, you may have to fall back on the other tiller tenders that are made more for beating with strong weather helm.

While we are on the subject of remote tiller tending, you might be interested in a rig that lets you sail your boat from the bow while lounging in the cool down-draft of your foresail. Personally, on *Nomad* I always enjoyed sitting up in the bow pulpit with legs over the side watching for sharks and rays as I cruised shallow sand bars and flats in a favorite Florida bay. You could always read the consternation on others' faces as you sailed by at full tilt, perched all by yourself on the bow. Most people must have thought I had one heck of an automatic pilot on my little sailboat, especially when I sailed serpentine courses past them. Nobody noticed that the boat's entire control was in my thumbs on the deck beside me. They were in padded thumb loops on a pair of lines that ran aft, passed through port and starboard blocks on lines looped to the port and starboard stern cleats, and then tied off on the tiller. With the sails set and the boat moving on a light breeze that could be depended upon not to do anything tricky, it was fun steering from the bow. I only had to remember to cross the lines running forward so that when I wanted to steer to starboard, moving my right thumb actually drew the tiller to port, and vice versa. The rigging arrangement is detailed in Fig. 38. Sometimes as you lie back with your feet propped up on the pulpit and eyes almost closed while you sail single-handedly past the yacht club, it is not unusual to hear someone's voice drift out from the rocking chair crowd on the upper deck, "Hey! Who's sailing the boat?"

Boarding Ladders

Some kind of ladder for getting on and off the boat from the water is a necessity, even on small pocket cruisers such as my Com-Pac 16 that you can climb aboard in depths where the keel is not even touching. However, if that boat is in deep water and my head and shoulders are now at her waterline, climbing aboard is not that easy. The bigger the boat and the more freeboard it has, the less easy the task is. Eventually you may want to install a permanent folding ladder on your boat's stern as I did on *WindShadow*. The marked advantage of fixed boarding ladders is that they are not only sturdier than any others, but they are always there when you need them.

If you were single-handing at sea and fell overboard on a lifeline, your folding ladder stowed below decks wouldn't do you much good. When I realized this potential danger with

A folding permanent boarding ladder as shown mounted on the transom of my Com-Pac 19, *WindShadow*, provides easy access to the boat on the land or in the water. Before it was added, however, I mounted an emergency step (shown unfolded) on my rudder blade. It was intended to simplify my getting back aboard the boat if I ever fell off while sailing.

the Com-Pac 19, which has considerable freeboard, I corrected it in a hurry. But not with the permanent ladder I presently have. I did it with one step, a fold-up chrome plated brass step that was mounted by through-bolting stainless steel bolts to *WindShadow*'s long kickup aluminum rudder blade.

I used a stepladder beside the boat and trailer to establish just how high the step needed to be. The step served its purpose nicely and with the boat's backstay handy for grabbing onto one can climb aboard quite easily. Essentially, however, this single rudder step is mostly for emergencies. My crew mates are often scuba divers and although we tie off our heavy tanks for hauling aboard from the boat, the rest of our cumbersome garb makes it tough negotiating the single step. Hence the sturdier stern boarding ladder.

Plastic Ladders: If you get one with enough steps, these are quite serviceable as boarding ladders for swimmers. Be sure that you get one that is securely made and not so flimsy the steps will break. Also, be sure the folding legs that go against the hull of your boat are not partially folded or cocked when you come aboard. Otherwise your weight may wipe them out permanently. Fold-up plastic ladders usually hook over the side. Though they fold for stowing they still manage to hook everything in sight when you try to drag them out from below. I finally bonded large wooden brackets to the fiberglass bulkhead inside the cockpit seat lockers. They keep the ladder secure and out of the way until needed.

Rope Ladder: This is another simple item to construct. It consists of steps of thick-walled three-quarter-inch PVC pipe and a length of nylon rope. How many steps and how long the rope must be depends on the amount of freeboard you need to cover. But Fig. 39 shows the rigging procedure. On my big boat, *WindShadow*, I hooked the ladder over a starboard winch. On my smaller Com-Pac 16, I mounted mid-cockpit cleats outboard the coaming for rigging a boom-vang. This is just a line that end loops onto my boom's outhaul cleat and

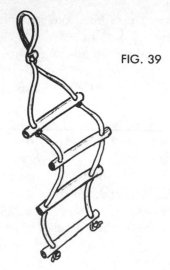

FIG. 39

—•— A ROPE AND PVC FOLDING LADDER

cinches down on the port or starboard cockpit cleats to keep the boom end from riding up on a beat or run. Initially the starboard cleat also supported my rope ladder until one day, with me on it, cleat and all pulled free of the bulkhead. To resecure it I had to through-bolt it to a backup block I installed inside the coaming. It never failed after that.

Climbing a rope ladder is somewhat tricky unless you do it the way trapeze artists do in the circus: heel, toe, heel, toe, alternating up the ladder. This method pushes the ladder away from the hull when you heel it; otherwise its difficult to get your foot into the rungs.

Anchor Hanger

Boat anchors either end up lying loose with chain and rode on the foredeck while sailing, or draped over the pulpit if one exists. Neither is good. When your little ship is blasting along at full speed in an angry sea, you don't want your anchor bouncing overboard and causing all kinds of unmentionable mayhem. Better to secure it in a more seamanlike manner and avoid the possible trouble.

Anchor hangers are made for that purpose. Most marine supply outlets have them for a price. Again, you can make an even better one with no more than a length of clothesline and two thimbles (stainless steel loops that come in various sizes at marine supply outlets). Here's how to make your own hanger:

Materials: Seven feet (more or less depending upon pulpit size) of quarter-inch braided cotton clothesline. Two stainless steel thimbles large enough to enclose the stocks of a lightweight type (Danforth style) anchor.

(1) Hold your anchor outboard of the bow pulpit with the anchor centered and the stocks about an inch below the railing.

(2) Mark the rail of your pulpit at a point midway between the end of the stock and the anchor fluke on each side.

(3) Wrap the rail with tight coils of the line, beginning by overwrapping the end at a point that will wrap a little over two feet of the bow pulpit rail equidistant from both sides. Make the coils tight. Wrap them to the first mark, then stop.

(4) Here, wrap one of the coils around a thimble, hold it in place if necessary with Scotch tape at the small end of the loop, and continue wrapping tightly to the next mark. Again, wrap a coil around a thimble. Continue wrapping to the end of the line.

(5) Finish off the wrapping by again overwrapping, tucking the loose end back through several coils and after pulling it tight, snip off the excess and force the coils back over the cut to conceal it.

(6) Make sure that the stocks of your anchor fit equidistantly between the thimbles in a position where the stocks can only be removed from one thimble or the other by shoving the anchor to one side and forcing the thimble around a stock end.

(7) Now remove the tape at the base of the thimble and wrap it tightly with nylon line. Either sew it through the rope to secure the end or tie it securely and melt the tips of the ties to prevent fraying.

Once the anchor is in its hanger, it is shackled to chain and rode and will remain there for easy deployment. Then unshackling the chain and rode from the anchor, you can secure its shank with a light line to some fitting on the bow for trailering. Since the mast on my Com-Pac 16 rests across my bow pulpit when I secure it with shockcords, the tie-down in turn secures the lightweight anchor to the bow pulpit.

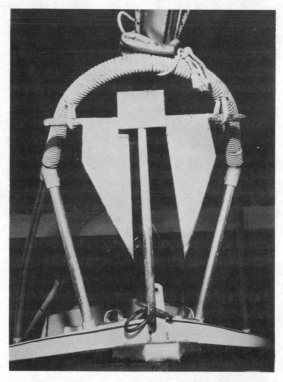

A bow pulpit is a handy place to secure one end of the mast when trailering. A length of line and two thimbles make a convenient hanger for the bow anchor.

Double-Duty Windscoop

In the summer, many of us stay overnight in small boats whose unventilated cabins can get uncomfortably hot. Living in tropical Florida and spending up to two weeks aboard my Com-Pac 16, *Nomad,* often pointed up the need for an effective windscoop. Windscoops are those colorful devices made of thin ripstop nylon with a scoop shape that can be hoisted over a boat's hatch to funnel prevailing breezes into the cabin for refreshing ventilation.

I owned one of these commercial scoops but at that time I had only a main hatch where it could be erected. This always necessitated removing the Bimini top which was then sorely missed when the morning's hot sun beat down on us. Moreover, the boom had to be disengaged from the mast and swung over with its furled mainsail to be lashed onto a side stay. Then I could hoist the windscoop on the main halyard.

To circumvent all this and still have an effective windscoop, I solved the problem by putting three brass grommets in a standard sized bath towel. One grommet went into each of two corners on the long side of the towel and one went in the middle of the opposite side. Short cotton lines attached to each of the corner grommets were then tied to the boat's port and starboard stays just under the Bimini. The middle grommet was clipped to a shockcord leading inside the cabin where the other end hooked to the handle of a water jug. Once the loose corners were clothespinned to the inside of the companionway, the air passing under the Bimini was scooped directly into the cabin, gently fanning us with cool breezes all night long.

The nice part was how easy the towel air scoop could be disengaged and used for its regular purpose. Moreover, we appreciated having the shade of our Bimini when we got up each morning. The scoop works equally well without a Bimini or overhead awning. Should your side stays be farther forward than those on the Com-Pac 16, merely extend the length of the lines securing it. Different sized towels make this speedy scoop adaptable to practically any size of companionway. If your boat has a forward hatch already then this kind of miniscoop will increase its ventilating capability when the lower part is pinned inside and the two corner lines are angled up and tied off to each side of the bow pulpit or lifelines if these are available.

Foredeck Hatch

Eventually the need for better ventilation in the cabin of my Com-Pac 16 started me thinking about how to add a hatch on the foredeck. Putting a straight edge across the deck told me there was enough curvature there to make proper bedding of the hatch somewhat tricky. I priced several small commercial hatches but found none of them to my liking. The area I was dealing with was relatively small and most hatches were too large. Short of starting from scratch to build a hatch to fit the area I had to work with, I decided the boat's lazaret cover was exactly the shape and size of the hatch I would like on the foredeck.

When I contacted the Hutchins Company and told them about it, they kindly sold me a spare lazaret cover and had their carpenter shape a teakwood frame to fit the curve of the deck. All I had to do then was to position the woodwork, draw the area to be sawed out, and take it from there.

The point where I really sweated was when I started sawing the hole in my deck. If it didn't work there was no going back and doing it over again. Once the hole was cut, I bedded the wood frame in silicone sealant and drilled and through-bolted the frame in place, filling all drill holes with plastic wood. A pair of nylon hinges were incised into the wood and properly lined up with the back edge of the lid for bolting in place. Then, finally, a proper size chrome hatch lifter was purchased from a marine supply store and along with a secure chrome-plated hook and eye, these items completed the assembly of the forward hatch. To make sure that the edge sealed satisfactorily to the wooden frame I added contact foam insulation all along the upper edge of the frame. The hatch can be opened to any position and held there with the lifter adjustment screw. It is hard to imagine how much improvement this makes to the comfort inside a cabin, both day and night. Better than installing an air conditioner. If your boat suffers from ventilation problems, consider adding a forward hatch.

Boat Names

There are several different ways to put your boat's name on her. If the name is not too long, it can be painted across her transom, or perhaps it can be put on with conventional

Block vinyl letters obtainable at most hardware stores can be enhanced by strip vinyl highlighting when applying a name to your boat's transom. Note also use of the striping as decoration around the coaming and rudder.

More artistic vinyl lettering designs such as this can be customized for you by Boat Graphics of Southfield, Michigan. This gold-and-brown boat name was easily attached to the Com-Pac 19's beam.

adhesive vinyl letters. These are available from hardware and builder's supply shops in a variety of different size block letters. Vinyls weather well and seem able to last almost indefinitely. They can also be enhanced by highlighting letters with vinyl striping for a three-dimensional effect.

However, if you prefer a more quality look with a touch of individuality, you should check with the professionals. Some cruisers have their names customized in large eye-catching letters just abaft their beams. One company that comes highly recommended because of the overall quality of its work, is: Boat Graphics, Suite 314, 19777 W. 12 Mile Road, Southfield, MI 48076. Tel: (313) 358-3150. They will work with you to develop the right graphics for your boat's name. They make custom designs and have standard typestyles and graphic images that are handcut from top quality adhesive vinyls. You can have anything you like in a choice of twenty colors that can then be applied to your boat in or out of the water.

Name Boards

Another way is the name board, often a nicely finished piece of wood with the letters painted or sometimes carved into the surface and set off by contrasting gold leaf or paint. Still others have worked out their boats' names by stapling their letters in lengths of rope on appropriately weathered pieces of driftwood. Most such boards are attached to the sides of the deck house, room permitting. When I decided to do a somewhat different style of name board, it was because the Com-Pac 19's name, *WindShadow*, was too long for the room I had on her stern.

I wanted something that could be attached to the boat's bow pulpit that would look more distinctive than just a painted name board. This gave rise to the idea of a shadow board—a piece of nicely finished teak shaped especially for

Routed teak name boards attached to *WindShadow*'s port and starboard bow pulpit provide an alternative way to display a boat's name.

the foredeck position it would occupy, with stylized lettering incised into the wood with a router. As the wood aged, the incised lettering would weather and turn silver-gray against the well-oiled background of the rest of the board.

Any other wood but teak would have worked and been far less expensive. However I wanted a name board that would be as durable as possible considering the weathering and seas it would take and yet provide the long-lasting beauty of aged teak.

Once the boards were selected, shaped, and sanded, I located a commercial sign painter who was also an experienced sign router. After the design was decided upon, it was pounced onto the board with blue chalk, darkened with grease pencil, and this became a guide for the free-hand routing.

After this was done I used cotton swabs and household bleach to start bleaching the incised letters, rinsing after each application. Repeated applications of the bleach were necessary to start the normal weathering process. The surface of the wood was treated with teak oil to maintain the darker color and enhance the grain texture.

Brass screws and aluminum metal straps secured the boards to the port and starboard sides of the bow pulpit just abaft the anchor chocks. Surprisingly, I found that the name boards provided an additional feature: They helped to keep rode, chain, and anchors secure on the foredeck when they were not in use. As the lettering takes on its contrasting silver sheen, the boat's name is always interestingly set off by the shadow effects of oblique sunlight, shadows that change depending on the different angles of light.

Louvered Hatch Doors for Large Boats

Few things add so much to a sailboat's appearance as louvered hatch doors. Not only do they look "salty" but they provide both privacy and free-flowing ventilation. Removable louvered doors will provide you with the double advantage of a ventilated hatch when you want it, or you can exchange the doors for the solid, lockable hatchboard(s) when your boat is left unattended.

Unfinished, inexpensive fir louvered doors are available in many sizes at home supply, hardware, and do-it-yourself shops. To determine which size will fit your hatch, take your hatchboard(s) to the supply shop and select a pair of doors that will fit within the measurements of your board. Since your hatchboard fits into a hatch slide, allow for at least a couple of inches clearance between the back of the doors and the edge of the board at the bottom. If the top of the doors extends beyond the top of your board a couple of inches, don't worry. The excess can be sawed off.

Other materials needed include: four solid brass strap hinges and screws; sandpaper; a piece of marine plywood the same thickness as your hatchboard and large enough to fill up the side spaces between your doors and the hatch slides; wood stain of your choice and a spray can of satin sealer such as clear polyurethane Defthane Satin #2; fine steel wool; paint brushes; and paste wax.

(1) Measure across the top and bottom of your hatchboard and mark it with a pencil.

(2) Lay your hatchboard flat and place your doors over it so they meet at the top and bottom marks. Move the doors up or down so that any top or bottom parts to be sawed off appear equal. Now tape the doors to the hatchboard.

(3) Carefully turn over the board and doors and, using the edges of your top and bottom hatchboard as guides, draw a line along the parts of the doors to be sawed off.

(4) Untape the doors from the board and saw off the excess with a saber saw. If much of the bottom is removed you will have to reattach the remaining piece to the doors. Since this is a key piece that holds the door's louvers

together, this must be done securely. Carefully drill through the sides of the door into the ends of the piece, using a bitt slightly smaller than a 2″ × ⅛″ casement nail. Glue the pieces together with strong wood glue; then tap the nails into place and allow the joints to dry.

(5) With the sawed doors once more in place on the hatchboard, lay an oversized piece of cardboard on those areas not covered by the doors. Trace around the edge of the hatchboard until they are outlined on the cardboard. Cut out these pieces with scissors and use them properly marked as port and starboard sides to act as templates for drawing the same size pieces on the marine plywood the same thickness (half or three-quarter inch) as your hatchboard, which you purchased for this purpose. Saw out each piece and sand.

(6) Sand the doors and stain all parts with penetrating oil stain. Since I was unable to find the exact shade of teak stain to match my woodwork, I mixed my own. It is almost the same shade as my teak. To get that color I mixed one-third light walnut stain, one-third honey maple stain, and one-third Watco Marine Teakwood Finish (a penetrating resin oil that acts as a sealer). This combination was brushed on and allowed to dry. Then three coats of the clear satin polyurethane were sprayed on. When dry the doors were lightly smoothed with steel wool, paste wax applied, and they were buffed to a hand-rubbed finish.

(7) All parts should now be fitted into the hatch slides to make sure everything will match. Light trimming may be necessary. Position the hinges, noting where the lower ones must be attached to avoid conflict with the hatch slides. Then screw them in place. The doors and side pieces can be tucked snugly in the hatch slides by contact cementing two-inch-wide strips of leather-like Naugahyde over their edges. Both louvered doors should fit neatly together when in position. When positioned exactly right, make sure that the companionway hatch adequately clears their top edges; then screw them in place using three-quarter-inch (or longer)

brass screws in holes you drill through the slides into the edges of the door frames inserted into the slides. These screws should be spaced equidistant from the top and bottom and merely hold the doors in position so that they are less likely to slip out of the slides while in use. The screws and the doors are quickly removed when you wish to replace the doors with your regular hatchboard. Both doors easily fold for convenient stowage when not in use.

Louvered Doors for Small Hatches

The smaller hatch opening of the Com-Pac 16 required a slightly different arrangement. The two unfinished louvered

Louvered hatch doors for your sailboat are simple to make. All materials are available from most do-it-yourself shops. Note that the size selection of the doors depends on the size of the original hatch cover.

The finished louvered doors as designed for the Com-Pac 16 are removable when the main hatch is in place and locked.

doors that best filled the opening measured 9″ × 20″ each. These were just tall enough to allow the companionway hatch to close. As described earlier, the necessary size frames to support the doors and fit the slides are sawed out, one for each slide. Since the hatchboard in the Com-Pac 16 is half an inch thick, this was the thickness of the piece to fit the slot. But since the doors had to be mounted flush to a frame, I measured their thickness, then sawed out the pieces to fit between the hatch doors and the slides. These sections were placed over those with the half-inch lips for fitting the hatchboard slots and the two were bonded together with Resorcinol Waterproof glue. This liquid resin bonds like iron. Before it set I also smeared the glue around all edges of the plywood to ensure their being waterproof.

When well set, all pieces were ready for the finishing touches—sanded smooth, stained, and given the final coats of polyurethane. Again, the louvered door frames that fit into the slots of the hatch slides were covered with heavy leather-like Naugahyde contact cemented in place. Four brass screws secure them in the slides and are easily removed so that the door may be replaced with the lockable hatchboard.

12

Customizing for Comfort: Inside

If you plan to use anything electrical on your boat, probably the first thing you will want to install will be a storage battery. Because of its weight, try to stow it somewhere amidships but within easy reach. The older Com-Pac 16s have a space under the cockpit sole just large enough for an automobile battery in a plastic dishpan. Heavy duty gator clamps make it easy to connect or disconnect your wires for charging. In its snug position aboard *Nomad*, the battery cannot move left or right because it is blocked by the berths on each side, nor can it lift out of its container because of the cockpit sole overhead. The only way I can get it is to slide out the Thetford head, then slide the dishpan and battery forward. It was a nuisance just to check the condition of the charge.

To eliminate it, I wired in an invaluable little item called a Battery Condition Tester and mounted it within easy view on the after bulkhead. Then all I had to do to tell at a glance what kind of condition my battery was in was to punch a button and watch the needle on a tricolor gauge tell me whether it was good, fair, or low. Good battery condition gauges are not that easy to find. This one came from the auto parts house of J. C. Whitney & Co., 1917-19 Avenue, P.O. Box

8410, Chicago, IL 60680. Their catalog lists an assortment of other things such as high intensity aircraft type lights that make small but bright reading lights for inside the cabin.

When I first started work on *Nomad,* I was primarily interested in having running lights so that I could sail at night, and a pair of bullet type lights in the cabin for reading. The boat's mahogany pressure post was just right for a pair of these. An electrician friend helped me with the proper wiring diagram and I tried to run the wires in as unobtrusive a way as possible, hiding them in corners and holding them in place with plastic clips from the electrical supply store that were contact cemented to the fiberglass.

When you have nothing but a fiberglass hull to attach things to and you cannot drill holes through it, it becomes quite a challenge, as I soon learned in designing and trying to hang port and starboard book racks. The racks themselves were easily made out of 2″ × 3/4″ fir with 2″ × 1/4″ lathing. My dimensions enabled me to also support in that rack an automobile type FM stereo/tape combination to work off my twelve-volt system. I was asking the rack to hold up quite a lot of weight, which was where the trouble began. I tried a variety of glues and epoxies. Some held for a while but after a few trips they all eventually let me down. Ultimately I decided the only secure way to do it was with fiberglass cloth and resin.

It was a messy business but it succeeded. When I finished, the racks were bonded to the bulkhead forever. To bond them well, all paint in the contact areas was ground off with a rotary grinder right down to the bare fiberglass roving. When that was done I decided it might be best to paint the bulk-heads. The basic color of the interior at the time was a speckled shade of charcoal. I wanted something lighter that would help illuminate the forepeak and be a bit more uplift-ing to look at.

I first experimented with a shade of light blue but that gave everything such a cold look I quickly removed it. I chose instead a combination of warm yellow, green, red, and orange colors, sort of an interior Tequila Sunrise. I painted it with flat Latex paint.

It worked great. On each after bulkhead I left room for a pair of stereo speakers, one on each side over the berths. These were large speakers and contained heavy magnets. I first traced their form on a piece of half-inch plywood. The plywood was then contact cemented to the bulkhead. Before doing this both the bulkhead and block of wood were sanded clean of any paint and were crisscrossed with knife cuts to ensure a rough, better holding surface for bonding. Once the wooden speaker supports were glued and dried in place, I screwed the speakers to them and wired them to the stereo.

To me, few things are more enjoyable on a sailboat than good music. Imagine being anchored under a full moon on a balmy summer night in the Florida Keys, dining on a freshly caught lobster garnished with cool slices of ripe mango and washed down with chilled white wine, while a Chopin nocturne is playing softly in the background. That is one of the purely enjoyable moments that cruising is all about.

Electric cabin lights are nice when you need them. But when you are on an extended cruise in which you will have no opportunity to recharge your battery, you find yourself avoiding their use. Brass oil lamps have a charm all their own and one of these proved to be one of the best battery savers we could ever have thought of.

At first we started with a very tiny oil lamp, with a wick half an inch wide. This was fine for an atmosphere light but you would not try to read by it. The small kerosene lamp allowed us to see sufficiently for general purposes at night, especially in a cabin as small as ours where everything was centrally located. Once you entered the cabin of our Com-Pac 16 you got into your berth. There was no place else to go. Over your left or right shoulder was the compression post with its small brass oil lamp. It was great for everything but reading.

The battery saving aspect of any kerosene lamp is that you avoid using precious electricity. Though kerosene is more expensive than ever, it is still a pretty cheap form of illumination. But if you want to be serious about oil lamps, judge them by the width of their wicks. If you plan to use one for all-purpose illumination including reading, get nothing less than a one-inch-wide wick. Large though this brass lantern might be for a small cabin, it will allow you to use your battery for far more important things, such as running lights at night and Chopin concerts, for up to two weeks on a standard automobile battery before requiring charging.

If your boat provides enough room for you to be able to ship a deep cycle marine battery, then by all means do so. This type is much longer lived than the standard auto battery and is designed to provide maximum voltage for a long period of time before weakening and requiring recharging.

All your electrical systems should be wired through an easily accessible fuse panel but be aware that if this is near your main hatch and you sail around salt water very long, some of your systems may suddenly not work, solely because corrosion on one of the fuses has broken the circuit. Usually all you have to do is turn the fuse in its holder and the circuit will again be completed.

Berth cushions are often not the most comfortable kind on stock production sailboats. The main problem is that when you sit on them you bottom out fast. Some are worse than others. When you lie on them you may not be aware of their hardness until around 3 A.M. when you suddenly discover there is not a soft place to be found anywhere on them. Most of the standard berth cushions are covered with vinyl—not the coolest kind of material for a hot summer night. Sheets help considerably. But if you want a more permanent arrangement, I suggest that you try cushion covers. Fabric shops sell tubular terry cloth. This is simply cloth shaped like a cylinder. Moreover, it is stretchy. If you want your vinyl berth cushions to suddenly feel better than they ever did before, buy a length of this cloth, sew up one end of it, and stretch it down over your cushion. To hide the seam, turn it inside-out for sewing, then reverse it as you put it on the cushion. It not only looks fine but feels just as good, especially when you lay your sunburned self down on them after enjoying a hearty day's sail. Your second mate will like them because they are so easy to remove and wash. If for some reason you cannot find the tubular terry, then purchase a stretchable terry (or a soft substitute) wide enough to sew your own cushion covers.

Despite their added comfort and coolness, the fact that you still hit bottom on the cushions will eventually drive you to make some additional changes. The cushion covers are the key to deeper cushioned comfort. Here's a trick that backpackers know: all you really need for total sleeping comfort is to be able to cushion yourself from your head to your hips. Arms or legs need not be on this diminutive bed. With that in mind, the addition of another two and a half inches of polyurethane foam to your present cushion, held in place by your stretchy cushion cover, will provide you with the kind of sleeping comfort you may have previously enjoyed only at home. I stressed the head-to-hip length of foam because in the Com-Pac 16 there is not a lot of distance between the hips and the after cockpit bulkhead over your legs.

So the cushion that is added is actually contoured or sloped down to the original cushion in the hip area. And if your sailboat is anything like mine with the empty V space between berths, then there is an opportunity to make the small boat sleeping area larger than it actually is.

We did this aboard *Nomad* by making a polyurethane foam plug that fits the area perfectly (cut the foam larger and squeeze it in). Naturally, it has its own cover of stretchable material. The open end of the plug cover overlaps and is secured with a strip of sewed-on Velcro. The accompanying photograph shows the plug in place and the surprising

The removable foam plug that fits between the two V-berths of the Com-Pac 16 widens the sleeping area considerably, adding to the comfort of the small pocket cruiser.

additional amount of berth space it creates in the Com-Pac 16's small but comfortable cabin.

Actually, the only bad thing about making these berths so comfortable is that in the morning, when you really should be up fixing breakfast and getting ready to make sail with the first decent light, there is an overwhelming tendency to settle deeper into your oversized berth, wiggle your toes, and snatch a few more moments of sleep.

When you are off on a cruise for several days, a nice refreshing shower in the morning isn't bad. Not to mention how great it feels at the end of a day, especially if you have been swimming in salt water.

But whoever heard of such luxury aboard a sixteen-footer?

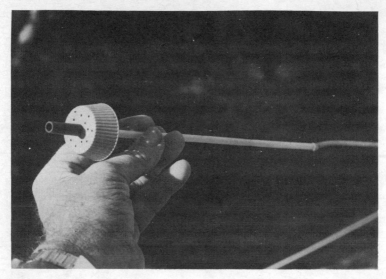

This breather tube and perforated cap when attached to a Clorox bleach jug of fresh water provide a conservative gravity feed shower.

It took me a couple of sailing seasons to solve that problem adequately. I knew there was a simple gravity feed shower on the market. With this you fill a black plastic bag with fresh water and allow it to spray out of a flexible shower head. Sailing in the summer tropics, however, about the only time you want to hang up a black plastic bag of water in the summer sun is when you want almost boiling water for some purpose such as washing dishes. You surely wouldn't shower in it at the risk of a pretty bad burn.

Instead, I played around with ideas that made use of items normally found aboard my boat. Clorox bleach jugs, for example, are marvelous containers. They enable you to stow away gallons and gallons of drinking water in any nook or cranny large enough to hold a jug. These containers are superior to most because of their durability. Moreover, the few drops of Clorox left in the bottom of the jugs after they have been emptied are just enough to help keep your drinking water nice and pure for a long time. Since you do not consolidate all the weight of your water supply but are able to distribute it evenly around the boat, you are better able to carry the load.

So, naturally, when I began thinking of a freshwater shower I began to eye my Clorox jugs. First, I drilled many tiny holes in a spare cap and tried squirting the water out over my head. This failed because there was no way the jug could breathe as the water was forced out. But the idea was basically sound and all I had to do was figure out how to make the jug breathe without putting a hole in its bottom. The solution was remarkably simple. I inserted a thin plastic tube through the cap, connecting it by a short length of rubber tubing to another length of plastic tubing that went to the bottom of the bleach jug. Spray holes were drilled in the cap all the way around the breather tube. This unit, consisting of no more than a Clorox jug cap and the breather tube, became my portable shower head. When not in use it was placed inside a plastic bag and tucked away. But when we wanted a shower all we had to do was open up a water jug, screw this "shower head" on it, hold it overhead, and receive just enough water to be able first to soap and second to rinse off. Squeezing the jug helped increase the force of the spray.

Conserving the amount of water used for a shower in this manner, two people can get a remarkable number of showers out of a single gallon of water. When Julie, my wife, and I sailed together in the fall when the weather is much colder, then we needed something black to solar heat our container of shower water. I tried spray-painting the white plastic jug black, but this never lasted long. The jug of water invariably got pushed against other gear and the black paint flaked off. The final solution, however, was to set the white jug in a black plastic bag and place the whole thing on deck in the sun for about an hour before the shower. By then the black bag had worked its magic: it had gathered sufficient heat from the

208 / Handbook of Trailer Sailing

sun to warm the jug of water inside. Such luxury of course always depends upon having sufficient fresh water. Even though only a small amount is used for a shower, eventually there is a need to replenish it.

Normally, this is no problem for most trailer sailors unless you happen to be sailing in areas where fresh water is in short supply. This is often the case in the Florida Keys after a summer of drought. Again, it was from the need to conserve fresh water that cruising sailors came up with a solution by which one can take a shower and come out feeling just as comfortable as possible—and not use a single drop of fresh water. A saltwater shower is just as refreshing and we never bother using our shower head for that one. All it involves is dipping up a bucket of sea water, adding to it one-half capful of the commercial fabric softener, Downy, and surprisingly, after the shower you will not end up with the stickiness you would with the salt water alone. Instead, you will feel refreshingly clean as you would after a freshwater shower. Once you try this you will save your fresh water for drinking and cooking.

All our showers take place in the cockpit. If you object to wearing a bathing suit, take your shower at night. Incidentally, on any lengthy live-aboard cruising we do, we always ask that whoever accompanies us bring swimming suits entirely of nylon. I realize we live at a time when youngsters enjoy swimming in cut-offs but such items, damp with salt water, almost never dry out. Wearing them slightly damp leads to quick discomfort. Nylon swimwear, on the other hand, even under the most humid conditions, dries in a few minutes. On tropical cruises, it can be worn day and night quite comfortably because there is hardly much change in temperature.

Similarly, saltwater sailors have discovered that the lemon-scented detergent Joy is aptly named as far as they are concerned. Joy lathers beautifully in salt water; consequently, all dishwashing is done in salt water using it, with a light freshwater rinse afterwards.

Speaking of washing them brings up the question of what kind of dishes are best for your sailboat. You will find that marine catalogs show a variety of nesting cookware and dishware, all usually of aluminum. Others can supply a line of quality plastic dishware or, more appropriately, dishware that appears to be ceramic but is made of unbreakable plastic. And of course there is the old standby: paper plates.

Being as small as it is aboard our boat, we opted to avoid a lot of dishware. Some people dislike paper plates because they are not very sturdy and they create a problem of disposal. Using them means having a lot of refuse to stow aboard between meals. Since most such items are rather bulky, the volume of this throwaway material can be quite considerable.

Any aluminum pots or pans or dishes around salt water eventually take on a speckled kind of corrosion that is not only unsightly but rather distasteful when you eat off the dishes. Aboard both my cruising sailboats we have adapted to a type dish that again is a favorite of back-packers—the Frisbee! The advantages of the Frisbee are well worth considering. The disc is the right size. It has sides that make it good for stew or anything juicy that you would not want running off into your lap. It is durable, yet flexible enough not to be easily cracked or broken. Several Frisbees nest together so nicely that we keep them inside our covered frying pan, thus eliminating an extra stowage problem. Frisbees clean up quickly after a meal, and if you should go ashore to a beach, your "dishware" turns into an invigorating source of fun for all. Even by yourself, with a brisk sea breeze you can fly your "dinner dish" Frisbee off a sand dune and have it boomerang back to you. Indeed, the company's motto should really read, "For Feeding and Family Fun There Is Nothing Like Having a Fling with a Frisbee."

Along with the dishware is the question of your boat's galley. How much you make of this depends upon how much boat you have to make it in. Larger boats have counter areas with built-in double burner alcohol or kerosene stoves. As the boat shrinks in size, so does its galley. In some boats about twenty-two feet long the galley is hidden and the same two-burner stove sits on tracks under a bulkhead over a berth. When needed it can be slid forward into its work position and then pushed back out of sight when not in use. Even smaller yachts have no apparent room for a galley, so it falls to the ingenuity of the boat owner to devise one.

You too can custom-make a sliding galley stove if you wish, or some trailer sailors simply carry a small fold-up stove that can be set up wherever the cooking is to be done. With the exception of extremely miserable weather, most of the cooking we do is over a small stove set up on the floorboard in our cockpit while we are at anchor. When sailing, we use a Forespar Mini Galley that is supported by our main hatch step. This remarkably compact stove is fired by a container of butane gas. It is a swinging unit that holds its several components—coffee pot, soup or stew pot, and frying pan—securely in its bracketed frame while cooking. The nice thing about this type of stove and other swingers is their size and the smallness of space required to use them. Like other marine stoves, they are available through marine catalogs and marine supply outlets.

Any cockpit cooking is convenient because the stove is shielded from the wind by the sides of the footwell. Of course there are times when the wind is so brisk that even the footwell will not contain it. I fabricated a windshield for just such times that does the trick nicely. Several corrugated cardboard panels were cut to the required height and, when laid flat, they were taped side-to-side with duct tape on both sides of the panels. The panels were then sprayed with quick-drying adhesive and sheets of aluminum foil pressed onto them front and back. The shield can now be shaped

Forespar's Mini Galley shown attached to my hatch step is a natural swinger capable of holding pots and pans in a gimbled unit fitted to the butane stove at the bottom. The small cooking unit fits tight places and is removable.

around your stove and pot to concentrate the heat within. I estimate that it cuts cooking time by at least 50 percent. It stows flat under a berth cushion.

The total contents of our galley aboard our sixteen-foot *Nomad* fit into a plastic dishpan. The single-burner stove, which fits into its own container/cook pot, nests with frying pan, coffee pot, and the usual culinary tools in one plastic container. Toweling, condiments, and canned goods occupy a second dishpan that has been laced at its seams behind the first.

These units occupy the after end of our eight-foot-long starboard berth. Naturally, since they are that far aft on the

The contents of an entire small boat galley will fit into a pair of laced-together plastic dishpans. This one is pushed to the after end of the boat's eight-foot-long starboard berth. Note also the stereo speaker and book racks on the bulkheads.

berth the unit would seem to be difficult to retrieve easily. By adding a long line to one end of the galley container, we can easily pull it within reach.

Putting it away, we use a boat paddle stowed alongside the berth that pushes it back to the after end out of the way.

If you keep your needs basic, the actual cooking aboard your boat need not be a complicated affair. While we carry sufficient canned goods and backup supplies for many days of cruising, they are infrequently used because much of our food comes from the sea or the lake or wherever we happen to be sailing. (More about that later.)

Sooner or later you will have to decide on what kind of cookstove to use aboard your boat. No one ever advocates using any kind of gasoline stove because of the potential danger of explosion. While units employing bottled LP gas (liquid propane) may not be as inexpensive or as hot, they are considered safer. So are alcohol and kerosene stoves. Some trailer sailors even use small cans of Sterno and Sterno stoves for cooking. All stoves, no matter what kind they are, should be handled with utmost care and caution when in use aboard a boat where a sudden wave can upset things.

To be on the safe side, go with the tried and true marine stoves. If you are planning only a weekend excursion it might be better to prepare your meals in advance and simply warm them if necessary. Or you can carry the basic ingredients and have them all sliced, or diced, or grated, to minimize actual work so that nothing but the combining and cooking need be done. For example, one of our favorite seagoing dishes that we cook at anchor is a Swiss fondue. Whether we make it in the cabin or in the cockpit the ingredients are all pre-packaged in plastic bags at home. The Swiss cheese, pre-measured and grated, is added to a pre-measured cup of white wine and cooked over a low flame until melted and then the pre-measured shot glass of Kirschwasser and table-spoon of cornstarch is added. Even the crusty French bread has been pre-cut to bite size and bagged. So it is just a matter of combining and simmering the basics, dipping the forked bread into the mixture and, with glasses of chilled Rhine wine, the feast is on!

One of the safest and nicest little stoves we have ever seen for cooking fondue or any other simple meal for that matter is the Keny pressureless alcohol stove. There is no pre-warming necessary as on other alcohol or kerosene pressurized stoves. The fuel for the Keny is absorbed into material that looks like cotton batting, so it is unspillable. The stove has a high and low control and a shutoff. Though not as hot or as

One of the simplest and safest boat stoves available, Kenyon's pressureless Keny alcohol stove is ideal for small cruisers. The stove's wide top accommodates large cookware and its low profile makes for easy stowage.

fast as pressurized cookers, it gets the job done cleanly. The Keny is made by Kenyon, P.O. Box 308, Guilford, CT 06437. Tel: (203) 453-4374.

There is quite an art to storing foods, living without ice afloat, and managing such things as one-pot meals, but these subjects are worthy of books themselves and you should read up on them whenever you can. One of the best books recently published contains a wealth of information from live-aboard cruising people around the world. It is *The Best of People and Food Cookbook* edited by Barbara Davis and published by The Seven Seas Press, 524 Thames St., Newport, RI 02840. Even if you are not planning any serious cooking aboard, this book is filled with valuable tips and time-savers on the subject of eating afloat.

All boats—trailerables as well as large ocean-going cruising yachts—no matter what size they are, share a common
problem: insufficient room to stow things. The smaller your
boat is, the bigger the problem. One consolation is that if you
have only "x" amount of room, you are only going to carry "x"
amount of gear.

The trick is in knowing how to distribute the gear so that it
is not underfoot all the time. Fuels of all kinds should be
stowed on deck somewhere, preferably in a compartment or
lazaret of their own in the stern so that if there is any leakage
or seepage it will go out through the cockpit hawse holes.

Aboard our small sixteen-foot Com-Pac, we found that
cargo nets or stowage hammocks, made for this purpose and
sold through marine outlets, took care of a remarkable
amount of gear. Again, I went through the usual problems of
trying to figure how to attach them to a fiberglass bulkhead.
The only absolutely satisfactory method was to attach fiberglass hooks and wood blocks to the bulkhead, then stretch
the hammocks between them. We have hammocks on the port
and starboard sides in the forward compartment of *Nomad*.
When these overflowed I began to look for other areas to be
enclosed in a net.

Import-Export shops often sell decorative nets. We found
some of the finely woven nylon commercial shrimp net that
was perfect for attaching under the forepeak deck of our
small boat where two-inch-square wood blocks with screwed-
in brass cup hooks strategically spotted around the under-
deck enabled me to suspend a section of netting extending all
the way aft to our foredeck hatch. In this area we stow our
life jackets. They are up out of the way and yet easily reached
in case of emergency.

Pieces of this stretchable netting can also be attached in
the same manner to such things as the underside of the side
decks over quarter berths where innumerable small flat
items can be stowed, the kind that are often likely to get lost

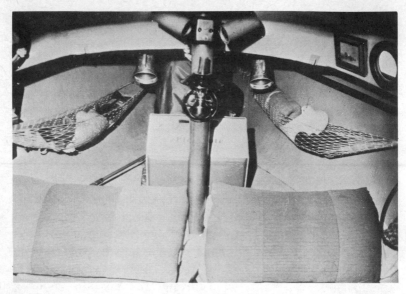

Forepeak stowage nets as I have used here aboard *Nomad* can be hung from small wood blocks and brass hooks fiberglassed to the bulkheads. The nets hold a remarkable amount of gear. Note the small kerosene lamp mounted below the cabin's electric lights on the boat's pressure post. The two tankards are also supported by cup hooks in epoxied wood blocks.

aboard a boat. It is the handiest stowage netting arrangement aboard *Nomad*.

Wherever there is space available we have tried to install small shelves. Once you start hunting for places to add a shelf you are surprised at how many places there are. On the Com-Pac I mounted the battery condition tester in a small block of Styrofoam painted black. This immediately presented a flat upper surface for a plastic lid that was secured in place and is now used for such things as keys, fuses, spare change, etc.

Aboard *WindShadow,* our larger cruiser, taut stowage netting has been cup-hooked to the mahogany woodwork over both the port and starboard berths.

Canned food, cooking gear, and the galley itself all go into the well-made plastic containers called StorageMates. This type of modular storage system has a variety of differently shaped containers made of sturdy, colored plastic. Those about one foot square are handy for pots and pans and larger items needed in the galley. The smaller modulars with a little modification become stowage containers or racks for books. Tucker Housewares, of Leominster, MA 01453, makes the containers we are using. They can be found in most department stores handling housewares.

Since we use our trailerable sailboats as land/sea live-aboard yachts, it quickly became necessary to bug-proof the boats' interiors. Bug sprays, bombs, and ointments are limited in their effectiveness. Strong defenses are needed against an after midnight attack of "No-see-um" black gnats or a swarm of mosquitoes. The alternative is either to seal

Small plastic storage modulars such as this can be adapted to a wide variety of uses aboard your sailboat. This is *WindShadow*'s portable bookcase.

yourself inside your cabin and stifle, or head for the nearest store that sells mosquito netting by the yard. This is finely woven nylon netting that will be just right for sealing off all your boat's openings against the hungry hordes that might try to eat you alive.

First, measure around all openings such as the companionway hatch, foredeck hatch, and portholes to determine how many square inches of netting are needed. Then add up all the linear measurements around the perimeter of these openings for the purchase of the miraculous fabric that sticks to itself—Velcro. Basically, here is what you will do:

Cement the fuzziest side of the Velcro about two inches to the outside around all your hatch openings. (The reason for using the fuzzy rather than the hook portion of the Velcro is that the hooks like to snag everything within their reach, be it a wool sweater or a watch cap. The fuzzy half of this one-inch-wide hook-and-eye Velcro material that you will be using will not do this.) Contact cement is used for this job. Since some amount of pulling will occur on the material I suggest you give it a double coat of cement, allowing the first to dry before applying the second. Then put up your Velcro strips.

When making the proper sized covering for the hatches, tape an over-sized piece of netting over the hatch so that all angles will be included. Then, with chalk or Magic Marker, draw straight lines to mark the outer edges of the hatch covering, remembering to allow at least two inches overlap of netting beyond the edges of the hatch. Masking tape will help hold the material smoothly in place for marking.

Cut the netting to size and then sew on a brightly colored strip of two-inch-wide cotton bias tape available when you purchase your Velcro, at most fabric shops. I suggest using a bright color to make these edges more visible in the semi-darkness when you may be putting up or taking down these screens.

The hook part of the Velcro stripping is now sewn onto this bias material so that it will mate with the fuzzy or looped Velcro strips around your hatches.

These screens easily roll up and stow in a small area. They can be quickly put up simply by pressing them in place.

To cover the opening ports on that boat, I made circular pieces of netting larger than each port and used small dots of Velcro sewn directly onto the netting. They mate with their counterparts contact cemented around the perimeter of the port. Dots were used here because the port's bolt heads provided the best places to anchor the Velcro. You may vary this method for your own ports.

Anyone with opening ports will realize that they will have a small problem about what to do with the couple of tea-spoonsful of rainwater that puddles in these ports after a shower. Since the ports open to the inside, you have to be fast to catch the water before it falls on the berth. This problem is easily solved on a sunny day by contact cementing a two- or three-inch length of oil lamp wick of one-half- or one-inch width to the bottom lip of the porthole. Now, when rainwater puddles there, it is quickly absorbed by the wick and drained out onto the side decks.

It seems that there is no end to the number of things you can think about that will make your sailboat more comfortable or practical. Experience is often the best teacher on how to utilize the amount of small space you have. It will not take many trips to tell you that traveling light is the best way to go, no matter how big your boat is. You quickly learn that bags are better than boxes for stowage and that there is really no need for a great deal of superfluous clothing. With the exception of cold weather sailing, where heavy sweaters and lightweight nylon or foul weather suits are necessary for warmth, most summer sailors find that everything they need will fit snugly into one of those small, sausage-shaped nylon duffle bags, preferably with a nylon or nonrusting zipper.

If you have a problem and you come up with an idea of how to solve it aboard your boat, don't be afraid to try it out. Think creatively. When I found puddles of condensation under our vinyl berths on *Nomad,* all I could think of was to put something under those berths that would absorb it. Several layers of folded newspapers did the job perfectly and we have never again had any problem with mildew there.

The stub keel of our Com-Pac 16 always allowed us to get within wading distance of shore, but in the wintertime no one cared to wade. Also, there were times when I wanted to leave the boat anchored in deep water and come ashore.

The answer of course was a dinghy. But where do you find a dinghy that will stow aboard a sixteen-foot boat without

Normally stowed in a backpack on the after end of *Nomad's* port berth along with its collapsible oars and foot-pump, this small one-man inflatable can be pumped up in minutes and serves us well as a tender.

Intended as a backpacker's boat, the inflatable has multiple air chambers and is used on a trolley system to get more than one person ashore.

being in the way, yet be capable of carrying several passengers ashore?

The problem seemed unsolvable, until I found a small inflatable boat to do the job. It is a one-man inflatable that fits into a backpack along with its take-apart oars and bellows foot pump.

This entire pack fits neatly on the after end of our sixteen-foot *Nomad*'s port berth and, like the galley on her starboard side, can be retrieved with a draw line.

The way we use this one-man dinghy to get more than one person ashore is to rig it like a trolley. A telescoping paddle holds a small saltwater fishing reel whose line terminates in a clip. The line is clipped to the stern of the inflatable and the first passenger rows ashore while the second stays aboard the boat, feeding him line from the reel. When the first passenger gets out of the boat, the second then reels the inflatable back to the boat and rows ashore himself, taking the rod and reel along. The process is repeated for each passenger and the same procedure is used in returning to the sailboat.

Quite possibly there are several inexpensive one-man inflatables that will do this job. However, the Sea Eagle pack boat inflatable we selected has features not normally found in the inflatables sold inexpensively as beach toys. Here are some of the Sea Eagle pack boat specs: Inflated length: 5' 8". Deflated size: 8" × 12" × 14". Weight: 8 pounds. Weight capacity: 1 adult or up to 250 pounds. You can see from these facts just how practical such a boat is even for the smallest of cruisers. Using the foot bellows on your minicruiser you can inflate a minidinghy in from three to five minutes. Not bad. If you would like further information about this little boat, contact Leisure Imports, 104 Arlington Avenue, St. James, NY 11780. Tel: (516)724-8900.

With our Com-Pac 19, we often carry a Thompson hard dinghy of sandwiched glass and rubber that has served us well in all respects for many years. This is a standard eight-foot dinghy that we carry atop our towing automobile on a boat carrier. When we are sailing, it follows behind the big boat so well we hardly know it is there. On long coastal cruises it serves admirably as our tender.

Every time a question arises in your mind as to how to do something to improve your life afloat, reason out a solution and follow it through. This is as true for the big things as for the little. For example, when stick matches, despite their being carried in waterproofed containers, sputtered and often failed more times than they worked, we eliminated them. They were replaced with inexpensive gas lighters for cigarette smokers. They never fail. Moreover, they can be adjusted to shoot a long flame into the wick of an oil lamp and seem to last forever. Load up on them.

Another simple cure took care of another small matter: when you wake up in the morning after swinging at anchor all night in some quiet cove, it is nice to know at once which way the boat is heading and where the wind is now coming from. All we have to do after waking up is look up. Overhead I have attached one of those small spherical automobile compasses for mounting on windshields or car dashes. This tiny telltale compass makes an ideal direction finder when mounted upside down on your overhead. The small suction cup that comes with these inexpensive compasses is seldom adequate for long-term mounting. I glued and stapled it to a small wood block, painted everything but the contact surface, and epoxied it overhead. Incidentally, I have tried many epoxy adhesives and found the fast-setting kind to be the least reliable for holdability. The best I have ever encountered is a two-part paste that winds up holding like iron. So far it has never failed me. You might like to check it out. If your hardware store does not have it, the product can probably be ordered from its source. It is called PC-7 Multipurpose Epoxy Paste made by Protective Coating Co., Allentown, PA 18103.

Finding ways to customize your boat for comfort is one of the enjoyable things about owning a boat. The only bad part is when you reach the saturation point and run out of things to make for it. Then I guess you have to buy another boat and start the fun all over again!

13

The Care and Feeding of an Iron Wind

Once upon a time, not so many years ago, sailboats made their way in and out of harbors without engines. Today, thanks to the necessity of sailboats having to work their way through often crowded marinas, some kind of power other than sail has become a must. For most trailer sailers that source of power is an iron wind, an outboard motor.

On most sailboats today, it is carried on a spring-loaded wood motor mount and aluminum brackets that can be lowered to put the outboard motor at its proper operating depth in the water. Because most large sailboats have high transoms, the outboards designed for sailboats usually have longer shafts so that the propeller unit is deeper in the water than it is on a standard or short-shafted outboard. This is to avoid cavitation or the lifting of the foot of the outboard out of water so that the prop spins wildly when the boat encounters waves or choppy waters. To obtain maximum drive and power the foot of the motor needs to be submerged at all times.

When not in use, the outboard and its mount are raised out of water on the spring-assisted lift bracket and the motor tilted forward so there is no drag.

The question that confronts all trailer sailors is: how large an outboard will I need?

Your boat, no matter what size it is, can be moved along by the smallest of outboards. This might be all right for getting in or out of a marina. But your motor will also be used to get you out of trouble. There may be times when storms catch you far from your home port and you decide to secure all sails and motor home. Winds and waves may be considerable so that now, instead of the small horse engine that got you in and out of port, you need something with drive, something that will power your big boat through the more severe weather conditions.

Most authorities on this subject suggest that you get the outboard motor that is the largest and most powerful that can adequately be carried by your boat. In other words, it is better to have more horses than you need rather than less. The reasoning behind this is that it is more economical to operate a larger outboard at half power than it is to run a small one at full power.

Sailboats that have heavy displacement hulls will go no faster than their hull speed, anyway. To determine your boat's hull speed, multiply the square root of its waterline length by 1.3. The answer will be your boat's hull speed in knots. This will be about the top speed that you can expect from your boat either under sail or power.

Even an outboard that might make a runabout boat double its speed will get nothing more than the hull speed out of a displacement hull sailboat. So, in selecting an outboard, go for one that will provide more horses than you actually think you will need. By that I mean keep the number of horses within reason based on some of the information that will follow.

With the exception of the small outboards, those featuring gear shifts that will enable you to shift from neutral to forward or reverse are distinctly advantageous. Of course, outboards that lack this feature will have power heads that can be turned 360°. Just remember, in starting up one of these outboards, as soon as they fire up, your boat will start moving.

In choosing a motor, be sure it is a make that is well enough known in your area so you can be sure you will be able to have it serviced and that parts will be available.

As for what size outboard will be best for your particular boat, I suggest that you ask your local sailboat dealer about this. He can suggest just how much horsepower he feels is necessary for the kind of boat you own. He may be a dealer for certain kinds of outboards, but just because he is, it may not be to your advantage to let him push off a certain kind of outboard on you. Check around first and if possible get another opinion. I know of one instance in which the dealer was pushing a certain make of outboard motor designed for sailboats, but made abroad. A friend bought one of these for his sailboat on the suggestion of his dealer and a year later the dealer stopped selling this line. My friend then had problems obtaining parts and service for the foreign-made outboard.

When purchasing a used sailboat that obviously originally had an outboard motor with it, inquire about the possibility of purchasing the motor with the boat, provided of course that the motor is in good shape. Often, you will get a good buy this way.

If the boat has been used in saltwater, ask the owner what kind of regular maintenance he employed to keep it in good working order. I hope he will tell you that after every exposure to saltwater he flushed out the water pump with fresh water and saw to it that corrosion did not occur. Usually the general exterior appearance of an outboard used in saltwater will be a tip-off as to how well the interior was maintained.

If the paint is chipped and there is excessive corrosion

around the foot, you can assume that the inside of the motor may be just as bad.

If you are unable to obtain any information about what size outboard will be best for your boat, here are some suggestions resulting from tests with sailboats of different sizes and weights and the outboard motor sizes that provided these boats with adequate performance in reasonably calm conditions.

For monohulled sailboats, they are as follows: 10 to 12 feet long, 2.5 to 3 horse; 12 to 14 feet, 3 to 4 horse; 14 to 16 feet, 4 to 5.5 horse; 16 to 18 feet, 5.5 to 6.5 horse; 18 to 20 feet, 6.5 to 9 horse; 20 to 22 feet, 9 to 12 horse; 22 to 28 feet, 12 to 20 horse.

The slender light displacement hulls of small catamarans and trimarans enable them to achieve higher speeds under both sail and power than the heavy displacement monohulled boats. Therefore, small cruising catamarans capable of handling larger size outboards will achieve higher rates of speed. Instead of mounting an outboard on each hull, most such boats have a single outboard mounted on a transom or through a deck opening on the centerline of the boat.

Heavy trimarans and catamarans that comprise the majority of the large cruising boats in this category may not develop any more speed from their higher powered outboards than would their counterparts in monohulls because they fall more in the category of heavy displacement hulls.

In performance tests in which three long-shaft Chrysler outboards of 6-, 12.9-, and 20-horsepower were tested on a twenty-two-foot Hirondelle catamaran, here are the results: The 6-horse achieved a top speed of 4.8 knots; the 12.9-horse of 5.8 knots; and the 20-horse of 5.9 knots.

To achieve this the 6-horse used a little over a gallon of gas an hour, the 12.9 consumed a little over two gallons of gas an hour, and the 20-horsepower consumed a little over two and a half gallons of gas an hour.

The 20-horsepower motor obtained six miles per gallon at

a speed of 5.9 knots; the 12.9-horsepower achieved seven miles per gallon at 5.8 knots; and the 6-horsepower motor achieved eight miles per gallon at 4.8 knots. For this boat the 12.9-horsepower motor would be the most cost effective of the three. The 6-horse lacked sufficient power if it were needed.

Hull speed of the Hirondelle cat is 5.8 knots. The reason why there is so little difference between the speeds obtained with the 12.9-horsepower motor and the 20-horsepower motor is that no matter how many horses were pushing the boat, when it reached its theoretical hull speed, nothing would make it exceed that point.

WindShadow has a waterline length of sixteen feet six inches. This gives her a hull speed of 5.2 knots. Recently, in running mileage checks over a measured mile in calm water with a 4-horsepower outboard on this 2,000-pound displacement hull, I found that at 5 knots the 4-horse outboard would give me 6.1 miles per gallon but if I cut back the throttle to 4 knots, the motor gave me 13.3 miles per gallon, better than twice the mileage when the motor was run at reduced throttle.

In his book, *The Outboard Book* (Motor Boating and Sailing Books, The Hearst Corporation, New York, New York, 1978), author Nigel Warren says, "The best mpg consistent with reasonably fast progress is achieved at a speed (in knots) corresponding roughly to the square root of the waterline length (in feet), and this rule applies to any displacement boat, whether cruising cat, monohull, or motorboat. . . . Forcing a boat to go faster rapidly diminishes the miles covered on a gallon of fuel."

This substantiates my findings on *WindShadow*'s motor mileage trials. The square root of her waterline falls exactly at the 4-knot figure which gives her her best mpg rating. While the 4-horse does well with this 2,000-pound boat, it is a better size motor for the 1,100-pound sixteen-foot *Nomad*. I power *WindShadow* with a British Seagull 170 that turns out an equivalent 7.5-horsepower and is equally economical.

The propeller that comes with your outboard motor may not be the one that will provide the best performance for your size sailboat. Unless the outboard is specifically designed to be used on a heavy displacement hulled sailboat, its propeller will be more suitable to move a smaller, lighter displacement boat. Most sailboats are heavy for the relatively small outboard motor that will be pushing them. It is essential therefore that the propeller on that outboard is pitched in such a way as to allow the motor to achieve its fully rated rpm.

For sailboats, three-bladed propellers are more efficient than two-bladed, and four-bladed are more efficient than three-bladed. Most American outboards will have three-bladed propellers. Stock props, on which the edges curl back, away from the blade, are not shaped for maximum efficiency when pushing a heavy sailboat. These are made for lighter displacement motorboats. A sailboat propeller will have no such curve to the edges of its blades. Generally, the best propeller size for your boat will be the smallest pitched prop that will fit your outboard. An improperly pitched propeller can overload or overspeed an outboard, both conditions resulting in power loss. Outboard motor manufacturers—and some have a hotline that will answer your specific questions—can be your best source of information about proper propellers and pitch for the size sailboat you wish to power it with.

Sailboaters should remove an inadequately pitched propeller that comes with their motor and either trade it in at the time of purchase for a better pitched prop, or simply keep it and store it away aboard the boat as a reserve. Chances are you will never have to use the spare because, the way outboards are built and used today on sailboats, the propellers are usually long-lived.

Basic Trouble-Shooting

Many reasons exist for an outboard motor to either stop running or to run poorly. If it has been performing all right, suspect something simple has gone wrong rather than something really bad. Solving the mystery of an outboard's problems is simply a matter of following the clues and eliminating the possible problems until the trouble is found.

Begin this process of elimination with the fuel system:

(1) Check for fuel in tank.

(2) Be sure fuel shutoff valve is open.

(3) Be sure air vent on fuel tank is open.

(4) With a remote fuel tank be sure to squeeze fuel pressure bulb on hose.

Pull the choke on and try to start the motor. If it fails to fire off after several tries, push in the choke and keep trying. If you smell fuel the motor may be flooded. Let it rest awhile and, with the choke in, try starting it again.

If the motor starts and stops and continues to remain stopped after you try to start it again, this may be due to fuel starvation. If you are on the water and unable to bring the motor into the cockpit footwell for repairs, an emergency procedure might be to continue squeezing the bulb on your remote tank hose to keep pressuring fuel into the carburetor.

Fuel starvation may be caused by fuel blockage to the carburetor, possibly a clogged in-line filter which should be removed and cleaned or replaced. However, if the motor does not start at all, then proceed to check out its ignition system:

Take out and inspect the spark plug(s). If a plug is in good condition it should be dry and colored grayish-brown at the spark gap. If it is wet and grungy and you have no replacement, clean it up with a small wood splinter, toothpick, or knife blade, picking out any carbon or sludge. Clean the gap and all surfaces to remove any fouling material. Wipe it dry with a rag. Check and regap it with a feeler gauge if necessary.

If the old plug is wet with fuel, that indicates too much of it is in the cylinder. With the plug removed, turn over the engine a few times with both throttle and choke wide open. This should dry out the cylinder.

Replace the plug(s) and reattach the leads. Try starting the motor again. If it fails to start, take out the plug and leave it attached to its lead, lay it on the cylinder, and spin the engine again. If you shade the plug with your hand you should see a healthy spark jump between the plug and the cylinder. If the spark looks yellow and weak, hold the lead by its insulation and, while positioning it a quarter inch away from the cylinder, slowly turn the engine over. A spark should jump from the lead to the cylinder. If the lead is capped with a rubber protector, insert the end of an insulated screwdriver into the protector, making contact with the metal terminal there and, while holding the insulated handle, place the screwdriver near some metallic part of the motor while you turn over the engine. If you get no spark, suspect a faulty plug or serious internal ignition problems that will probably require the attention of a qualified repairman.

If you have a good blue spark and the plugs are not fouled and are properly gapped, the engine should now fire off and run.

If it does not, you will have to pursue the problem inside the motor. If you are at sea, do not try to dismantle your motor over the water except in the direst of emergencies on outboards that are just too heavy to lift aboard.

Otherwise, bring the outboard into your cockpit footwell and remove the cowling. If you seem to be getting fuel all the way through your fuel line to the carburetor, dismantle the carburetor, empty and clean it out, then remove its needle valve. Blow through the orifice. Make sure the float is func-

232 / Handbook of Trailer Sailing

tioning properly, then reassemble the carburetor and, after making sure all the fuel is turned on and you have waited for the carburetor to refill, try starting the motor again. By all rights it should fire off and perform the way it is supposed to.

If it doesn't, don't lose your cool. Outboards can be notoriously temperamental and sometimes need coddling. When all else fails, ignore it for about ten minutes. Have a cool drink, relax your nerves, then attack it again. Try various combinations of throttle and choke adjustments. If your slow speed needle valve has been moved, reset it to the proper position as described in your outboard operator's manual.

After several starting attempts, recheck your spark plugs to see if they are wet or dry. Eventually your efforts will be repaid by a sputter and a roar as your iron wind finally decides to cooperate and comes to life.

Along with the above steps, be sure that nothing is fouling the outboard's propeller and that your fuel is fresh and properly mixed. These two suggestions are so obvious that they are sometimes overlooked.

It is wise to run a preliminary check on your outboard before any trip to be sure that fuel, plugs, and everything else is in proper working order. Never run an outboard out of the water because it may quickly overheat and be damaged. If you have used the motor in saltwater and do not have one of the devices that are made to clamp over the water pump intake so that fresh water can be hosed through the system to flush out the corrosive saltwater, here is an alternative: Run your outboard in fresh water for a few moments. If it is inconvenient to back your boat into a freshwater lake or pond, then try this: Lower the unit on its motor bracket and raise a plastic garbage can high enough on a table or wagon where it can be filled with fresh water and the motor run awhile at low speed to flush it out.

Always carry with your outboard a spare set of plugs, a plug socket wrench, spare shear pins, and a small assortment

After running your outboard in saltwater, if you lack a flushing device, lower the unit into a container of fresh water and run it awhile to get rid of the corrosive salts.

of tools. They should include a screwdriver, pliers, wrench, an old jackknife for scraping contacts, and a set of feeler gauges for properly gapping the plugs. Put these items in a small plastic fishing tackle box with some clean rags, nails, plastic hose, electrical tape, and the outboard's service manual and you should be able to handle most superficial problems that may arise. One nice thing about an outboard on a sailboat: you always have a backup system to get you home.

Winterizing

One thing most of us tend to overlook is the care an outboard motor requires while it is laid up through the winter months. Doing a good job of caring for your motor at this time is pretty good insurance for its being in top working condition for the next season. Failure to properly care for your motor at this time can cause just the opposite result: it can fail you when you need it. So here is some advice for preventive maintenance:

(1) With the motor immersed in fresh, clean water, remove the cowling, start the motor and, while it is running about half throttle, spray some rust-preventive oil slowly into the carburetor intake until the motor chokes and stalls.

(2) Remove the motor from the water, drain carburetor, fuel line, and tank. Spray the inside of the fuel tank with lubricating oil, then screw the cap back on.

(3) Disconnect the spark plugs and turn the flywheel with your hand to empty water from the water pump.

(4) Remove the spark plugs and turn the flywheel so that the piston will lift halfway up the cylinder (you will see its wall through the spark plug port). Leave it that way. Clean or replace the spark plugs.

(5) Spray everything under the cowling with a lubricant such as WD 40. Replace the cowling, spray it with lubricant, and wipe away excess. Do the same with the lower unit.

(6) Wrap the outboard in a plastic garbage bag and store it in a dry, well-ventilated place.

Most outboard motor manufacturers recommend that you check your outboard motor's gearcase oil level and change it after the motor has been run for at least ten hours. After that, the oil level should be checked after every 30 hours it is run, and the oil changed every 100 hours, or once every season, whichever comes first.

Since sailboaters seldom run their outboards as frequently as motorboaters, a once-a-year gearcase oil change should be adequate.

By inspecting your outboard's foot near the propeller you will find a screw-in type of drain plug. Several inches above it will be another screw plug port. This is called the oil level plug. When checking the oil level, stand your motor upright and remove the level plug. Normally the oil should come up to this hole. If the motor has sat in an upright position overnight, it might be a good time to remove the drain plug (the bottom one) and check for any water contamination. The water will have separated from the oil and will trickle out first, if any has managed to seep into the gearcase through a possible worn propeller shaft seal. If you find water, take the motor to a repair man and ask that he repair the leak to avoid possible gear damage in the future.

At season's end when you drain and change this oil, remove both the level plug and the drain plug so that the oil can easily drain out from the foot of the motor. Do this on a warm day and there is less chance that the oil will be thick and reluctant to drain.

Obtain a container of outboard gear oil especially made for this purpose and refill the unit by injecting the oil through the lower drain plug hole while the motor stands upright. When the oil appears at the level plug hole, screw in *that* plug. Then you can remove the oil container nozzle from the lower hole and replace that plug.

This procedure is followed to prevent air from becoming trapped inside the gearcase and giving you an incorrect oil level.

Any major problems with your outboard should be taken to your outboard service center. But if you take good care of your motor and keep it properly maintained, there is no reason why your iron wind won't be ready to give you the benefit of all its power whenever you need it.

14

Open Boat Sail-Camping

The pleasures of long-distance cruising and overnighting are not limited solely to sailboats that have cabins. Wherever sailors can get a trailerable boat into the water, they are going to enjoy the double-barreled benefits of sailing and camping. For sail-camping has advantages that many big boat cruisers never even thought of. Instead of being restricted to deeper water as are some of their bigger boat brethren, open boat sail-campers can go virtually anywhere just as long as there is enough water to float their boats.

Ponds, lakes, canals, rivers, bays, and the oceans are their waterways. All of their boats are not only trailerable but many are car toppers, capable of being carried on boat racks over the family vehicle. No matter how they reach the water, essentially they all share the same desire to combine the challenges, thrills, and fun of sailing with those of camping and to do it as efficiently as these smallboaters can, considering what they have to work with.

Sometimes ingenuity is the name of the game. Six people I know, comprising two families, solved their needs by creating a catamaran with their two canoes. Separating their hulls by several feet and lashing them to two-by-fours, they rigged a common sail, packed aboard all their duffle for a camping trip and, with the assistance of a single outboard mounted between the hulls, they often spent summer vacations sail-camping the coasts. Not only were they sail-camping but the evening I saw them sail into their campsite they had been sail-fishing—both families trolling up a long stringer of delectable looking bluefish that they intended cooking on the beach that evening for supper. Four adults, two children, a couple of canoes, and a homemade sail, and these folks have the time of their lives. All it cost them was a canoe apiece and some clever rigging.

No matter how large your boat, where there is a will there is a way. My Hobie Cat 16 to some might appear to be nothing more than a very fast sailboat, suitable only for day sailing. But looks are deceiving. The catamaran is ideally made for short- or long-distance sail-camping expeditions.

The first expedition I made plans for was to sail my cat westward, paralleling the beaches of the Gulf of Mexico, sailing from the northwest Florida panhandle on past the beaches and bayous of Alabama, Mississippi, Louisiana, and Texas.

Considering how fast the Hobie Cat went—Hobie Alter, the daddy of that popular cat, told me the 16 had been clocked just under thirty knots an hour—I did not believe it would take very long for me and my companion to reach Texas. There, we would phone for our wives to drive out with the boat trailer and bring us home.

A lot of planning went into that anticipated trip. I felt that by paralleling the coast we could always pull ashore anywhere to refill the few bleach jugs we planned to carry with fresh water. The gentle sloping sand beaches being what they were, we could easily push our cat up the shingle and get it high enough above the tide mark to enable us to camp high and dry each night on shore.

For that purpose, we planned to carry two rolls of three-foot-wide polyethylene plastic which would serve as "runners." The idea was to lay the plastic on the sand where the hulls would slide more effortlessly. We would wet the plastic to make it easier to push the boat well up on the beach.

Basic food supplies would be carried in waterproof plastic bags tied to the boat's trampoline. Snug-fitting, long-billed hats with fold down flaps would keep the sun from cooking our noggins too badly during the day. And as for a shelter at night, nothing could be more convenient than the protection of the trampoline of our boat. It would make a perfect roof between the hulls. We would sleep under it on inflatable mattresses and carry mosquito netting and insecticides to ward off any flying varmints.

When Coast Catamaran Co., which makes the Hobie Cat, was apprised of our intended long-distance sail safari, their representative, Sandy Banks, thought it was a great idea. He suggested that we scrutinize all our standing rigging and fittings to be absolutely sure that everything would stand the stress of such a trip. This of course we did. Our target month was June.

That June turned out to be the worst June in a decade. A hurricane completely devastated our plans. It threw everything out of whack so badly that our anticipated long-distance cruise never got launched along the coast, so we never had our shot at Texas. Instead, that August we spent a week sail-camping on the catamaran along the northwest Florida coast and bays.

My companion was a chap who had sold his business on the West Coast and bought himself a West Wight Potter. He was trailering his little sailboat to south Florida from where he could sail over to the Bahamas.

It was his first trip to Florida. One look at the Gulf Stream and he decided not to tempt the fickle currents of that river in the sea with his sailboat. He decided instead to join me for some Hobie Cat cruising along our northwest coast where things are a bit more benign.

It was a complete success. Along with our waterproof

plastic bags of gear we carried a small pop tent as a permanent base camp for my camera equipment and a few food supplies. But for the next week we kept ourselves pretty much satisfied with fresh fish, crabs, scallops, and oysters that we were able to forage from the waters where we sailed.

The catamaran was a highly efficient and fast boat to cruise on. We sailed among the deserted sand and sea oat barrier islands scattered along the coast east of Panama City, Florida. Fins, face masks, and snorkels, along with the pole spear I lashed to our cat's dolphin striker, were all we needed to be assured of having fresh seafood whenever we needed it.

A single-burner Coleman gasoline stove, its container (cooking pot) and lid (frying pan), and a roll of Reynolds wrap aluminum foil largely comprised our galley. A pocketknife shaped driftwood utensils whenever we needed them. Coffee, coffee pot, and mug, along with a medicinal bottle of brandy, took care of our other needs.

Our clothing was minimal. Our bathing suits were the uniforms of the day. Jeans, T-shirts, and lightweight nylon windbreakers became our more formal attire at night. Footwear, when we absolutely had to wear it, was flip-flops. At night we clothespinned the big canopy of mosquito netting to the underside of the cat's trampoline, using sand to seal and weigh the edges. Whenever it rained we rolled away from the centerline of the tramp where it was lashed together and managed to keep quite dry by avoiding the runoff. And since this was still the hurricane season, that week we had some runoffs—torrential—the kind all too common in the tropics that time of year. But once the sun came out and everything steam-dried, things were nice again. Each morning when we awakened we shared cups of coffee with a touch of brandy, hugging the cool shadow of the draped jib sail, between the cat's bows. Without the shade of the trampoline we could not have spent many days in that sun without severely dehydrating. Normal air temperatures that time of year are in the humid high nineties in the shade. You can imagine what it is in the sun.

One nice thing about sail-camping on a Hobie Cat is that you can cover distances so quickly that you are always within reach of civilization when you need it. One of our main campsites was about seven miles away from a state park where we occasionally bought ice. On the cat we made that trip in minutes.

In subsequent years of sail-camping open boats I purchased what was then called a Hobie Hilton. This is a gold-colored nylon boom tent made especially for the Hobie. It fits perfectly, entirely enclosing the trampoline. Now we sleep on the king-sized roominess of the trampoline, which on the Hobie 16 is designed to lift slightly in the foredeck area. This is intended to cause a hydrodynamic wing-like lift when sailing full out so that everything begins to go airborne as the boat develops even greater speed. At rest, this feature pro-

Either ashore or afloat, a boom tent can turn your boat into an instant overnighter. This nylon tent fits into a bag no larger than a grapefruit.

vides a head rest and the give of the tramp makes for some heavy sleeping.

I have enjoyed overnighting on cabin cruisers and overnighting on open boats and I honestly have to say that both provide somewhat different but equally enjoyable experiences. Open boat camping is a bit more basic and might appeal more to men and boys than to women and girls. But I would be hard put to choose which I have enjoyed more.

As I mentioned earlier, these experiences are not limited to one or two different kinds of boats. Practically any kind of boat that is big enough to carry a few basic camping and survival supplies can be your magic carpet that will get you away from the congestion of public camping sites and off into the wide open spaces where your view is not cluttered up by people and things but confined more to the natural beauty of nature. The water, the skies, the sand, and the forests; the wildlife, the soaring sea birds, the hidden bays and coves, the untracked beaches, the unobstructed sunrises and sunsets, these are yours to savor once you have the wherewithal to sail away and enjoy them.

Almost all sailboats are satisfactory for sail-camping. You could do it on a Sunfish with your goodies in a plastic bag, and I believe a good enough wind surfer could do it with a waterproof pack on his back.

If family is involved, your boat will have to be bigger. Beamy day sailers, with or without decks, can be adequate. Just remember that everything should be secured in waterproof bundles, and not everything in one big bag. Plastic garbage bags, the heftiest of the lot, maybe even one inside another, make nice lightweight, weatherproof gear bags.

The beamier the boat, of course, the more room for everything and everyone. Do not try to overcrowd too small or slender a sailboat. Boats that have shallow draft and easily raised or tilted keels and centerboards can be sailed right up on shore. You see how efficient all this is when you realize what a great load carrier a sailboat is. You don't even have to backpack to your pristine campsite. It is right there not far from the beach where you land. Chances are too that that beach will be littered with driftwood (i.e., firewood) for the taking.

Experienced sail-campers soon find that the fun of it all is not in how many things you can bring from home that will make camping in the wilds more like living at home but how nicely uncomplicated it can be if you keep it simple. Those who know not only how to make do with little but how to do a lot with what little they bring are the real winners. They are the ones who will have the least work and the most fun and end up feeling the proudest about their accomplishments.

There is no need to bring everything but the kitchen sink into the wilderness to be able to live comfortably. Quite quickly you and your family can learn how easy it is to cook over a wood fire, how easy it is to create a really comfortable campsite. But don't expect to be able to do these things without first learning how. Doing it well is an art. You can learn some of the tricks by reading such books as *Roughing It Easy* by Dian Thomas (Brigham Young University Press, Provo, UT 84602, 1974). It is a unique idea book about camping and cooking from scratch with creative techniques that not only work but prove to be fun for the entire family to participate in. Similar books on camping will teach you all the tricks.

Probably not everyone is ready to go back to basics in this respect, but such books show what can be accomplished with not much more than a little knowledge. You learn quite quickly that you can survive quite well in the wilderness without an electric can opener. Or, for that matter, without ice. Those who have learned most about performing this seemingly miraculous accomplishment are the deep-water sailors who may be at sea for weeks and months. They have discovered some of the tricks for getting along without ice and if you read about their experiences in such publications as *Cruising World* magazine, you will learn some of their secrets for yourself. In the next chapter I will discuss this in more detail.

Lakes and reservoirs make ideal areas to sail-camp. Newspaperman sailor-camper Frank Miles, who has for years used a Lightning sloop for many of his sail-camping adventures, speaks highly of such places as the Tennessee Valley Authority system as being ideal for this.

"The TVA lakes that I know best have almost no restrictions," says Miles. "A person can pitch his tent just about anywhere. But these lakes, like other man-made water systems, do have locks. The best preparation for locking through is to have plenty of fenders and mooring lines." Those not locking can use sites closer to their parking areas.

In some areas of the country, coastal sailors may have a problem with tides. Most are not as fortunate as Florida sailors whose tides are seldom more than a few feet. But elsewhere, if you sail your boat ashore along a seacoast and forget about the tide after you unload and set up camp, you may find that a few hours later the waterline has left your boat high and dry and is now thirty feet or more away from where it was.

How to get your heavy boat back into the water?

The answer to that one is not to get stranded in the first place.

Dory sailor Stephen Groppe solved the problem in a unique way. Groppe, who has cruised his sixteen-foot dory for thousands of miles, said, "Our boat is too heavy for us to pull up and down the beach; so when we go ashore to camp, we use an 'outhaul mooring' to keep the boat safely off the shore."

Groppe uses a sturdy anchor, chain, and a 100-foot nylon rode for his boat. For his outhaul mooring he has two lengths of 150-foot-long polypropylene 3/8-inch or 7/16-inch line, a net float, and a nylon thimble spliced onto a three-foot line. The float can also be an empty one-gallon Clorox bleach jug. Here's how it works:

THE GROPPE OUTHAUL MOORING SYSTEM

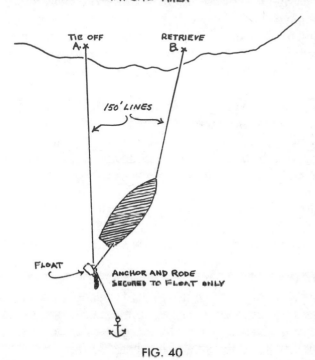

FIG. 40

Anchor your boat securely in deep water opposite your campsite. When sufficient anchor rode is out, tie it off securely to the handle of the bleach jug. Any excess rode should be coiled and secured there too. Next, pass one end of your 150-foot-long polypropylene line through the handle of the jug and tie it on to a stern cleat on your boat. Now, while letting this line run through your hand, go ashore with your boat. Once you have unloaded it, bend one end of the *other* 150-foot line to the bow and by pulling on the bitter end of the first line while paying out the second line, you can "trolley" your boat back out to the float. Secure both bitter ends of the trolley line well above the tide line ashore and your boat will remain in deep water no matter how low the tide drops, yet will be easily retrieved when you need it.

Sail-camping is not limited to the small boat sailor. The light-displacement day-sailing crowd probably makes up the majority of sail-campers, but even big boat trailer sailors, especially those with large families, are aware of the benefits of spending some time ashore so that the youngsters can let off steam.

The Alden F. Whitehead family that trailer sails the Long Island waterways in their O'Day 23, *Pixie,* has found that their family of four can have just as much fun, if not more, on a twenty-three-foot trailerable sailboat as on a thirty-five-foot yacht. For the last half dozen years, the Whiteheads have spent weekends and vacations cruising aboard *Pixie.* Usually the Whiteheads try to do most of their sailing while the children are napping or resting below. Then, as Alden says, "One of the beauties of a trailerable boat is the capability to beach the boat or anchor close to shore. This permits us to relax in the cockpit while watching the children play in the sand. Another benefit is gunkholing to beaches not accessible to large boats drawing over two and a half feet of water.

"A beach gives us extra living space like a backyard at home. It enhances the size of our boat."

Although not actually camping on the beach, the oldest child can accompany her father on beach scavenger hunts while the mother sits in the shade of the sun awning and their youngest plays in a "pool" (the cockpit filled with three inches or so of water).

After dinner the family often goes ashore to have a fire, toast marshmallows, pop corn, and recount the events of the day.

Other families I know use their trailer sailers strictly as a means of transporting their tents and camping gear to distant islands for weekend campouts. The sailboat is always available for recreation when needed. Since some of these campsites are many miles from their launching sites, and many families during summer vacation may spend up to a week or longer enjoying this life, it is obvious that they are sharing an extremely economical summer vacation, far more fun-filled than most people's vacations ashore. Sail-campers even eliminate the need for much boating fuel in order to reach the solitude of their private camping sites.

It is interesting to see some of these families enjoying the sand dunes, pines, and seven-mile-long virtually unmarked sugar-white sand of a barrier island on the Gulf of Mexico, a short sail across a ship's channel from the congested razzmatazz of a state park public camping area where people and campsites are packed side by side all season long. One can only hope that all those congested campers keep on being content right where they are.

If you are curious about how long and how far you can go with sail-camping, you might ask Hobie Cat sailor Kenneth Henwood:

"The traditional way to cruise the Gulf coast of Baja California has always been to pack a large cruising boat with gear and proceed to sail from anchorage to anchorage with an offshore view of the coast," said Henwood. "All very comfortable, but you have to pass up small isolated coves in favor of well-worn paths."

Watching the Mexican fishermen, who always seemed to be ashore in bad weather, gave Henwood an idea.

"In my fast, beachable sixteen-foot Hobie Cat, *Olu*, using lightweight camping gear for living on the beach, I could poke into places previously seen only from a distance."

In this way, sacrificing some "necessities" for the freedom to put into shallow out-of-the-way coves and make their camp, Henwood and his buddy, Ed Prorock, sail-camped their way along 350 miles of Baja's Gulf coast from near Santa Rosalia to Cabo Pulmo, south of La Paz. They made the trip in January and February, a time they chose because the prevailing winds are from the north then, blowing moderately hard each afternoon. This meant they would have a good run whenever they wanted to sail.

So the next time you want to try something different in trailer sailing, you might like to see how far you can go on a beach-hopping summer vacation of sail-camping. It's a combination hard to beat.

For more information on the subject, read *Camping By Boat* by Dan and Inez Morris (The Bobbs-Merrill Company, Inc., New York, NY, 1975).

15

Cruise Planning

The beginning of any cruise of consequence starts with lists. Lists of things that have to be done, that have to be included, preferably categorized so that at a glance you should be able to separate the wheat from the chaff. Or more accurately, keep your food requirements out of the clothing department; your camera gear out of your boating supplies. List them all separately but in the same notebook. I've found that the yellow legal-size pads make for good lists. Don't spare the ink. Think out carefully what you will require and get it down on paper. And don't expect to get it all down at one time either. Good cruise planning and list-making should take several days if they are done right. Just keep the notebook handy so that you can jot down additions when they occur to you.

If I plan to be cruising where I am just a short sail away from supplies or assistance, my lists are short and concise. But if I will be cruising where I may be several days away from any source of supplies or any hope of assistance whatsoever then I have to consider how to handle an emergency myself. If a mast stay were to snap, for example, I had certainly better be prepared to repair that break with some

kind of backup stay. Maybe it need not be any more complicated than a couple of bronze screw clamps and a length of
tiller cable, but I surely would plan to have something.

The same would be true for a first aid kit for the boat. If
you are going to be sailing somewhere out in the back forties,
consider all the things that might go wrong in which you will
need some kind of first aid treatment to protect yourself and
your crew. Naturally, if you are cruising along Lake Michigan, possibly you might need first aid items only to take care
of sunburn and minor cuts. But if you are cruising in the
tropics, you may want to include in that first aid kit such
things as a small bottle of diluted ammonia to counter the
burn of fire coral or the chance encounter with sea urchin
spines. You may even want to include such things as antibiotics, pain-killers, and disinfectants, along with tourniquets,
large bandages, and even a suturing kit in the event of a
major accident.

Of course one can imagine all kinds of off-beat accidents
that might occur, such as an attack of appendicitis, for
example. Or how about something as seemingly far-fetched
as a shark bite?

Though the latter may seem about as unlikely as appendicitis or as being struck by a bolt of lightning, both things can
and do happen, and if you are unprepared to cope with them
the results could be fatal. Lightning strikes may be avoided
by grounding your sailboat as well as possible. Short of more
elaborate preparation, aboard a boat with no backstay, you
can clamp a jumper cable to the forestay and let the other end
remain in the water. Ideally at least a square foot of metal
should be attached to the ground. That's why, on a boat with
a backstay, the jumper cable can be clamped to it and to the
aluminum rudder blade if such is available. At least this
provides some measure of comfort when you get caught out
on an open body of water in a lightning storm and your mast
is the tallest object for miles around.

As for shark bites, the worst I saw occurred eight miles offshore when a three-foot-long shark we had caught was being held up to have its picture taken and it swung up and tore a chunk out of a teenager's shoulder. Tourniquet, pain-killers, disinfectant, and bandages were the only things that saved the boy from going into shock before we could sail him ashore and get him to a doctor.

If we had been a week away from help, that doctoring, which included suturing, would have had to be done by ourselves.

On a lengthy cruise I always carry a Tupperware type flexible plastic box measuring 12″ × 10″ × 6″ that contains all the medications and bandages necessary to cover most accidents that might occur aboard our boat. Many of these are prescription drugs obtained through the suggestions and assistance of our family doctor. The very first item in the box is a copy of the soft-cover book, *Advanced First Aid Afloat*, by Peter F. Eastman, M.D., published by Cornell Maritime Press, Inc., Cambridge, MD 21613, in 1972. This is an excellent guide for the yachtsman and small boat skipper who venture beyond the range of immediate medical assistance. It tells you how to do everything from mouth-to-mouth resuscitation to (Lord forbid) how to perform an amputation. It also contains valuable suggestions about what to carry in a compact first aid kit. Before I leave this subject I want to mention that the discomfort of stinging caused by a variety of marine organisms can be eased by treating the area with some Adolph's Natural Meat Tenderizer. It contains papain that neutralizes the venom.

One of the first things you will need to think about in planning a cruise is a cruising chart of the waterways where you intend to sail. If you plan to cruise in salt water you will want to obtain charts from your local U.S. Coast and Geodetic Survey agent. If in doubt as to how to find him in your city, check the yellow pages of your telephone directory. Ask about a local source for the charts at a marina. They may even sell them there.

If you plan to cruise on a federal reservoir or similar waterway that falls under the government's jurisdiction, contact the U.S. Army Corps of Engineers for your proposed cruising area and obtain the necessary charts that may be available. All such publications are remarkably inexpensive and are sold at cost.

Recently, a friend and I cruised down a 106-mile northwest Florida waterway. It was part of a navigable river system which, like all such rivers and streams in the United States, falls under the jurisdiction of the federal government. The charts for that trip comprised a bound volume of low-altitude aerial photographs that was 14″ wide, 20″ long and ½″ thick. Not only did these charts provide us with a precise bird's-eye view of about three miles at a time, page by page, but all the major navigation features were indicated along with mile markers for the whole trip. The cost for this prodigious amount of work was five dollars.

Plan early to obtain your charts so you can plot your courses and know exactly where you intend to go. In the case of U.S. Coast and Geodetic charts, lay out your course ahead of time with all the compass bearings clearly indicated so there will be no need for you to do this while sailing.

If you are planning on a short weekend or overnight cruise, your list will be a lot shorter. In some instances you may decide to bring food that is already prepared at home. Precooked meals are excellent. All you have to do is keep them in a cooler. Such things as sandwiches and fried chicken bagged in plastic need only to be served.

If you are planning a more extensive cruise for a week or more, then you will be more concerned about keeping such things as fresh vegetables and eggs over a longer length of time. Normally, trailer sailors need not be as concerned about these matters as those sailing for long periods where they are unable to replenish their supplies. Most trailer sailors can easily replenish their water and food supplies when needed, without difficulty. So, many will be content with storing a variety of canned goods as a supplement to the fresh food items that will probably be used first.

We have found that a good way to keep everything in better shape aboard our boat is to bag it in plastic. It makes no difference what it is, if moisture can effect it, tuck it into a plastic bag and either twist-tie or Zip-loc it. The newer, easier Zip-loc plastic bags have been a boon to both campers and sailors.

If you don't want your clothes to take on a certain amount of dampness, bag 'em. This is also especially true of packaged goods such as sugar, salt, cornstarch, and even such things as packaged macaroni and cheese, not to mention all spices. Leave these items exposed to the air for a couple of days on the water and you may find they have turned into hard bricks.

Plastic bags will prevent this. No matter where you cruise, a certain amount of dampness will pervade everything on your boat. What the sea air doesn't get, condensation will, unless you protect it.

Clothing should be rolled and one or more pieces placed together in some kind of lightweight plastic bag that can be sealed. Sometimes you can line a duffle bag with a plastic bag and close off the moist air from these items in this manner. Fortunately a wide variety of lightweight to heavy duty plastic bags is available to fit any need. All our garbage and disposables go into a plastic bag kept aft in the cockpit locker. Not far from it will be found our oily funnel, container of outboard motor oil, and oily measure, combined in their own small plastic bag.

Have the kids collected a bunch of seashells, some with critters still hiding in them? Nothing works better for those soon-to-be-noxious treasures than to secure them well in a plastic bag. In time you'll wonder how you ever got along without these transparent, easily packed space age wonders.

I could expand on how invaluable they are for storing fresh meat or fish fillets in the cooler, but I believe you get the idea. One word of warning: remove any sharp fins from fish or the bags will be punctured and all their juices will mingle rather disagreeably with your melted ice water. If you are fortunate enough to cruise where fresh shrimp are available, avoid plastic bags for them or their sharp horns will do what fins do. Store the shrimp in some of those flexible plastic refrigerator storage containers and be absolutely sure none of their essence gets into your cooler or your crew may elect to abandon ship.

Plastic bags of the proper size are also great for protecting your camera and lens if you lay them down in the cockpit for a moment. Just remember not to close the bag tightly or it may sweat. The plastic will not only keep the gear from getting splashed, but if you sail in saltwater, there may be moisture on your cockpit cushion that will eventually show up as rust on your camera housing.

One of the weightiest problems confronting small boat cruisers is the stowage of food and water, and the best way to keep perishable things cool.

If you are going out for a few hours' sail, there is no problem. Crushed ice or ice cubes from home will suffice. If you are going off for a few days cruising, forget the crushed and cubed ice. It will last only a matter of hours. Think in terms of block ice.

If you are going off cruising to areas where ice is unobtainable, or simply too difficult to get, think in terms of dry ice. Here's how my dentist and his crew of seven work it on a week-long cruise: they take two coolers—one with block ice that can be ice-picked into smaller chunks for cooling beverages, and one for frozen food to last for the entire trip.

All the food is prepared in advance. It consists of such dishes as beef stew, chili con carne, beef Stroganoff, and spaghetti and meat sauce. These combinations go into two-pound coffee cans topped with snap-on plastic lids and frozen (a two-inch space at the top is left for expansion).

These containers of frozen food go into a pre-cooled cooler and are taken to a meat-packing business that sells dry ice. The dry ice people will tell you how many pounds are needed, depending on how long the food is to remain frozen. The dry ice is then wrapped and placed atop the frozen food cans and the cooler is taped shut.

On the cruise, this cooler gets opened briefly only once a day when the cook takes out a can of food in the morning so it will thaw out for use by noon. In this manner, the cook has nothing more complicated to do than warm up the meal every day for a week.

A variation on this is to bury a block of dry ice in a pile of ice cubes in the center of a cooler, then stack food around it. The dry ice will weld the cubes together and provide a longer lasting block of ice than if it were nothing more than plain ice. Just remember, when dry ice provides the only coolant, to make sure nothing is exposed to it directly such as un- wrapped fruit or vegetables or they will be freeze-burned and unusable.

For weekend cruises we often freeze water in advance in various sizes of plastic containers that fit our coolers. This way we have the refrigerant when we need it and as it melts we then have cold drinking water. Again the multipurpose Clorox bleach jug is a nice size and shape to handle for this purpose. If you need more room for food, stow the frozen jugs elsewhere. Just make sure not to stow it to thaw where it will drip on a wife's berth, as was once done by persons who shall remain anonymous. Thawing jugs sweat and will, I assure you, soak the entire foot of a berth.

Today, coolers come in all sizes and degrees of quality. Generally, you get what you pay for. It will pay to invest in a good one—a chest with thick insulation. Forget the basic styrofoam box kind of cooler unless you are willing to put up with its leaking. Large coolers such as the forty-eight-quart coolers with trays for keeping food out of the ice area are standard and good. Two coolers—one for food and the other for drink ice—may work more efficiently than one that needs to be opened repeatedly.

It seems to be a tossup among users as to whether it is better to leave melt water in the box or to drain it off. Some argue that the melt water causes quicker thawing, while others say the melt water maintains the box's coolness. If it is clean and fresh, I usually leave the water and keep the food sealed. I know in extreme cases the icy water without ice has prevented food spoilage in tropical heat for a day until we could replenish the ice.

A lot of coolness is often lost through inadequately insulated cooler lids. You can cut down on this by adding a plastic-wrapped piece of foam rubber inside the box. Some trailer sailors also help their box's efficiency by replacing used food items with blocks of styrofoam so less area has to be cooled. Any way that you can think of to insulate your cooler better will result in longer lasting ice.

After many trips, despite careful soap and water washings, your box may develop a disagreeable odor. You can freshen it immediately by wiping its inner walls with a small clean cloth that contains two or three drops of vanilla extract.

In packing an ice chest for a cruise, chill the box with ice several hours before you plan to use it and it will stay cool longer. To help keep such things as vacuum bottles hot, pour boiling water into them for a few moments and then empty and add your soup, tea, or coffee. A good glass vacuum bottle will keep the contents hot all day. Trailer sailors who might want a variety of beverages or soups can save themselves considerable trouble just by filling one or more quart vacuum bottles with boiling water. The water can be added to such things as instant tea, coffee, boullion cubes, and a variety of dehydrated products including soups and mashed potatoes.

All you need to serve a quick meal and beverage afloat is enough boiling water and the rest is modern-day magic!

On *Nomad* and *WindShadow* our noonday meals are kept simple. The fisherman's favorite combination is often a package of soda crackers, a flip-top can of beans and frankfurters, and a can of sardines. While sailing we often snack on these, too, since they are basic and easy. Crackers play a large part in many of our meals. They go well with fresh oysters and scallops for lunch and with the wine and cheese before supper at sundown. For years I tried to figure out the best way to keep crackers reasonably fresh aboard our boats. The tin container that takes an entire box worked well for a while, but being bulky aboard a small boat, it often lost its lid and humidity took over the crackers.

Recently, however, I discovered an ideal package that keeps our soda crackers crunchy for weeks on the water. We found that the containers for Pringles potato chips are just the right size for a single package of about 100 soda crackers. We tape the lids on with freezer tape and weeks later the crackers stored in these cans are still fresh. Since we use the containers over and over again and some rust began on the metal ends of the containers, we spray-painted them and ended the problem. Probably the next best thing about these containers is that you can stow them anywhere and they take up hardly any space. Several get tossed into the port and starboard cargo hammocks of our sixteen-foot *Nomad*, as well as anywhere else the long round boxes fit.

Cruising sailors enjoy a variety of snacks while they sail and few are easier to serve and more nutritious than dried fruits and nuts. An inexpensive source for these items is your local food coop. Some live-aboard sailors even take the time to dehydrate their own fruits and vegetables. They use solar dryers, often nothing more complex than a cookie tin and grill with reflective aluminum foil under the grill and a cover of mosquito netting to protect the food from flies.

One of the niftiest ideas I ever heard appeared in *Mother Earth* magazine not long ago. A reader reasoned that since campers and trailer sailors often left their vehicles parked all day long in the sun, they were hotter than ovens inside. So he suggested making good use of this fact. He made a small wooden rack, stapled nylon netting on it, and placed sliced bananas, apples, and any other fresh fruit onto the netting. Then he set it up on the dashboard on his parked car. By the end of the day he had dried fruit! Quite an idea. If you want to try making a collapsible model, put wing-nutted bolts in the corners of the rack.

We use fresh vegetables and fruits as often as possible on long cruises. But in the tropics, where air temperature during the day is often a humid 98°, it takes a bit of doing to keep everything for a week or more without refrigeration. But it can be done if you pack carefully. Fresh vine-ripened tomatoes, for example, should be wrapped individually in newspaper and placed in cardboard cartons, then stowed in the shade. The tomatoes will last for weeks.

Other vegetables can be handled in a similar way. Root vegetables should be kept as dry as possible, separated from each other in a ventilated compartment. On especially long cruises where supplies may be difficult or impossible to obtain, some sailors carry buckets of moistened sand and bury their root vegetables in the sand to keep them fresh. Most trailer sailors are not that anxious to take on the additional weight of the sand, but it apparently does the trick.

When you cruise with cameras and film, plan to carry them in their own weatherproof bags. I keep all the color film in a plastic bag that fits inside the large bag containing cameras and lenses. Since I use a variety of cameras and lenses and need a bag that offers me quick and easy access, I chose an insulated diaper bag with snap-open top. These bags often have built-in stiffeners in their ends and keep equipment from being crushed with other boating gear. Usually I reinforce these stiffeners with thin pieces of plywood contact cemented in place and then covered with soft material to prevent any possible chafing. Individual lenses are often wrapped with small hand towels to cushion them and the other equipment. Surface cameras and underwater cameras are never carried in the same bag. Each has a bag of its own to prevent possible saltwater contamination, even though all of this gear is given a thorough fresh water rinsing before being dried and stowed away.

Speaking of weatherproof bags for cameras, some companies package food in weatherproof (meaning rustproof) containers that are lighter weight than any canned goods. Moreover, these foods are specially prepared for backpackers, campers, and cruisers who want complete simplicity. You don't do anything but heat and serve.

I'm speaking of the foods in foil pouches, such as Backpacker's Pantry products produced by Dri-Lite Foods Inc. of Redding, California, and the retort packaged products of Yurika Foods Corp. of Birmingham, Michigan. There are other brands on the market but I mention these because they are most familiar to me. The Dri-Lite foods must be reconstituted with two and a quarter cups of boiling water after which they must be left to set for five to ten minutes. They can even be reconstituted in their foil pouches. The result is such a combination as no-cook Stroganoff with beef. Dri-Lite's 6½-ounce pouch of Stroganoff, for example, when reconstituted provides two 11½-ounce servings. The foil pouch can be crumpled into a tiny ball and there are no cans to contend with. Cost at this writing for the two 11½-ounce servings is $4.65.

The Yurika product is similar in that it is also contained in a foil pouch. But there the similarity ceases. The retort product is not freeze-dried or otherwise dehydrated. The food has simply been cooked and sealed in its own pouch. All you have to do to prepare it is to put the pouch in a container of water and heat it. Then tear open the pouch and serve. One advantage retort cooked food has over the dried products is

Dehydrated and pouch food have these advantages: lightweight packaging, simple preparation, and long shelf life. For these reasons they are popular with cruising sailors.

that no water need be added to the product itself, which means you save some fresh water in the preparation. Retort foods can be heated in salt water if necessary. Probably the greatest difference to many people will be in their taste. Some feel that the retort foods have more sealed-in flavor than the dehydrated products.

As far as comparable costs go, consumers need to consider the advantages or disadvantages of the foods and their packaging against the conditions under which they will be used. For example, if weight is a consideration you might not want to stock up with an array of canned goods. In any event, here is what you will currently get for your money:

A 10-ounce serving of retort prepared beef Stroganoff retails for $3.48. More than twice that amount, or a 23-ounce serving, of reconstituted freeze-dried beef Stroganoff retails for $4.65. In my opinion the 10-ounce serving of the retort product would be inadequate for two hungry sailors. But twenty ounces of retort beef Stroganoff would make that meal cost over $7.

Or perhaps you prefer beef stew. Retort prepared beef stew (two 10-ounce pouch packs) retails for $5.81; the dehydrated beef stew (two packages amounting to 12 ounces each after reconstitution) retails for $4.80; and canned beef stew (24 ounces) retails for $1.50. But the dried product weighs only four ounces!

So for these foods that require little preparation and are light to carry, with no trash of any consequence to dispose of, you pay a premium while often sacrificing flavor. But in exchange you get convenience and a long shelf life.

Along with food, water, ice, clothes, and charts for your cruise, make sure you have all your boating needs. Check out everything before you leave. Are all your flashlights handy and working well or do they need fresh batteries? Is your storage battery up to snuff? Trickle charge it before you leave to make sure. Are your anchor light and running lights all operating, or is there a problem that needs correcting? Have you remembered to put fresh water aboard? How about fresh outboard motor fuel? Is everything aboard that you need, or did you take out some important item to dry or repair and forget to put it back again? Check out all lanterns, clean their chimneys, and trim their wicks if necessary. Get spare wicks just in case you finally finish one in the middle of the night. How about your boat bumpers? Are they all aboard along with other gear in that category? Are all your life vests stowed within reach or are they still hanging on the clothesline to dry? Blankets and bedding all aired out and fresh sheets and pillowcases aboard ready to go? How about towels and swimming suits and binoculars and a million other things that you will surely need?

How to remember them all? Go back to your lists. Check off everything that goes aboard; circle those items that may have to wait until the last minute. Do everything long before your moment of departure, preferably at least no later than the day before you intend hooking up and trailing off on your cruise. That way, while you are driving along the highway mentally ticking off everything you planned to bring, you won't have to turn to your wife and say, "Oh, did you remember to bring . . . ?"

And hear her say, "My gosh, *no*. Didn't you put it in?"

16

Fun Afloat

Sailing is only part of the fun of being on water. A lot of other fun things can be done there, both on it, beside it, and under it. Trailer sailors who fail to take advantage of these things are missing half the show. After all, they are coastal cruisers who have far more opportunities to do these things than the big boat deep-water sailors. In their shoal draft boats they can sail far and wide along the ever-changing shorelines of lakes, rivers, bays, and seacoasts, exploring any and all interesting looking coves, deserted islands, meandering bays, or intriguing backwaters. Just looking becomes a favorite pastime. Just looking with a pair of binoculars from a quietly ghosting sailboat, one can watch wildlife without panicking it and often see sights seldom seen before.

One spring morning in a quiet cove on a Georgia reservoir I watched redwing blackbirds catching fragile-winged mayflies in their beaks, then walking to the water and dunking the flies repeatedly, making them easier to swallow. After a good soaking, some of the birds flew into the marsh with their beaks filled with the lacy-winged insects as if they might be carrying the pre-soaked and softened food back to their nesting young. I felt privileged to have seen this.

Many a morning while enjoying coffee in *Nomad*'s cockpit we have been entertained by the large black and white skimmer birds common to our coasts as they try to catch breakfast by flying just over the water with the lower half of their bright red beaks skimming the surface for minnows.

Another time we watched large swallow-tailed kites over the Apalachicola River as they fed themselves in mid-flight, reaching back to tear pieces of fish from their talons as they soared gracefully overhead. And once we were fascinated by a pair of playful eagles that climbed high above us one afternoon over a desolate Florida lake, came together, locked their talons, and free fell in tumbling unison with folded wings for several hundred feet before releasing each other and flying off in opposite directions. We had watched the mating of eagles!

Birdwatching is fun and watchful coastal sailors have an unprecedented opportunity to look in on an even wider variety of animal life. Sooner or later they will see gamboling raccoons, deer coming to the water to drink, stealthy stilt-legged egrets or herons fishing along shore, a family of skunks, pelicans, an army of comical sandpipers. They are all there to be seen.

As shoal water sailors we have the option to go ashore virtually anywhere we can beach our boats. When we do we are able to come into intimate contact with the wildlife we might normally have watched from afar. On certain barrier islands along the northwest Florida coasts there are skimmer bird rookeries. Ashore we are greeted by raucous cries of the adults who swirl overhead in a black and white cloud while some put on a comical display of "crippled bird" as they try to entice us away from the young. Both the young and the unhatched eggs are in the open, easily spotted on the bare sand beach.

In other instances, an encounter might be more startling. One evening a friend and I were sail-camping on one of the islands with my Hobie Cat. We had moved up into the sand

Outgoing tides will never maroon the shoal draft fixed keel Com-Pac yachts on a beach when they can be parked in wading-depth water. Going ashore to explore an isolated shoreline is one of the enjoyable things about sailing coastal or inland waters.

dunes after dark and built a small driftwood fire to cook hot dogs. The fire was reduced to glowing embers when my companion suddenly let out a yelp.

I stared at him in the darkness and saw, standing beside him and nuzzling his shoulder, a small deer. It was apparently looking for a handout. We fed her what we had—hot dogs and buns which she consumed with such relish I figured she had been panhandling campers before. She ate to her heart's content while we petted her and, when we ran out of food, she ambled off into the sand dunes and pine scrub behind us.

If you are overnighting anywhere along a coast in a sheltered cove where sea birds are active, it is a pleasure to watch the antics of seagulls. Start tossing them soda crackers and you will have a flock of them practically feeding out of your hands. For any of you photography buffs, that's a great time to shoot some seagull pictures. Just remember to use your fastest shutter speed.

After several hours of sailing, it is always fun to pull into a beach and let the family do some beachcombing. The islands we roam are backed by many miles of brackish bay and fronted by many miles of deserted Gulf beaches. One finds a variety of bay marine life along the brackish water sawgrass and sand flats on one side, and then a short walk over the sugar-white dunes brings us to the ocean-flanked beaches where we swim, look for seashells, driftwood, and bits of bleached coral. A handful of plastic bags is all one needs for collecting. It might be wise to take with you also a visored cap of some kind, a pair of sunglasses, and sunburn cream along with the awareness that you need to be careful not to soak up too many ultraviolet rays.

Sometimes, in a particularly pleasant place, we might gather driftwood for an evening fire on the beach, with hot-dog roasting or popcorn popping over the embers.

One day, on one of our explorations of a barrier island, I spotted a piece of string. The string was frayed as if it had had a lot of use. It lay across the top of the sawgrass and stretched inland as far as I could see.

I began to follow it and it led me over several low sea-oat crested sand dunes. Finally, in a small valley, I found the other end of the string attached to a large red and white plastic bat-wing kite with a long yellow tail.

I picked up the kite, tossed it into the air, and it immediately flew high over my head as I let the frayed string slip through my fingers.

I was so enthralled watching this marvelous find with its long plastic tail as it climbed steadily higher on the sea breeze that before I knew it the kite was flying over the bay and the end of the string slipped through my fingers.

I dived after it as the end dangled just inches above the sawgrass and just out of reach of my grasping hand. My wife looked up just in time to see me come kangarooing through the tall grass in my flip-flops until one stuck in the mud. After that I was bounding even higher because few things are more uncomfortable underfoot than the sharp blades of this grass.

Just as the string was following the kite out over the water, a final headlong dive nailed it. That kite is still part of the permanent gear aboard our sailboat. We fly it often. I

At your afternoon anchorage, flying kites from your sailboat is an enjoyable pastime for young and old alike.

changed nothing about it. The string is still frayed, the yellow tail has gradually lost a couple of feet of its length in the course of time, but after many an afternoon sail, while we are enjoying sundowners, our bright-colored plastic kite soars high above us. Sometimes I tie it off to the tiller and it flies above us all night long. Sometimes we have more than one kite flying at a time. In fact, kite flying became so much fun aboard our sailboat that we gradually acquired several different kinds.

One is a very fast and maneuverable fighter kite from India that is flown on a 100-foot length of strong nylon carpet thread. Different ways of handling the string make it fly in different directions. Another is a forty-five-foot-long Mylar dragon kite with a spool of what must be a mile of string on it.

We fly our kites at anchor. There are few better places to fly these fantastic shapes than on unobstructed waterways and along the beaches. It is really a sport for all ages. Everyone enjoys flying a kite.

Last summer from our anchorage in Largo Sound near Pennekamp Coral Reef State Park at Key Largo, I watched with my binoculars while a paraplegic in a wheelchair flew three kites in tandem. They were two-string manueverable kites. It was a pleasure to watch the fun he was having with them as he dived and swooped them over a large parking lot near the water.

On another day a short distance away I watched another sailor do something I had never seen done before with a kite. Not only was he apparently flying it underwater but he was also able to fly it up out of the water.

As any dedicated kite sailor knows, once his kite nose-dives into the drink, any further tugging on the kite string causes the kite to do just the opposite of what he wants it to do. It will sail hard for the bottom. Only by gentle steady pulling can one normally retrieve the wayward piece of plastic.

So, when I realized this sailor was flying a kite that

This Skipjack sailor in the Florida Keys designed his own two handed kite, one that flies underwater as easily as it does in the air.

appeared to be half fish, I jumped in my dinghy and rowed over to find out what kind it was.

He said he had designed it himself. He was living aboard an old Skipjack that he had purchased and been repairing gradually over the last seven years. One of his hobbies was kite flying. He had designed the kite he was flying but would not divulge how it was made to fly up out of the water. It resembled the manueverable two-string kites that were flown by the man in the wheelchair except that this one was larger and seemed to be more maneuverable.

Kites take up little room in a sailboat and flying them is a pastime that is nice entertainment for the entire family. If you would like more information about kites and their cost, write for a copy of the Spectra Star Kites Catalog, Spectra Star

More family fun can be had spinnaker flying if your spinnaker is big enough
and your wind strong enough.

Kites, 3519 Caribeth Drive, Encino, CA 91436. Tel: (213) 897-2979. Toll free outside California: 1-800-423-5614. Also, if you would be interested in reading more about the worldwide sport of kite flying, you will enjoy reading the quarterly journal, *KiteLines,* published by Aeolus Press, Inc., 7106 Campfield Road, Baltimore, MD 21207. Tel: (301) 484-6287. Subscription for one year (4 issues) is $9. It is a remarkably well-done magazine that tells you everything you might ever want to know about kites, kite flying, and current new designs in this sailing-related activity. Incidentally, one of the models that can be ordered through Spectra Star Kites is a Kite-A-Maran—a kite that looks like a catamaran. If flies in the sky and sails on the water! Even the ship's captain will be lucky if he gets to play with that one.

Fishing is another sport to pursue on the water. It makes no difference whether you are a fresh water sailor or a saltwater sailor, you can try your hand at fishing wherever you are. On fresh water lake and river cruises, it is no trouble to tie several cane poles on deck, curving them around the standing rigging well out from underfoot. For bait, you will have already stowed aboard a small container of worms that you have kept cool.

In the evening I try to drop anchor in a quiet cove where fish might bite. This often results in a fine catch of panfish for supper.

On river trips where there may not be still water areas, we rig the open-face spinning reels with slip lead (free-running) sinkers, and bottom fish the deeper water for catfish.

Quiet afternoons near sundown on reservoirs or lakes are perfect times to put out a long line or two from a casting rod and troll for black bass. While it might seem that your boom and sail will interfere with your long fishing rods, actually nothing could be easier. On *Nomad,* my sixteen-footer, I mounted a length of PVC pipe alongside the motor mount and when the butt of a casting rod is inserted, the pipe makes a fine rod holder for trolling.

A length of PVC pipe screwed to the wood motor mount makes an excellent fishing rod holder for trolling.

On *WindShadow,* with its stern pulpit, it was easy to screw on a pair of commercially available rod holders. These enable us to troll two rods at a time and both are clear of any sailing gear, yet always within sight and reach for instant action.

At certain times in the spring and fall, our Gulf coasts have runs of different species of gamefish. Some of these fish come quite large, such as the cobias that range up to eighty pounds apiece. Besides being excellent fighting fish, they are very good to eat. Usually traveling in schools along the Gulf Coast, they will strike trolled lures, especially those trolled behind a quietly sailing sailboat. Tackle for these gamesters is heavier than the usual saltwater fishing gear. Cobia fishermen use standard saltwater boat rods and level wind saltwater reels, or the eight-foot fiberglass surf or pier fishing rods with large spinning reels loaded with twenty-pound test or heavier monofilament. If you tangle with cobias, a strong gaff hook is needed to boat them.

Two of the most popular species of food fish that make their migratory runs along the Gulf Coast are Spanish mackerel and bluefish. When these species show up, so do flotillas of trolling anglers. Concentrations of fish can cause such traffic jams of boaters that they have to set up a traffic pattern to avoid collisions. Usually it moves in a big circle, a right lane of boats going one way, a left lane going the other.

Aboard their Com-Pac 16, *Drifter*, Jim and Kathy Pullen use ultralight cane poles and fish for the fun of it at sundown in a Florida bay.

Woe unto anyone caught in the wrong lane going the wrong way!

Despite this seeming chaos, if the wind is right, a sailboat makes a fine trolling boat. You can sail and troll at the same time, the reels' brakes set light so that striking fish will not break lines.

As soon as a fish hits the trolled lure, the sailboat turns up into the wind, moving out of the traffic pattern. All sheets are released to stall the boat. Then the fish can be played and brought in. As soon as it is boated, the sail-fisherman tightens sheets and moves back into the pattern for more trolling.

If you sail saltwater coasts, you may be interested in foraging for whatever shellfish are available in your area. Once you have sailed the coastal bays several times, noting where there seems to be a concentration of boats and foragers, and after you talk to locals about where to look, you will learn where the best foraging sites are.

There are two ways you can do it. Either you anchor (or beach) your boat and wade around the shallows or dig around in the mud, hoping to come up with clams, scallops, oysters, or whatever; or, you can get into the water and hunt them.

Where bay waters are clear and unpolluted, donning face mask, snorkel, and fins is the much more fun way to forage. All you have to do is search out the shallow waters for your seafood supper. And probably your crew members will all be doing the same with you.

If you do it this way, it is mandatory to have an easily seen dive flag displayed on your sailboat. And to be doubly safe, tow one on a float with you in the water so that power boaters can easily see you. Such flags and other diving equipment may be obtained at dive shops.

When we get in the water to go foraging, I try to be ready to take several different kinds of seafood—crabs, other shellfish, and fish. So the basic gear besides mask and fins is a pair of cotton work gloves, a nylon "goody" bag for catches,

While inland sailors may enjoy snorkeling from their sailboats just to see what they can see, coastal sailor snorkelers can dive for oysters, scallops, and crabs. All such sailboaters should fly the Divers Down flag to warn other boaters of their activity.

and a pole spear, the latter items available at dive shops. The spear is a shaft with a special point on one end and a loop of surgical rubber tubing on the other. It is "cocked" underwater by hooking your thumb into the loop, pulling the spear back and grasping its shaft. When firing, release the spear and it will be launched.

An alternative to the large pole spear is a three-foot length of brass welding rod that has been sharpened on one end. A similar but lighter weight loop of rubber tubing is whipped onto the other end. This makes a good blue crab spear. All you have to do is shoot the crab and slip it off the barbless shaft into your goody bag.

Our barrier islands in the summer are good foraging grounds for oysters, scallops, a variety of whelks, stone crabs, blue crabs, mullet, and flounder. To find them you slowly propel yourself along the surface watching the bottom anywhere from two feet to six feet below you. Sometimes you encounter a bed of scallops and stop to pick them up. Other times you might find a large horse conch that you drop into your net bag along with the scallops. Awhile later you might come upon a concentration of oysters from which you select some of the nicer sized ones and add them to your collection.

Sometimes in the eel grass you will see a blue crab lifting his claws threateningly at you. You skewer him on your brass rod spear. He too ends up in your catch bag. Sooner or later you may see a concentration of old oyster shells heaped up around a hole in the bottom in an effort to camouflage it. Look closely and you will see a large crab turned sideways in the hole. Be sure it is a stone crab and not a blue crab. Stone crabs have claws almost the size of a human hand. They can easily do painful things with one of those pinchers, but if you have hunted them regularly, you know that the first thing they do when you reach into the hole to grab them is to clench their claws in front of them. In that instant you have to lock both claws with your one hand and bring the crab out where you can grab each claw. Then, with a slight twist of the claws in opposite directions, you will feel the crab actually release them. You then return him to his hole where he will regenerate other claws. Stone crabs can replace their pinchers in this manner at least nine times in their lifetime. Since one claw will usually be much larger than the other, we generally take only that one. On a stone crab, all the meat worth eating is in the claws. Boiled and cracked, the tender sweet morsels dipped in melted butter, the fare is mouth-watering. And if you are curious about what it is worth, check out the prices for stone crab claws on a Florida restaurant menu sometime.

Foraging toward shore and shallower water you will see places where powerboats have been running aground, scarring the bottom as their outboard propellers cut sandy paths through the eel grass. When you find such paths you swim along them watching carefully for a hidden flounder. Flounder (flatfish) like to lie in these open patches and cover themselves with sand so that only their eyes appear. If you come upon a hidden flounder you have to look carefully. All you usually see will be his outline. Or possibly his eyes. Once you determine where his head is, a downward thrust of the pole spear will pin him to the bottom. Carefully ease him into your goody bag because this is one of the choicer fish to be found along the coasts. Some may weigh seven or eight pounds. By the time you add a couple of these to your catch, you will have all you can do just dragging the goody bag back to the boat behind you.

That evening, when you cook up your catch, it is a nice feeling to know that you are completely self-sufficient. Your boat is powered by the wind, you have caught your seafood by yourself, and have been able to enjoy a feast literally fit for a king at no more cost than the effort to get it.

On a long cruise in an area where the coastal waters are clean enough to support a variety of marine life, you should have no problem supplying your needs in seafood. This kind of foraging is fun for the whole family. It requires a minimum of equipment and is carried out in the safety of shallow water. All bays should provide a variety of seafood for the taking. Just be sure it is not a polluted area and that there are no restrictions on taking shellfish.

Since most sailors enjoy swimming, most of them also know how much fun it is to use mask, fins, and snorkel. Have you ever stopped to think how similar sailing is to flying and the fact that sailors and aviators share a lot in common? How about flying? Haven't you ever yearned to dive like an eagle, hover like a hawk, or soar like a seagull?

I have and so have you. Now, thanks to someone's similar yearnings, you can do all these things: dive, hover, and soar like a bird, doing it from your sailboat without the slightest fear of falling.

The "flying machine" and techniques for accomplishing these things are so simple that you won't believe how much fun it is until you try riding a sea-sled. The sport is sea-sledding. All it amounts to is being towed through the water while you hang on to a specially shaped board. A downward tilt of the board and you go underwater; an upward tilt and you surface again. Same principle as a flying wing or a submarine's diving vanes. Add one enthusiast in mask, fins, and snorkel with a yen to soar through inner space and you have the sport of sea-sledding.

No telling when or where the idea originated, but in recent years divers use sea-sleds to cover long distances in searching for shipwrecks, preferably old Spanish treasure wrecks. You may not have that opportunity, but at least your sailboat—either under sail or power—provides an excellent way to tow a snorkeler on a sled, provided you can keep the speed down to one to two knots.

A sea-sled can either be home-built or purchased. Essentially it is nothing more than a piece of well-sealed and painted (or fiberglassed) marine plywood with the shape and dimensions as shown in Fig. 41. In this case handles were hammered out of thin-walled aluminum conduit pipe and bolted in place, then wrapped with cotton line to provide a grip. An eye bolt near the center of the board provides a point for tying on the tow line. For best results a standard ski tow harness with rollers should attach to the tow boat. Length of line depends on the depth a sledder wishes to go. It should be at least three times the depth. Thus, to sail to a depth of ten feet underwater, the tow line should be thirty feet long.

Commercially made sea-sleds may be obtained through your local dive shops. One company makes what it calls a Manta Snorkel Sled of molded high density polyethylene that can be partially flooded to better adjust the buoyancy of sled and diver. The Manta comes with 100 feet of braided tow line that ends in a harness with an easy quick release mecha-

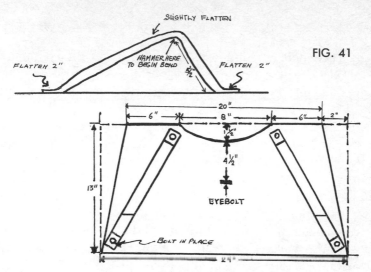

SLIGHTLY FLATTEN

HAMMER HERE
TO BEGIN BEND

FLATTEN 2"

FLATTEN 2"

FIG. 41

5½

20"

6"

8"

6"

2"

1½"

4½"

EYEBOLT

13"

BOLT IN PLACE

24"

(top) Fig. 41 shows the plan for making a homemade sea-sled.

(bottom) The finished product is shown with tow line and other optional items such as a depth gauge and a quick release buckle.

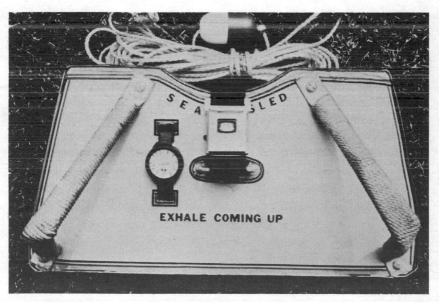

S E A   SLED

EXHALE COMING UP

279

nism. The whole rig sells for $59.95 from Tracy International, P.O. Box 1435, Pompano Beach, FL 33060.

Sea-sledding is simplicity itself. Initially you might think that it will be tiring to hold your breath. Not at all. Since you are doing nothing but holding on and not expending any energy, you will be surprised at how long you will be able to stay underwater. And with a flip of your wrists, you porpoise swiftly to the surface for a breath through your snorkel. Once you have the feel of it, you will be going up and down without even bothering to lift more than your snorkel out of the water.

To start, grasp the sled's handles and hold it out in front of you on the surface with its leading edge tilted slightly upward. Once the towing begins, you will continue riding the surface until ready to dive, then tilt the board slightly forward. It will dip below the surface and take you with it.

By tilting the sled one way or another you can sail in a serpentine path or do a series of dips. On the surface your hand signal—a thumb up or a thumb down—will tell the tow boat whether to pick up speed or to slow it down. When we use a sled in the keys for hunting lobsters behind our sailboat, we furl the sails and motor. But out on the reef for underwater sightseeing, we sail, maintaining as closely as possible, a one- to two-knot speed. If the wind is too strong, we power. But on those days with steady breezes, it is almost easier doing it under sail. Speed can be maintained by sheeting in or feathering the main.

On a 100-foot-long tow line a sea-sledder can dip down to thirty feet underwater without the slightest difficulty other than perhaps the need to clear his ears by pinching his nose and blowing to equalize the pressure. But usually the sights to be seen will be in much shallower water. There he can soar over walls of coral and dip down into sandy valleys at leisure. It's a great way to spot fish!

Of course you would only use a sea-sled in water with good visibility. But once you have tried it you will be amazed at how versatile this simple idea is for providing you and

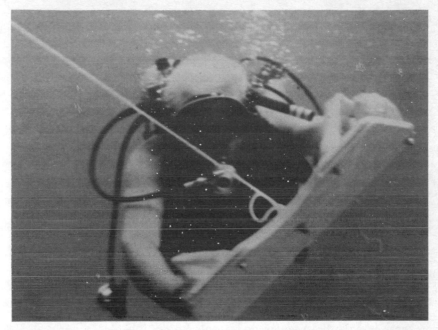

A diver can snorkel or use scuba to enjoy sledding behind his sailboat while under sail or power.

your crew with many hours of enjoyable underwater flying time.

Another nice thing about it is that after your flight, you can wind your line around your "flying machine" and stow it below just about as easily as you can your kites. See what I mean about the similarity of flying and sailing?

17

Keys to Adventure

Picture yourself in a tropical island setting, cruising water so clear that you can see lobsters flicking their antennae ten feet underwater. Picture yourself pulling ashore to explore deserted isles lush with vegetation, then anchoring offshore to partake of an icy rum punch while lobsters you have caught simmer in salt water moments before you dip them into melted butter and enjoy an unparalleled epicurean delight. See yourself slumbering beneath star-studded skies while being fanned by balmy tropical breezes. Better yet, picture yourself doing these things year after year at a cost of little more than your basic investment in your passport to paradise.

That passport is a seaworthy trailerable sailboat with live-aboard capabilities. Size is of no great consequence as long as you have made it comfortable enough to live aboard for an extended period of time.

The tropical island setting I have described is not in some remote corner of the South Seas. It is in our own backyard: the Florida Keys, 100 miles of islands scattered like white stepping stones off the southeastern corner of the United States, curving in a long archipelago, with some of the clearest, warmest, tropical waters available to trailer sailors in our Northern Hemisphere.

My passport to this Eden was my Com-Pac 16 pocket cruiser *Nomad,* fully loaded with cameras, diving gear, and food to sustain my sailing companion, Mike Wisenbaker, and myself for two weeks of cruising on land and sea.

I had customized the Com-Pac for the kind of land/sea cruising we had in mind. In the water or out, it was to serve as our home away from home. Small as it was, we wanted the boat to provide us with at least basic comforts. Fully aware that we would be living in intense sunshine for those two weeks, I had designed the lightweight Bimini top for the boat that I described earlier. The carpeted cockpit floorboard, when raised and supported over the footwell, would give us additional sleeping space in the cockpit whenever we wanted to sleep topside. Our iron wind was a 1½-horse outboard. *Nomad* was equipped with a 12-volt electrical system for powering running lights, spot light, reading light, and an anchor light I had wired through the mast and which sat atop it; plus an FM stereo radio/tape system. Food and compact cooking units were stowed aft on our two eight-foot-long berths. Book and chart racks, bulkhead storage nets, a solar shower, self-steering and bow pulpit steering gear, plus all the basic coastal navigation charts and instruments, spare parts, tools, fishing gear, etc., that one might need for a 1,300-mile land/sea safari, was just the beginning of what went inside the boat. Along with those items were cases of canned food, several gallons of drinking water, loaded ice chest, bedding, chemical toilet, clothing, walkie-talkie and weather radios, safety equipment, a large first aid kit, motor and lantern fuels, scuba tanks and diving gear, spear guns, camera equipment, and a saltwater condenser, to mention all the large things. Somehow, magically, the boat swallowed it all up and still left room for me and my companion. Moreover, when friends Jim and Kathy Pullen saw what kind of capacity the Com-Pac had, they promptly purchased one exactly like it and accepted my offer to join our sail-camping safari.

Jim, who, like Mike, is also a diver, customized his Com-Pac *Drifter* like *Nomad*. Since this was to be Jim and Kathy's honeymoon, they added a refinement to the Bimini top on their boat: a wrap-around sunshade. Mike, with a snicker, claimed it was really a honeymoon curtain, whatever that is.

Just as we had done, Jim and Kathy loaded their Com-Pac with all the essentials. And that August our twin-boat Com-Pac expedition hit the highway in north Florida bound for the tropical delights of the Florida Keys.

After the first few hundred miles of trailering, one of the bonuses of Com-Pac boat and compact car cruising became apparent. Despite the 1,900-pound load we were trailering, the finely balanced long-tongued trailer and the Com-Pac's aerodynamic shape enabled us to average twenty-two mpg with my Pinto. Moreover, having that much load behind us helped stabilize the compact car so that it felt as if we were really driving a much larger vehicle.

Florida is a long state and we drove straight through to Key Largo, the northernmost key, covering 650 miles in twelve hours of continuous driving. We had chosen Key Largo because it is the site of a most unusual park: the John Pennekamp Coral Reef State Park, the first underwater state park in the United States. It and the adjacent Key Largo Reef Marine Sanctuary cover approximately 178 square nautical miles of coral reefs, sea grass beds, mangrove swamps, and all the unspoiled natural wildlife one would expect to find in such a preserve. Florida established this underwater park several years ago to try to salvage at least a small portion of the natural offshore reef and maintain it in as pristine a condition as possible.

Here was paradise on our doorstep. Tropical vegetation, shore birds, and marine life, an environment protected from the encroachments of civilization. Tropical life as it was before man changed it.

The park provides camping areas, picnic shelters, concession buildings, nature trails, and one of the best marinas and boat launching facilities in the entire Florida Keys.

Our interest, however, was in the offshore coral reef park: eight and a half nautical miles into the Atlantic and twenty-one nautical miles in length.

Pennekamp is an ideal place for beginning any keys sailing safari. No other offshore reefs or areas outside the sanctuary are anything like this. On Pennekamp's reefs the coral formations are undamaged and flourishing. Fish life is so abundant you think you are observing one of the world's largest natural aquariums (which it is). The water is so clear that depths are almost impossible to judge accurately. Underwater visibility of over 100 feet is normal.

The reefs range from shallow to deep, and there is enough area for everyone to explore whether they are visitors aboard the park's big glass-bottom boat, snorkelers on a guided reef tour, or scuba divers seeing it all on their own.

Scattered among the reefs are the remains of shipwrecks from the era of wooden sailing ships, with little remaining but their ballast rocks, iron cannons, and anchors, all coral encrusted. There are also modern-day wrecks near the outer edge of the park where divers can descend to see the remains of a World War II tanker.

Oddly enough, fishing and lobstering are allowed in this enormous marine sanctuary. But do not even think of doing any kind of spear fishing or shell or coral collecting. These things are forbidden.

For a small fee you can park your car safely at the park's marina, launch at their double concrete ramps, and follow the canals through the mangrove swamps about two and a half miles to the Atlantic Ocean. This is the take-off point for various parts of the fringing reef that parallels the coast about six to eight miles offshore, or for coastal cruising. We generally power through the canals and establish an anchorage in the nearby Largo Sound.

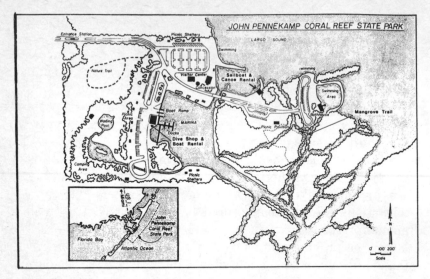

Excellent launching ramps at Florida's Pennekamp Coral Reef State Park and ample protected anchorages in Largo Sound make this a jumping-off spot for sailing or underwater exploring in the park's coral reef preserve.

This enclosed body of water is about a mile long, half a mile wide, and provides excellent protection from the weather. It has an average depth of six feet but the bottom is not very good for anchoring. It is an iron-hard bottom of lime rock covered by marine grass and seaweed. To be absolutely sure of good holding, we always swim out our anchors and drive them in, using the two-anchor Bahamian method of mooring.

Since the boat is near mangroves, our mosquito netting over all hatches and ports sometimes becomes necessary on still nights when the mangrove mosquitoes and foraging no-see-em black gnats are about. But usually breezes are pleasant and brisk enough at night to keep the insects at bay.

Those not used to extremely high humidity and high temperatures day and night will get their first taste of the tropics here. Summertime air temperatures are in the high nineties. The water temperature of Largo Sound matches the air temperature most of the time. The water will be so warm it is often uncomfortable for swimming. But a sudden rain-storm can cool it off quickly. Tropical rains are frequent, especially in the late summer. You can expect torrential rain, lightning, and thunderstorms with possibly frequent squall lines and high winds. Between these weather fronts, how-ever, sailing and cruising along the coasts and the reef will be idyllic.

There are other anchorages along the coast but I suggest you study the U.S. Coast and Geodetic charts for these areas before investigating them. All such charts are available at the park marina. So is ice. You can replenish your food supplies at grocery stores just outside the park. Don't be surprised if there is a water shortage; there often is in the keys.

After spending a delightful week savoring the sailing, sea-sledding, snorkeling, lobster hunting, scuba diving, and un-derwater photography that we were able to do there, we reluctantly hauled out our Com-Pacs and headed south again. We trailed the rest of the 100-mile overseas highway past dozens of other islands and intriguing cruising waters to reach the southernmost tip of the United States: Key West.

This was our main target, our jumping-off place for yet another virtually unspoiled cruising area—the Marquesas Keys clustered in the middle of a desolate stretch of ocean some thirty miles west of Key West. It was here that all our efforts to be self-sufficient aboard our small sailboats, a long way from any immediate assistance, would be put to the test. And here, I want to describe in detail what occurred because it was our first venture into comparatively long-distance cruising in tropical seas where it was important that we quickly learn such things as how to read the color of the water to avoid grounding. Or what a mirage on the water looks like, or how to tell which of several distant islands are closest to you, lessons that were to be invaluable aids to coastal navigation on other tropical cruises. To us all at first, however, it was a bit baffling.

I had plotted our round trip of about sixty miles of sailing

The author shows one reason why the warm waters of the Florida Keys are so popular with foraging trailer sailors—a spiny lobster.

to take us through a series of ocean shallows called The Lakes, where the water was seldom more than six feet deep over the banks. But, too, it was an area of unpredictable crosscurrents and tidal cuts flowing swiftly to the open sea.

Since this was our first sailing trip of any distance and duration, we wanted to be sure of our bearings right from the beginning. Despite our charts and navigation instruments, we were unprepared for orienting ourselves to the peculiar "landmarks" we found west of Key West. Nothing we saw on the horizon seemed to fit the pictures of scattered mangrove keys on our charts. Then we discovered why. It seemed that we could see forever! Far more islands met our eyes than were on the charts because of an odd tropical mirage boaters experience in such waters. It lets them literally see *over* the horizon, seeing islands that sometimes appear to be floating in the sky attached to tiny wavy tendrils. These, we finally guessed, were trees.

Also, we had to learn that islands closer to us appeared brighter gray-green than those that were perhaps two miles farther away. But once we realized this and oriented our charts to Marker "17," we were off and running on a light southerly breeze, the bows bubbling musically as gulls cut crescents across our azure wakes.

As the sun rose high in a cloudless sky, we basked in the shade of our Bimini tops and let the sea miles slide by.

Leaving Mule Key to port, it was a pleasant reach across one of the lakes while Archer Key grew larger and greener as we approached, steering well clear of the long tongue of yellow sand reaching offshore in the shallow water. The eel-grass bottom seldom changed its depth or texture, the long slender blades streaming southward with the outgoing tide.

Just north of Barracouda Keys I shot a line of position with the hand-bearing compass, taking a sighting off the east side of Barracouda and the northwest side of Woman Key, then triangulating those bearings on the chart. We were right on course.

By late afternnon we reached Boca Grande Key and the six-mile-wide channel separating us from the Marquesas. Since the loaded sailboats drew only two feet of water, we dropped anchor within wading distance of the beach, planning to spend the night moored offshore of Boca Grande and making the channel crossing in the morning.

Mike set off to explore the island while Jim and I slipped on face masks, fins, and snorkels to investigate the mangrove channels for a possible seafood supper. Kathy wisely enclosed *Drifter*'s cockpit in its honeymoon curtain—a bedsheet to shield it from the slanting rays of the still hot sun. Later, as we rafted together, the sheet clothespinned to the edge of the Bimini top served as a welcome wind break for our fish supper cooked over stoves in the cockpits, the

(top) Moored for the night off Boca Grande Key on their way to the Marquesas Keys, *Nomad* and *Drifter* have their cockpits shaded from the intense tropical summer sun.

(bottom) As the two Com-Pac 16s rafted side by side, we cooked the fish we caught in our cockpits.

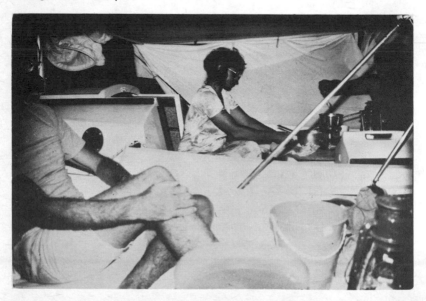

grouper and mangrove snapper fillets from the fish Jim and I had speared while snorkeling under Boca Grande's tangled mangrove roots, enhanced by Kathy's tossed salad.

Boca Grande channel tides sweep out so swiftly that one glance at the water streaming by our hulls that night was enough to make us think we were dragging anchors. But the key's stationary silhouette quickly dispelled the illusion, aided by the knowledge that we had dived down and buried the anchor flukes deeply in the hard sand and eel-grass bottom twelve feet underwater to doubly secure our position. And to be sure they stayed where we put them, we deployed all 100 feet of our anchor rodes.

Shortly after breakfast the next morning, on a southeast breeze, we hoisted sail and made our way across choppy Boca Grande Channel toward the Marquesas over the horizon. Named for the Spanish Marquis de Caldereita who arrived there in 1623 with a salvage party searching for the treasure galleon *Atocha* that foundered in those waters in 1622, the cluster of ten mangrove islands and shoals encircle a three-mile-square area of shallow emerald-colored waters whose August temperatures average in the nineties.

Running downwind briskly, we hated to break our gait as the islands grew large and lush ahead of us. Instead, we aimed for the narrow dog-leg-shaped channel into Mooney Harbor where depths average three feet. We gambled on being able to sail through the islands. It was a lesson in water reading.

Inside, depths shaded from brown to amber-gray, the latter being sparsely grassed marl flats. The trick was to stay in the meandering narrow channel. Occasional groundings sent us over the side into knee-deep water and a crusty marl bottom. A hearty heave on the boat would break the crust and slurp us into hip-deep marl reeking with the hydrogen sulfide odor of rotten eggs. Needless to say, we quickly learned to avoid grounding. Behind us, Jim and Kathy picked their devious way through the same odoriferous shoals.

After three miles of tricky maneuvering, we emerged on the northwest side of the Marquesas and sailed northward. Noon found us beaching the boats in the shallows of a tidal swash between islands. Lunch over, we went ashore to explore. Surprisingly, there was no sandy beach—only a hard, flaky marl. Thick, bushy growth dotted with occasional spider lilies flanked the forest of mangroves. One tall coconut palm leaned askew over the water's edge as the sea slowly but surely worked to claim it. Sea birds abounded, mostly gulls, terns, and anhingas. Although the islands are a wildlife refuge, they offered little refuge for the occasional pelicans we saw dangling lifelessly from tree limbs, their feet hope-

Working our way through the complex Marquesas Keys, *Drifter* is framed by mangrove growth as we stop for lunch at one of the deserted islands.

lessly entangled in monofilament fishing line. The birds, apparently already ensnarled in the fishing line somewhere along the mainland, must have flown in to the perch, tangled on it, and were unable to leave. This common wildlife tragedy points up the danger to these sea birds caused by an angler carelessly discarding some of his tangled fishing line into the water where the birds are snared by it.

Late that afternoon, we sailed onto the northernmost beach of the main island to find a single rickety wood dock backed by a pair of lonely palm trees. Again we explored, trying to reach a hidden lagoon through an impenetrable jungle of mangroves. Defeated, we returned to the beach, where I picked up a piece of broken pottery later identified by underwater archaeologist Duncan Mathewson as the same type of pottery found offshore where Mel Fisher's Treasure Salvors Company was searching for the mother lode of the *Atocha.*

What was this fragment doing on the north shore of the Marquesas?

Part of the *Atocha*'s bow was known to have washed ashore in 1623 on the Marquesas. Could this fact and the finding of the pottery shard mean that the main treasure was perhaps located closer to the island than the treasure hunters suspected? It was an intriguing thought.

Instead of continuing on around the main key, which on the chart showed no interesting break in the miles of continous mangroves, we decided to sail back the way we had come that day, perhaps ending up by dark at a particular west-end peninsula we had passed.

The amber sun was already low in the sky as we sailed on a light breeze back toward deeper water. In the process, Mike and I ran aground so securely that, with the outgoing tide, Jim had to swim over and help push *Nomad* into deeper water. Shortly afterward, we were ghosting along together less than a mile offshore when I glanced down through the

Beside the only dock and the only palm tree on the north side of the main key in the Marquesas, our boats swing at anchor while we explore the shores of this deserted island.

clear ten-foot depths and spotted rocks and ridges along with something else.

Mike must have thought I had lost my mind when I lunged forward to kick over the anchor. I shouted one word—"Bugs!"—and Pullen didn't have to be told twice. Later, Kathy said he dropped the anchor with one hand, snatched up his fins, mask, and gloves with the other, and rolled over the side with all canvas flying and the boat not even settled to her hook.

Mike and I were equally quick about getting into the water. The next fifteen or twenty minutes were a blur of frantic diving, grabbing, chasing, gasping, struggling activities that bagged us each several fine spiny lobsters before we ran out of daylight.

We spent the rest of the night right there. After toasting our success with pewter mugs of rum punch, we fired up the lantern and, in its comforting amber glow, began a ritual so simple it is always hard to believe the results are so delightful. We dropped the lobster tails into a potful of seawater simmering over our single burner stove, slid a bar of butter into the inverted lid over the pot, and gave it a squirt of fresh key lime juice.

Minutes later, the cracked tails were served on Frisbees with tossed salad and crusty Cuban bread. Dipped into bubbling lime-tangy butter, each bite was incredibly delectable.

Stretched out on his cockpit cushion, a pile of cracked lobster on his Frisbee and another one dripping with butter about to be consumed, Mike managed to mutter, "I wonder what the poor folk are doing tonight!" Judging from the sounds coming from *Drifter* anchored just astern of us, the Pullens, at the height of their lobster supper, may have been wondering the same. They sounded pretty ecstatic. We all agreed it was a feast to be remembered.

The Pullens put up their nuptial curtain and turned in early. The ocean was glassy still, mirroring the full moon that bathed everything in ivory light. It was a night made for diving.

Mike looked at the water and decided it was not for him. I think he was too full of lobster, too contented to move. But I was curious to see what kind of sea life might be wandering around on this bottom so far off the normal beaten track.

Slipping on mask, fins, and weight belt I eased into the water with my underwater light for a look around. Finning down through a setting made to order for *Jaws*, I swept the yellow cone of light back and forth slowly through the inky water. No night-walking lobsters were in sight but what I did see I could hardly believe.

Pullen's anchor rode lay across a trench about four feet long and two feet wide. Fitted tightly in that trench was a

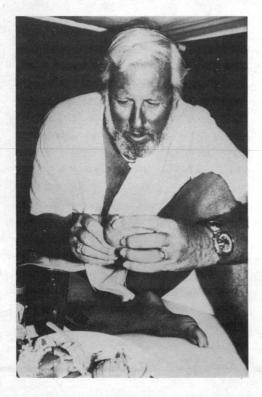

Lobsters for the catching provided much of our fare each night as we sailed our way through the tropical islands. It was always a movable feast!

huge gray-mottled grouper that must have weighed close to eighty pounds. It would have been senseless to have speared the fish; we needed no meat. But what was he doing there?

As I eased closer to see how long this goliath would hold his ground, he slowly disappeared before my eyes! All it took to accomplish this was a gentle fin movement that eased his big frame forward into a cave at one end of the trench. What an escape artist!

For the next few days we explored different areas of these desolate islands, sometimes one or more of us going ashore to beachcomb for miles along the untracked beaches. At one time there was a tall lookout tower on the main island. Now, all we found was its remains covered by the fast-growing undergrowth. It had apparently been dismantled to discourage visitors to this natural wildlife refuge. Sometimes we explored inland, finding such bizarre things as an old park bench propped up between tree stumps as if someone had once used it as a piece of furniture.

Along some coasts we found hundreds of small vase sponges washed ashore that looked like something Robinson Crusoe might have used for a sun hat. Each was a perfect fit.

The mangroves abounded with snappers and groupers available for the spearing. And we dived up lobsters whenever we found bottom rocks and crevices exposed by the tidal wash or wherever there were undercut grass banks beside large sand flats. Invariably by snorkeling along these undulating lines of grass we would see the telltale antennae of our next seafood supper waving at us.

Much the easiest way to catch the "bugs" is with a crab net whose handle has been sawed short to a length of about two feet, and a tickle stick. The latter need not be anything more than a slender piece of bamboo or the brass welding rod spear. When the antennae of lobsters are sighted, you dive down and will usually find the crawfish watching you from a rock crevice or an undercut grass ledge. The tickler is eased out and used to reach behind and tap the lobster on his tail.

When this happens he will come out of his hole and that's the time to immediately pop your hand net down over him. With gloved hands you then hold him tightly and measure him with a lobster measure tied to your goody bag. To be legal the lobsters must measure over three inches from between the eyes to the back edge of their carapace. Anything less than that is let loose as are any lobsters bearing yellow egg clusters under their tails. Using this net and tickle system we seldom lost a keeper. Each night we usually feasted on as many as we could consume.

Eventually, however, we came to the end of our stay in the Marquesas. Throughout, our Bimini tops were worth their weight in gold. Without them our trip would have been virtually impossible due to the daily intensity of the sun and heat. The shade these tops provided over our cockpits was what made it all not only bearable but quite comfortable.

On our next to last day in the Marquesas we sailed back around to the point where we had entered the complex of islands and turned in early. That night we were hit by a torrential thunderstorm that had us hoping that our jumper cables were providing us with the protection that would keep us from taking a hit from the many bolts of lightning streaking around the sky that night.

About 3 A.M. the storm ceased and so did all air movement. The only thing that moved were millions of mangrove mosquitoes and black gnats that swarmed bloodthirstily out of the swamps and onto our boats just before dawn. Mike and I were caught sleeping in our bathing suits on the cockpit berths. All we could do to fend off those hungry hordes was to pull light blankets over ourselves and swelter. Fortunately, the pests left with the first gray light of dawn.

Not long after sunrise the wind picked up from a quarter that no longer favored our sailing back through The Lakes the way we had come unless we wanted to tack and beat every foot of the way. This would have been tricky with the shallows flanking both sides of that area.

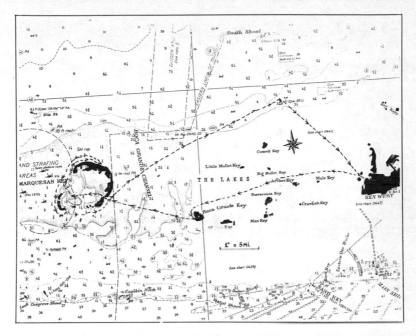

Our 1,300 mile land/sea safari with the pair of Com-Pac 16 sailboats was highlighted by our sail through The Lakes to the Marquesas Keys thirty miles west of Key West. It was a trip any small trailerable sailboat can easily make.

Hastily I plotted another course, a longer one that was more favorable for us to sail but one I knew would eventually have its disadvantages.

We set off from the red buoy "2" beside the Boca Grande Channel and spent a large part of the morning sailing toward our midday course change at the Northwest Channel bell buoy. It was a long, uneventful trip. The real fun began once we passed our marker, angled southward toward Key West, and then beat hour after hour against the strong incoming tidal currents. Repeatedly, Key West seemed within our grasp. Then, as the breeze calmed, it slipped away from us as we were pushed back up the channel.

Trying to figure out different strategies and angles of tack against the currents, we let our boats become widely separated until we were miles apart. Still, we kept in contact by the walkie-talkies which had served us well in this respect throughout our entire cruise when we were often sailing far from each other.

Finally, after nine hours of battling wispy breezes and being bullied by the tides, I nursed *Nomad* as close to Key West as possible and, as the tide once again began pushing us back, I fired up the faithful 1.5-horse outboard and chugged into port. Not long afterward, Jim and Kathy did likewise.

For the next couple of days, while getting better acquainted with Key West, Mike and I used *Nomad* as a live-aboard camper on its trailer at Boyd's Campground on Stock Island just outside of Key West proper. Apparently having enough of sailboat living for a while, the Pullens elected to move into a motel.

For our trip to the Marquesas we had launched at a small ramp at the end of Simonton Street opposite Wisteria and Christmas Tree islands. Another outstanding launching ramp can be found at Ocean View Marina on the north side of Stock Island reached by continuing on out the road on which Boyd's Campground is located. No one ever has any trouble finding such places in the keys. All they have to do is read the sign boards.

At Ocean View Marina, security guards take care of your vehicle and trailer while you are cruising, and the local waters along this coast are equally good for sail-sledding and lobstering.

Trailering once more back up the 100-mile length of the keys, we joined other fast-moving traffic on the toll Sunshine Highway and were soon home. Our land/sea safari of over 1,300 miles had been a complete success. Our two-and-a-half-week vacation cost was minimal. Overnight commercial camping fees averaged less than five dollars (expect to pay more today). Off-the-track camping areas were free. Since

(top) At Boyd's Campground near Key West, Mike and I camped in the sailboat between sailing trips.

(bottom) Each morning we awakened in our cockpit berth to the sight of tropical trees and flowers overhead and the sounds of tropical birds.

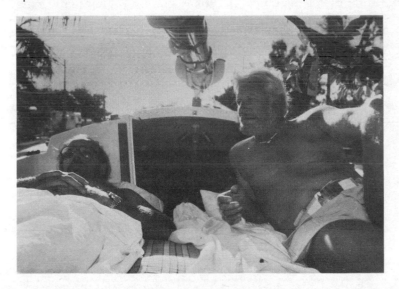

302 / Handbook of Trailer Sailing

we were self-contained on land or sea, the statement, "Sorry we are filled," never bothered us so long as a launching ramp was handy. Once afloat, overnight mooring sites were unlimited. Our sailboats made excellent mobile campers, the kind that we could easily haul out and wheel to any change of scene that tempted us. This, of course, is the tremendous advantage enjoyed by all trailer sailors.

Many mornings we awakened to the fragrance of tropical flowers wafting through out cockpit berth because where we were parked on our trailer we were often shaded by trees and tropical flowers.

With no motel costs, our only real expense was food and drink—mostly fresh juices and salad items. We provided our own seafood. Meanwhile, we successfully combined all the pleasures of a camping vacation with a cruise to exotic tropical islands—an adventure easily within reach of any small boat trailer sailor. If there are disadvantages to this way of traveling, we have never found them. What we did find, however, was that the greatest advantage of compact car and sailboat cruising can be summed up in one word—economy. Economy of both money and fuel. That feature may prove even more valuable to tomorrow's trailer sailor. But, no matter what the future brings, trailer sailing is a way of life that, once you have sampled it, is hard to exchange for any other kind of sailing.

18

From a Bare Boat

When you buy a stock production sailboat you get just that, a bare boat. You get cockpit seats but no cushions. You get no anchor, no lines, no lights, no battery, no compass, no motor, nothing but what you paid for—a bare boat; a pretty naked one at that.

Everything else you must add yourself. As detailed in earlier chapters, some of these things you can build yourself. Other things you will buy. They are called marine accessories. Of course you can sail your boat without them, but not nearly as comfortably or safely. If you plan any kind of cruising, don't scrimp on the necessary accessories. Your sailboat service center will have them. So will marine hardware stores and mail-order marine catalogs. What you buy and what you build will turn your basic bare boat into a well-equipped sailboat to be proud of. The few additions I have selected here are especially outstanding and valuable. With today's cruisable trailer sailers, these are currently leading in their field:

Outboard Motors

For the first time in twenty-five years, manufacturers of the world-renowned sailboater's outboard, British Seagull, have released their first totally new outboard motor design and it is a beaut! It is their most powerful model, called the Seagull 170, rated at 7.6-horsepower and capable of powering sailboats up to twenty-five and thirty feet in length. The reason why Seagulls are so much more efficient than many standard outboards is their gearing ratio. Seagulls are especially geared to move heavy displacement hulls at their maximum hull speeds which rarely exceed seven knots. They are the workhorses of marine otboards. Year after year they perform so reliably and economically that this has resulted in the Seagull reputation for tough, dependable sailboat outboards. The new Seagull 170 looks and sounds different from any other Seagull model. It is especially quiet. Nothing has been sacrificed in the quality of materials; the motor is built of the top marine grade bronze, brass, monel, stainless steel, etc., that have always been the Seagull trademark. This single-cylinder water-cooled engine provides 170 pounds of thrust for its large, four-bladed propeller. Another new feature to please Seagull fans is its remote 2.5-gallon fuel tank. Average fuel consumption at half to three-quarter throttle is 3.5 pints per hour or a five-hour cruising range per tank of fuel. The Seagull 170 has a standard recoil starter, but if it should fail it can be easily removed to expose a starter pulley that can be spun to start with a length of line. Its sealed gearbox has a forward, neutral, and reverse control lever and the sealed CD ignition is so waterproof that the motor will actually fire in water. This is true for all Seagulls and should this model or any of them fall overboard, even in salt water, all that is necessary to get it going again is to pump the water out of the cylinder, clean the fuel system and spark plug, and the motor is ready for running again. Try that on other outboards! Seagull makes four other models that may interest the smaller trailer sailors: a featherweight 45 (2-horsepower), a Seagull 55 and 60 (both 3-horsepower), and a Seagull 90 (5-horsepower). One of the best features about all Seagulls is that they have been built simply enough that

The British Seagull 170 with its 7.6-horsepower, sealed ignition, and four-bladed propeller was designed specially for powering heavy displacement hulls at their maximum hull speeds. It is the workhorse of marine outboards.

owners with basic spare parts, the service manual, and a bit of do-it-yourself ability, can handle practically any problem that may develop. A twelve-volt alternator is optional equipment for the Seagull 170. For additional information about this model and any of the others, contact your nearest Seagull dealer: IMTRA Corporation, 151 Mystic Ave., Medford, MA 02155. Tel: (617) 391-5660; 126th Avenue North, Clearwater, FL 33520. Tel: (813) 576-2484; 1930 H Lincoln Drive, Annapolis, MD 21401. Tel: (301) 263-4553; Seagull Marine, 1851 McGaw Avenue, Irvine, CA 92714. Tel: (714) 979-6161.

Galley Stoves

Forespar has come up with a Mini-Galley that is ideal for any size trailer sailer. The unit, comprised of a small canister of butane gas attached to a special flame head, swings in a bracket that has side spring arms to hold a pot, a frying pan, or a coffee pot so that no matter what angle of sail you are on, this galley will always maintain its vertical position. The great advantage of this Mini-Galley is that everything is consolidated and very safe. I mount mine on a lower companionway step when in use. The mounting is a small metal piece that screws flush to the outer edge of the step. The whole Mini-Galley can be quickly slipped onto it and fired off. When not in use I hang the unit on a similar support in one of the cockpit compartments. The heat from this butane stove is like a blowtorch so you have to be careful to keep it low and stir your food to prevent it from scorching. The gas canisters are available at most marine hardware stores and sportsman supply outlets. Though small in size, the butane canister will provide fuel to burn steadily for four hours. West coast deep-water sailors tell me that six cans of the fuel were used in their Mini-Galley to feed their crew during a twenty-one day cruise to Hawaii. Cost of the canister of butane is about three dollars. The Mini-Galley is a Forespar product available at most marine supply outlets.

Trailer sailors interested in a small compact alcohol stove should check out the good-looking Keny by Kenyon. This pressureless alcohol stove, using a few ounces of denatured alcohol (available at hardware stores) as fuel, provides a safe flame for cooking, not as hot as gas. Optional side windshields enable the stove to be used outside the cabin, preferably in your cockpit's footwell. Aboard *WindShadow* we enjoy making Swiss fondue on our Keny because the wide top and gentle flame are ideal for our large fondue pot. This stove is available through most marine outlets or directly from the Kenyon Distributors: P.O. Box 308, Guilford, CT 06437. Tel: (203) 453-4374; 2734 S. Susan St., Santa Ana, CA 92704. Tel: (714) 546-1101; 2642 24th Avenue N., St. Petersburg, FL 33713. Tel: (813) 323-1616.

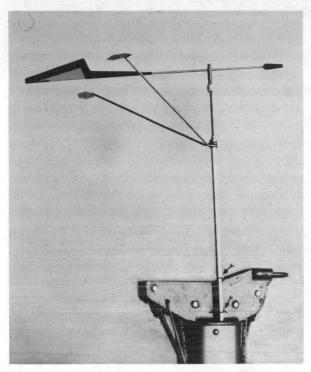

Especially for trailerable sailboats, Forespar's Point-Finder Windvane has one feature that puts it above the others: it can be removed easily from the masthead by pressing the two metal wings (see arrows) on the mounting.

Sailing Aids

Trailering is tough on masthead wind vanes. I have demolished so many commercial telltales this way that I found building them was cheaper than buying them. Then I found one with an added feature I had never seen before. Since then, my Point Finder wind vane by Forespar has never had to be replaced. The one thing they did that made a difference was to make their vane easily removable. Now I just snap it off, stow it in the cabin, and trail the boat without fear of losing my wind vane. By squeezing two metal ears, my Point

307

Finder is reinstalled before I raise my mast. Moreover, everything about this wind vane is first class. It is supersensitive, made of stainless steel, and painted for high visibility either day or night. The arrow is outlined in black to silhouette well against the sky. Two angled indicator arms on both sides of the vane show the maximum points for beating to windward. Reflective paint on all undersurfaces makes them easy to see at night with a light. Most sailboat supply houses carry the Forespar Point Finder and its easy to remove release fitting. For trailer sailors, it is a winner.

The same can be said for Forespar's anodized tiller extension. It lets you sit anywhere in the cockpit to steer your boat. A wrist twist on the rubber ball handle adjusts the telescoping rod to any length, locking it in place. Three kinds of tiller attachments are available. I like the quick release pin type. For a small additional fee you can make the tiller extension do double duty as a tiller tender. It is a preformed plastic pocket that screws into your coaming. It becomes a lock box for the ball on the end of the handle. Position your tiller, drop the ball of the extender in its box, and you can leave the helm unattended for a while and it will tend your tiller while you pour a cup of coffee or whatever. Forespar's tiller extension comes in three sizes: short—19″ to 32″; medium—27″ to 48″; and long—39″ to 72″. All work on the principle of a stainless steel universal joint.

Through the years I have bought several speed wand type boat speedometers—the kind you stick down in the water and read how high the ball rises in the tube. These are fine for slow-moving sailboats, but when things pick up and you find yourself sitting high above the water on a well-heeled sailboat, forget trying to stick a speed wand over the side. The conventional sailboat speedometers are best but, besides being expensive, they require through-the-hull mounting. For trailer sailors who want to bypass all that but still would like a reliable speedometer, I suggest you check out the

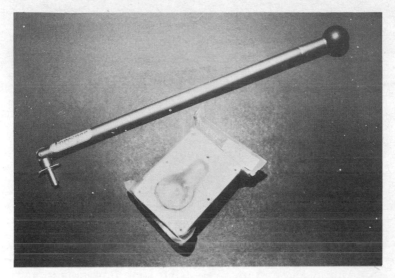

(top) Accomplishing two jobs in one, Forespar's tiller extension telescopes for easy handling and the unit can also be used to lock the tiller in any position with the optional lock box that attaches to the boat's coaming.

(bottom) Versatile, simple, and accurate are the words that best describe Knotstick, a device that trolls a disk and will tell you how fast your boat is traveling.

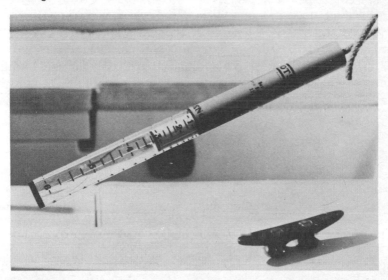

Knotstick. It is a calibrated plastic tube with one moving part and an elasticized line that pulls a specially sized weighted disk astern. For a long time I doubted this device would be any more practical than the dip-sticks I had been using, but once I tried it, I became a believer. Knotstick not only works but it is a highly accurate indicator of boat speed. Several scales and disks make it adaptable to a wide range of sailboats, including the speedy catamarans. If marine supply outlets do not carry it, you can order direct from Knotstick, P.O. Box 6340, Vero Beach, FL 32960. Tel: (305) 567-4445.

Part of the fun of trailer sailing is to be able to plot a course on your chart, then sail it and end up exactly where you plotted yourself to end up. As most coastal navigators know, this kind of piloting involves using such things as a marine chart with compass rose, a pencil, a pair of dividers, and a parallel rule. Essentially you may pencil in your desired course on the chart, use the dividers to determine how many nautical miles are involved, and then walk your parallel rule to the compass rose printed on the chart to determine your magnetic compass course. Each course change must be measured by walking the rule to the rose, then noting the direction on your course line. All of which is a bit of a bother, especially aboard a trailer sailer where your chart table may be a hatch board on your lap. But now, in the name of simplifying all this and avoiding the necessity for such things as dividers and parallel rules, an enormously practical little device called Compute-a-Course is made for the small-boat navigator. It is a calibrated movable plastic compass rose about eight inches square that takes all the trouble out of plotting. For course direction just align Compute-a-Course with your chart and your course line via the movable arrow and read off your magnetic compass bearing. Besides giving you a direct magnetic course readout, it will plot position fixes, measure distances on 40:000 and 1:80,000-scale charts, and solve time, speed, and distance problems. It is quick, accurate, convenient, and easy. Cost is about ten dollars and

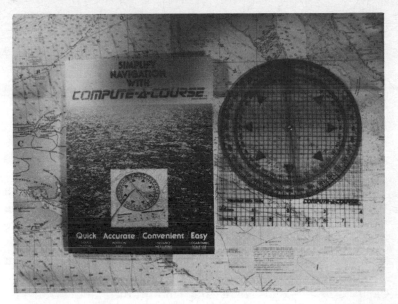

Made for the small-boat navigator, Compute-A-Course is a calibrated movable compass rose that simplifies charting your course.

it can be found at your local marine supply house or ordered direct from Compute-a-Course, P.O. Box 360, Shrewsbury, MA 01545.

No trailerable cruiser afloat worthy of the name should be without a weather radio and a good barometer. Radio Shack sells a popular brand of weather radio, and barometers come in different sizes and degrees of quality. If you have the bulkhead space and want something with a genuine nautical flavor, you might be interested in combining your weather instruments with an authentic piece of nineteenth-century shipwreck history. When I knew him a few years ago, diver/salvager Mike Dilts was scouring the bottom of the Great Lakes for the wreck of the Barkentine *New Brunswick* that foundered in a storm and sank with its valuable hardwood cargo in 1858. Mike found the wreck and salvaged the timbers from which he is now creating fine, hand-rubbed antique nautical gifts. One such piece combines a top quality barometer, thermometer, and hygrometer mounted on a rope-edged timber from the *New Brunswick.* Compass clocks and other items are also available. For more information, write: U.S. Saugeen Exploration, Ltd., R.R. 2, Lambeth, Ontario NOL 1SO, Canada. Tel: (519) 652-5921.

Teak Care

Large or small, trailerables today are usually trimmed in teak. How you take care of that fine wood is up to you. Some sailors have let it weather to a silver sheen. Others, like myself, wage an unending war with mildew and other maladies that make the wood look sadly neglected usually about two or three months after my latest teakwood bleach and clean treatment. Much of this frustration came to an end when I discovered a marine teakwood finish: Deks Olje (pronounced Decks Olya). The product cut my teakwood care time virtually in half. This fine wood finish originated in Norway over eighteen years ago. The miracle it wrought on the hard-used wooden decks of the Norwegian fishing fleet was not overlooked by admiring yachtsmen from other countries. Now the product is available in this country and is working its miracle for American yachtsmen who, like myself, have grown tired of having to constantly tend teak to keep it from looking scruffy. The Norwegian process is simple: The wood is cleaned and brightened with a mild acidic bleach called Dek Rens, then repeated wet-on-wet coats of #1 Matte Finish DO are applied until the wood will take no more. After these dry, repeated coats of DO #2 Gloss Finish are laid on with twenty-four-hour drying periods between each coat. After that, except for a few easy touch-ups, the job will stay good looking for some six to eight months before you may want to redo it. The Hutchins Company, manufacturers of the Com-Pac yachts, speak highly of another product handled by the same distributor. It is Marine Penetrol, made to restore faded fiberglass luster, polish

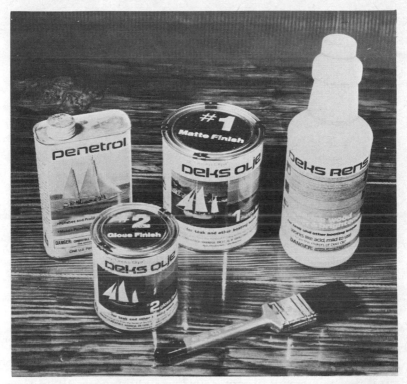

The Deks Olje products will solve many of your teak-care problems and provide a longer-lasting finish than usual.

metal, make painting and varnishing easier, and prepare old wood for painting. But they use it on the new teak trim of their boats, finding that touch-ups can be done quickly with the new coat dissolving the old and the final result looking like nicely oiled teak. In any case, these products work well and are time-savers compared to the usual short-term teak care treatments on the market today. If your marine dealer does not carry Deks Olje, contact the distributor: The Flood Co., Marine Products Division, P.O. Box 397, Hudson, OH 44236. Or call toll free: 1-800-321-3444.

Solar Power

Imagine placing a thin, flat item on your deck that is smaller than a bath mat, tough enough to walk on and to withstand any kind of weather, has no moving parts, requires no maintenance, lasts for years, and converts solar energy into electricity that constantly charges your sailboat's battery. Imagine having an unlimited supply of electrical power without needing to ever have your battery charged ashore. All these things are possible with PDC Labs International Inc.'s Solarchargers. They make space age marine and industrial Solarchargers that will provide a supply of electrical energy from the sun. Their marine models range from a 10-watt 0.6-amp 9.5-inch by 25-inch panel Solarcharger designed especially for the weekend sailor, to the 18-watt 1.0- to 1.2-amp panel for the multihull or bigger sailboat, and the largest marine Solarcharger: the 34-watt 2.1- to 2.3-amp model designed for the deep-water cruiser. PDC Labs has been making these Solarchargers for mariners for years, and know how rugged they must be. All the models are Bristol appearance, teak-mounted, with rounded edges in a sealed unit that will easily fit along decks or on hatches. My choice was the Model SC-10 Solarcharger, which is an excellent source of twelve-volt power for trailer sailors on a mooring or atop their trailers. This small unit can go on deck anywhere but I found it most effective when mounted on *Wind-Shadow*'s stern pulpit rail. Since it is not permanently mounted, when not in use it stows nicely out of the way against a cabin bulkhead. Moreover, for me, the nice feature is that I can interchange it between my Com-Pac sixteen- and nineteen-foot boats depending upon which one is being used. While trailerables are all usually able to find shoreside quick charging available, when I most appreciate what my Solarcharger does is on weekend or week-long cruises when I am sailing far from any quick charge shore stations. In the past, it involved lugging the battery out from below, easing it into a

Cruising trailer sailors will appreciate PDC Labs International Inc. Solar Chargers. The unbreakable units can either be permanently mounted on deck or temporarily clamped to the stern bow pulpit as this one is on *WindShadow*. All of them use the sun to trickle charge your boat's battery to its full capacity.

dinghy, rowing it ashore, loading it into the car, and driving to a filling station where it had to stay for several hours to acquire a decent charge. Now, this is no longer necessary. The battery remains in place aboard my boat, and the sun does the work for me. When you consider all the different ways there are to charge a boat battery afloat—outboard alternators, towed marine alternators, noisy gasoline generators, and thrumming windmills—absolutely nothing does the job with less fuss than the silent Solarcharger. For more information, contact: PDC Labs International, Inc., Box 603, El Segundo, CA 90254. Tel: (213) 374-7992.

Sea-Brella Bimini

Few things make sailing more comfortable, especially in the tropics, than a good cockpit sunshade, preferably one that can be left up, doing its job of keeping you shaded and cool as you sail. Such a shade is Sea-Brella, a unit with a heavy duty rain resistant cloth top and jointed PVC tube frame which combine to form a tough flex top that attaches to your boat's lifelines. The Sea-Brella was made especially for the Com-Pac nineteen- and twenty-three-foot sailboats but it will fit any sailboat with lifelines and similar dimensions (beams of seven feet to seven feet ten inches). In place, the Sea-Brella can be slid along the lifelines to shade most of a large cockpit, or it can be attached in a more forward position to cover the entire companionway hatch. Ours has kept us dry in some pretty heavy downpours, both under sail and on a mooring. When not in use, the Sea-Brella can be quickly dismantled, rolled up, and stored in its bag out of the way. For more information about it, contact: The Hutchins Company, Inc., 1195 Kapp Drive, Clearwater, FL 33515. Tel: (813) 443-4408.

Anchor Lights

In the past I have tried several different kinds of masthead anchor lights on my Com-Pacs. Invariably, however, corrosion either at the masthead light itself or at the electrical junction plug atop my cabin roof caused the lights to short out and be unreliable. If there is one thing you want to be reliable near a well-trafficked seaway, it is a highly visible anchor light. Eventually, I resorted to the always reliable oil lantern. Only once has it ever failed me and then I had burned the wick so short it no longer got fuel. As with all things aboard my sailboats, I try to include a backup system. One of the brightest and most efficient systems made for sailboaters today is the anchor light made by Guest Corporation. These long-lived battery-operated electric lights are cleverly designed for the job they do. Powered by a standard six-volt lantern battery, they seem capable of performing their task almost longer than any low-intensity incandescent bulb could be expected to burn. Atop the unit the light is enhanced by a special fresnel lens that amplifies it for a 360°-coverage and a two-mile visibility range. The unique feature about Guest's Model #452 anchor light is that it is automatic. An electric eye built into the light turns it on at night and off at daylight. This means that if you dinghy ashore in the afternoon, your anchor light will switch on automatically at dark and light your way back to the boat later that night. This feature is one reason why the light lasts so long.

This Guest anchor light sports a special feature—an electric eye that turns it on at dark and shuts it off at daylight. Powered by a six-volt battery, it is a long-lived light.

For more about it and other similar products, contact: The Guest Corporation, 17 Culbro Drive, West Hartford, CT 06110. Tel: (203) 525-5318.

Emergency Radio Beacon

Most trailer sailors are coastal sailors and seldom sail off into the wild blue yonder. But on those occasional cruises when you do, when you are out there alone far from any immediate help, wouldn't it be nice to know that if you *should*

Long-distance trailer sailors that sometimes sail off into the wild blue yonder should carry one of Guest's compact EPIRB systems. With a flick of a switch it sends out a continuous SOS radio signal that can be picked up by commercial aircraft and satellites thousands of miles away. It can be a lifesaver.

need help you carried a sure means of getting it whether you were sailing in mid-ocean or close to shore? I am talking about EPIRB, an Emergency Position Indicating Radio Beacon. The Guest Corporation now makes an EPIRB Class B model designed for pleasure craft. The whole thing is no bigger than a Thermos bottle with a short antenna attached, but the signal from this little unit can be picked up by such satellites as SARSAT, the Search and Rescue satellite that is monitored by the Coast Guard. The repetitive distress signal that enables help to pinpoint your location can also be picked up by aircraft. One nice feature about this unit is a diagnostic circuit switch that lets you check the unit and its battery to make sure they are good. Shelf life of the battery is six years. For more information about the Guest Model #630 EPIRB, write for the company's free catalog (see address above).

Helm Handler

There are many gadgets on the market designed to tend your tiller for a while so you can do something else. Few, however, are as well made or scientifically designed as the Helm Handler. It is instrument quality. Nothing flimsy. Top grade heavy walled anodized aluminum with stainless steel fittings. The control bar can be custom fitted to your size cockpit. It attaches about a third of the way up your helm from the rudder post and fits from your helm to your coaming. Swivel pins on each end enable it to be dropped in or lifted out easily. One of its nice features is micrometer adjustment made possible merely by turning a foam-padded section to fine-tune its helm handling characteristics. Works great when under power, too, relieving you of the tiresome chore of holding onto the helm on those long runs over the wide open stretches. Marine hardware stores have them, as do the mail-order catalogs. Otherwise contact the company: Recmar, 17875 Sky Park North, Suite B, Irvine, CA 92714. Tel: (714) 751-8774.

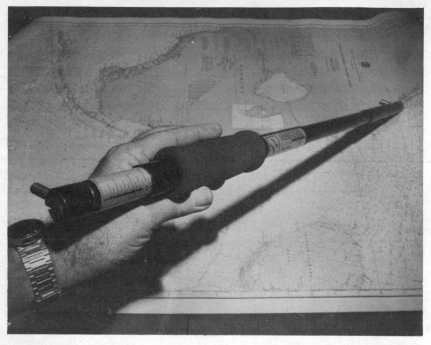

A precision instrument, Helm Handler's easily removed tiller tender has micrometer adjustments to enable you to fine tune its capabilities while you duck below for a cup of coffee.

Camera Afloat

Picture yourself sailing swiftly over the bounding main with decks awash, snapping photographs of the action left and right without a care about ruining your camera. Or, while on a mooring, picture yourself grabbing that same camera and dropping it over the side to photograph colorful scenes from another world, a watery one that would normally ruin any other 35mm camera. But not this one, not the all-weather Nikonos IV A. This camera is a sailor's delight—small, rugged, easy to handle above or underwater, fully automatic, and capable of handling all the popular 35mm films. With this one all you have to do is dial in the distance, point, and shoot. The camera does the rest, reading the light, automatically setting the aperture and shutter speed. It produces top quality photographs every time. No camera that fits in the palm of your hand can do better than that. It comes with a standard 35mm f/2.5 lens for above or below the water. If you really get interested in filming the underwater world, you can get several interchangeable lenses for the camera ranging from macro-closeup to ultra-wide-angle. Most quality dive shops handle the Nikonos U/W camera as do some photography shops, or you can contact the distributor: Ehrenreich Photo-Optical Industries, Inc. (EPOI), 623 Stewart Avenue, Garden City, NY 11530. Tel: (516) 222-0200.

Above or below water, the fully automatic 35mm Nikonos IV A is a sailor or diver's delight, picturing the action perfectly each time.

Appendix I
Trailer-Sailing Tips

Before they sailed off to Arizona, trailer sailors Carl and Nancy Zillmer sailed Michigan's Great Lakes in their twenty-two-foot Catalina, *Sea 'n Zee*. Some of the things they learned are worth passing on:

- Our neighbor had problems on gravel launching ramps. Since his boat outweighed his car, on wet gravel it wanted to pull his car into the drink. He needed the help of a four-wheel-drive vehicle to keep him dry. He drove a two-door Thunderbird and hauled a Catalina 25. We had no problem on such ramps, but it pays to watch out for wet gravel when launching.
- For heavy boats, use good air shock absorbers on your car to help support the load.
- We placed a foam pad on top of foodstuffs in our ice chest for extra insulation.
- Our Honda 7.5-horsepower outboard motor has an alternator for recharging the battery. It did the job nicely. Our neighbor uses a Honda generator to recharge a bank of batteries for the refrigerator on his twenty-five-foot trailer sailer.

- Be sure the weight of all gear—equipment, food, etc., is distributed so that your sailboat floats level.
- A Bimini top or some kind of cockpit cover is a must.
- Wear long-sleeved lightweight clothing for protection, especially if you are fair-skinned.
- Eggs, unwashed, keep fresh up to five weeks. Buy directly from the farmer if possible.
- Canned bacon is very good but it should be washed before cooking to remove excess salt.
- Potatoes, onions, and carrots in open-weaved bags keep longer than in plastic bags.
- Stock up before leaving home because marina prices are almost always higher. Take time in advance to plan a menu; it will be a happier cruise.
- Secure all loose halyards at night; make your boat as quiet as possible in consideration of others.
- Any electrical wires inside your mast that may clatter noisily can be silenced by tying chunks of foam rubber on a clothesline and stuffing it up the mast with a cane pole. A good night's sleep is important to the crew.
- Keep hot water in a *good* Thermos for cocoa, tea, instant coffee, etc. A cold body can ruin a trip.
- Place dirty dishes in a net bag and rinse them overboard. Joy detergent is the best when washing dishes in salt water.
- Clothes can be washed by giving them a squirt of detergent, putting them in a mesh bag, and towing them in your wake. Be sure the bag is well secured before tossing it overboard!

(And here are some others)

- A squeaky mooring or anchor line can be quieted with a few drops of liquid detergent where it chafes in the chock.
- If you run out of brass polish, a good substitute is Teak Brite. Occasionally wipe it on and rinse it off.
- A thin film of liquid detergent wiped on the inside of cabin windows will prevent them from fogging.

- Borax mixed with a little sugar makes an effective bug killer when sprinkled around the galley counter.
- If you equip your trailer sailer for cruising, to reach a more realistic figure for what your car will have to tow, plan on at least 1,000 pounds of extra weight. This will include such basics as outboard motor, fuel, water, anchor, battery, etc., but no personal gear, food, or bilge water.
- If you are unable to move your boat forward far enough on the trailer to have sufficient tongue weight, and all else fails, consider moving your trailer wheels and axle farther aft.
- If you have only so much to spend for a sailboat, think small but not cheap. Look over the sixteen- to nineteen-foot quality boats rather than twenty-two- to twenty-three-foot junk boats. Nothing can drain a boat budget faster than trying to repair a junker.
- If your boat has a bilge pump that can be operated from the cockpit, secure the pump handle to the inside of a lazaret or cockpit seat locker hatch where it can be quickly reached in an emergency.
- A boat in distress can best be located by EPIRB. Stow yours where it can be reached easily.
- Solder flowed into screw-head slots will prevent the screws from being removed from hatches or lockers by thieves.
- Bolt your outboard to its motor mount and conceal the fact with plastic wood or silver-color silicone cement.

Appendix II
Popular Trailer Sailers

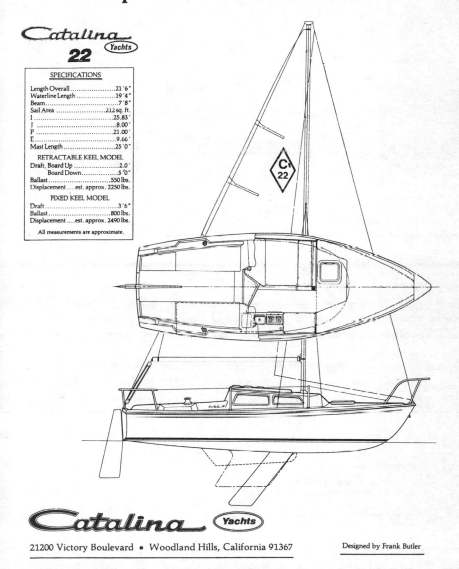

Catalina (Yachts)
22

SPECIFICATIONS

Length Overall ....21'6"
Waterline Length ....19'4"
Beam...................................7'8"
Sail Area ....212 sq. ft.
I ....25.83'
J ....8.00'
P ....21.00'
E ....9.66'
Mast Length ....25'0"

RETRACTABLE KEEL MODEL
Draft, Board Up ....2.0'
        Board Down................5'0"
Ballast.................................550 lbs.
Displacement ....est. approx. 2250 lbs.

FIXED KEEL MODEL
Draft ....3'6"
Ballast.................................800 lbs.
Displacement ....est. approx. 2490 lbs.

All measurements are approximate.

Catalina (Yachts)

21200 Victory Boulevard • Woodland Hills, California 91367

Designed by Frank Butler

SPECIFICATIONS

RETRACTABLE KEEL MODEL

L.O.A.	25'-0"
L.W.L.	22'-2"
BEAM	8'-0"
DRAFT Board up	2'-8"
Board Down	5'-0"
BALLAST	1500 lbs.
DISPLACEMENT	4150 lbs.
SAIL AREA STD. RIG.	270 sq. ft.
SAIL AREA TALL RIG.	295 sq. ft.

FIXED KEEL MODEL

L.O.A.	25'-0"
L.W.L.	22'-2"
BEAM	8'-0"
DRAFT	4'-0"
BALLAST	1900 lbs.
DISPLACEMENT	4550 lbs.
SAIL AREA STD. RIG.	270 sq. ft.
SAIL AREA TALL RIG.	295 sq. ft.
I.O.R. rating (est.) STD. RIG.	19.9

all measurements are approximate.

Patent numbers 3805724, 3648310 and 111523

- FLIP-TOP AVAILABLE. INCREASES HEADROOM TO 6'6"

- SELF-BAILING COCKPIT

- ADJUSTABLE TRAVELER WITH CONTROLS, STANDARD

- MOLDED IN SHEER STRIPE AND WATERLINE COLORS STD.

- FIBERGLASS RUDDER WITH LAMINATED HARDWOOD TILLER STANDARD

- SOLID TEAK TRIM

- HAND LAY UP DECK WITH DECK LINER

- HAND LAY UP HULL WITH HULL LINER

- ANCHOR LOCKER WITH DRAIN ON FOREDECK STANDARD

- NON-SKID PATTERN MOLDED ON DECK AREAS

- TWO COCKPIT HATCHES WITH SAIL LOCKER

- FLUSH FITTING FORWARD HATCH STANDARD

- STORM COVER FOR MAIN HATCH STANDARD

- STAINLESS STEEL CHAIN PLATES AND STANDING RIGGING

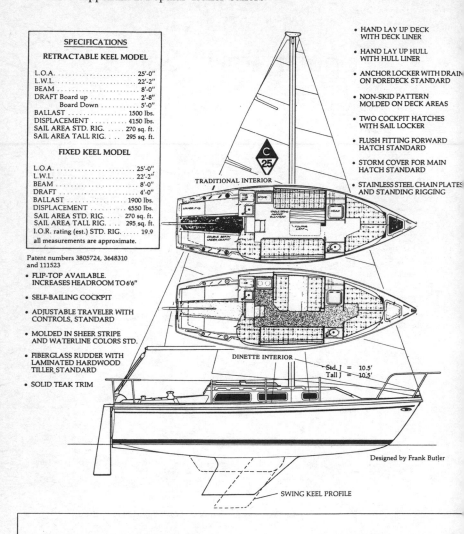

TRADITIONAL INTERIOR

DINETTE INTERIOR

Std J = 10.5'
Tall J = 10.5'

Designed by Frank Butler

SWING KEEL PROFILE

YACHTS

21200 Victory Boulevard • Woodland Hills, California 91367

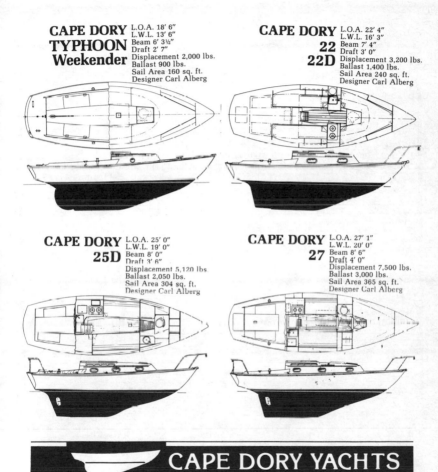

CAPE DORY TYPHOON Weekender
L.O.A. 18' 6"
L.W.L. 13' 6"
Beam 6' 3½"
Draft 2' 7"
Displacement 2,000 lbs.
Ballast 900 lbs.
Sail Area 160 sq. ft.
Designer Carl Alberg

CAPE DORY 22 22D
L.O.A. 22' 4"
L.W.L. 16' 3"
Beam 7' 4"
Draft 3' 0"
Displacement 3,200 lbs.
Ballast 1,400 lbs.
Sail Area 240 sq. ft.
Designer Carl Alberg

CAPE DORY 25D
L.O.A. 25' 0"
L.W.L. 19' 0"
Beam 8' 0"
Draft 3' 6"
Displacement 5,120 lbs.
Ballast 2,050 lbs.
Sail Area 304 sq. ft.
Designer Carl Alberg

CAPE DORY 27
L.O.A. 27' 1"
L.W.L. 20' 0"
Beam 8' 6"
Draft 4' 0"
Displacement 7,500 lbs.
Ballast 3,000 lbs.
Sail Area 365 sq. ft.
Designer Carl Alberg

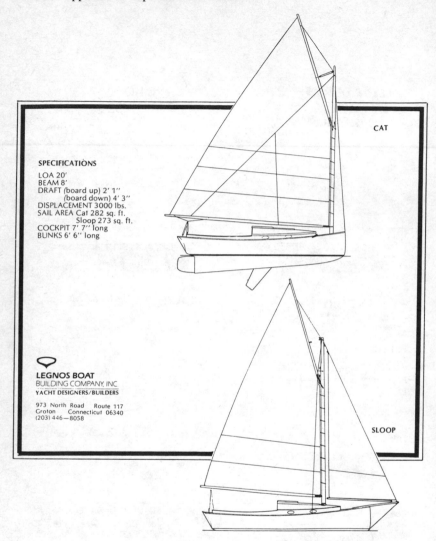

CAT

SPECIFICATIONS

LOA 20'
BEAM 8'
DRAFT (board up) 2' 1''
      (board down) 4' 3''
DISPLACEMENT 3000 lbs.
SAIL AREA Cat 282 sq. ft.
        Sloop 273 sq. ft.
COCKPIT 7' 7'' long
BUNKS 6' 6'' long

LEGNOS BOAT
BUILDING COMPANY, INC.
YACHT DESIGNERS/BUILDERS

973 North Road   Route 117
Groton   Connecticut 06340
(203) 446—8058

SLOOP

Neptune 16

L.O.A. .... 15'9"	SAIL AREA ... 137 sq. ft.
L.W.L. .... 13'6"	MAST LENGTH ... 19'6"
BEAM .... 6'2"	BOOM LENGTH ..... 8'
DISP. .... 900 lbs.	LUFF OF MAIN ..... 18'
BALLAST –	J 5'4"
S.K. .... 200 lbs.	
F.K. .... 275 lbs.	
DRAFT — KEEL UP –10"	— DOWN 4'
FIXED KEEL 26"	

neptune

88 SQ. FT.

49 30 FT

FLOTATION

8½' V–BERTH

OUTBOARD STORAGE

7' COCKPIT

Some items shown are optional.

CAPITAL YACHTS, INC.
NEWPORT ● NEPTUNE ● GULF
25914 PRESIDENT AVENUE
HARBOR CITY, CALIF. 90710
(213) 530-1311

CAPITAL YACHTS, INC.
NEWPORT • NEPTUNE • GULF
25914 PRESIDENT AVENUE
HARBOR CITY, CALIF. 90710
(213) 530-1311

SPECIFICATIONS

L.O.A...24'
L.W.L...21'
BEAM...7' 11³/4"
BALLAST (Fixed Keel) 1,200 lbs.
        (Short Keel) 1,000 lbs.
        (Shoal Draft) 1,200 lbs.
DRAFT (Fixed Keel)...4' 8"
       (Short Keel)...4' 0"
       (Shoal Draft)..2'to 3'6"
DISPLACEMENT: all models..3,200 lbs.
SAIL AREA (Standard Rig...250 sq. ft.
          (Tall Rig)......267 sq. ft.

NOR'SEA 27

THE PORTABLE HEAVY WEATHER CRUISER

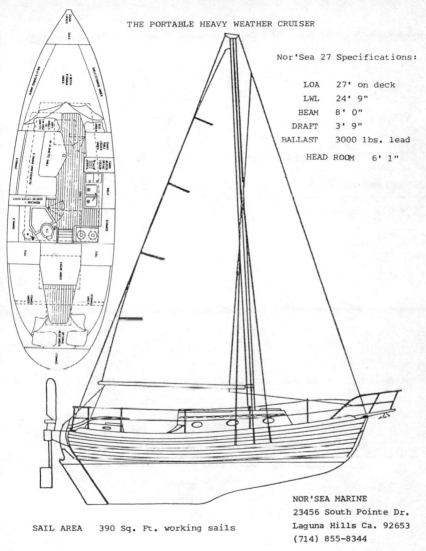

Nor'Sea 27 Specifications:

LOA	27' on deck
LWL	24' 9"
BEAM	8' 0"
DRAFT	3' 9"
BALLAST	3000 lbs. lead
HEAD ROOM	6' 1"

SAIL AREA   390 Sq. Ft. working sails

NOR'SEA MARINE
23456 South Pointe Dr.
Laguna Hills Ca. 92653
(714) 855-8344

O'DAY 222

LOA 21'9"

LWL 19'7"

BEAM 7'11"

DRAFT (BOARD UP) 1'8"
   (BOARD DOWN) 4'8",

SAIL AREA 100% 207 sq. ft.

DISPLACEMENT 2,200 lbs.

BALLAST 800 lbs.

I 22.75'

P 23.75'

J 7.75'

E 10'

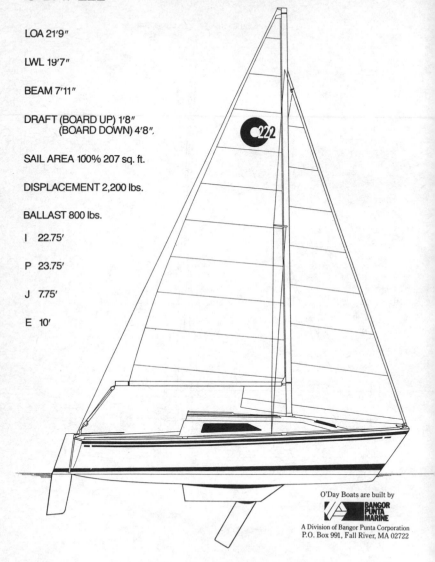

O'Day Boats are built by

BANGOR
PUNTA
MARINE

A Division of Bangor Punta Corporation
P.O. Box 991, Fall River, MA 02722

VAGABOND 17

VAGABOND SAILBOATS, INC.

3401 W. FORDHAM
SANTA ANA, CA 92704
(714) 979-9361

FAST, LIGHT, COMFORTABLE, SLEEPS 4, LARGE COCKPIT, AND EASILY TRAILERED BY A SMALL CAR. HARD TO BELIEVE?

The Vagabond 17 is a high quality, hand laid fiberglass overnighter ideal for a couple or small family. She comes complete with a double and two single berths, galley, private head compartment and a large, comfortable cockpit. And all at an affordable price.

At a light 950 pounds, she is trailerable behind even the small energy efficient car and her 17 foot length allows her to fit into the home garage.

A weighted swing keel locks in place and permits easy launching and even beaching in quiet bays and coves for shoreside fun.

The Vagabond 17 is a fast, roomy, safe weekender that you can afford.

Teak handrails, stainless bow pulpit, Harken blocks, dacron yacht braid sheets, kick-up rudder, positive foam flotation, anodised aluminum spars, bunk cushions, water system and dacron sails are all featured as standard equipment.

LOA	17'- 0''
LWL	15'- 0''
BEAM	7'- 3''
DRAFT K/U	1'- 8''
DRAFT K/D	4'- 2''
DISPL	950#
BALLAST	345#
SAIL AREA:	
MAIN	82 SQF
JIB	65 SQF
GENOA	87 SQF
SPIN	210 SQF

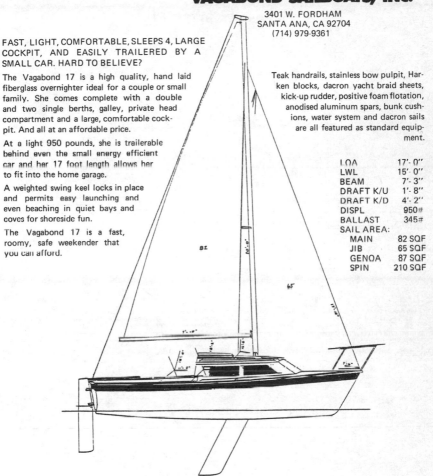

WEST WIGHT POTTER

15

19

L.O.A. . . . . 15'0"	Trailer Weight 180 lbs.
L.W.L. . . . . 12'0"	Aft Cabin Height . . 3'9"
Beam . . . . 5'6"	Berths 2
Draft:	Auxiliary . . . . . . 2-4 HP
Keel Up . . . . 7"	Mast Height . . . . . 17'11"
Keel Down . . . . . . 3'0"	Above Waterline
Sail Area:	Designer: H.E. Stewart
Main . . . . 68 sq.ft.	Price:
Jib . . . . 23 sq.ft.	Complete $3,795
Genoa . . . . . . 43 sq.ft.	Deluxe Trailer: $465
Spinnaker . . . 85 sq.ft.	
Keel . . . . 100 lbs.	
Boat Weight . . . 475 lbs.	

L.O.A. . . . . 18'9"	Keel Weight . . . 340 lbs.
L.W.L. . . . . 16'0"	Boat Weight . . . 1090 lbs.
Beam . . . . 7'6"	Trailer Weight 350 lbs.
Draft:	Berths 4
Keel Up . . . . 8"	Auxiliary . . . . . . 2-6 HP
Keel Down . . . . . . 3'7"	Mast Above Deck 22'0"
Sail Area:	Designer: H.E. Stewart
Main . . . . . . 83 sq. ft.	Price $6,495
Jib . . . . 32 sq. ft.	Sailaway
Lapper . . . . . 67 sq. ft.	Deluxe Trailer . . . $695
Genoa . . . . . . 98 sq. ft.	
Spinnaker 270 sq. ft.	

HMS MARINE, INC.
904 West Hyde Park Boulevard
Inglewood, California 90302
(213) 674-4540

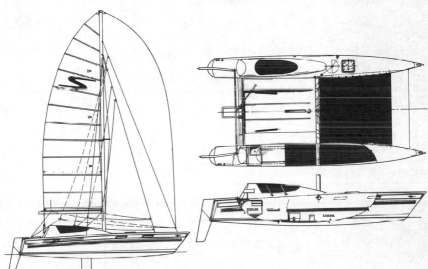

STILETTO

performance in cruising catamarans.

Specifications

LOA .... 26' 10"
LWL .... 24'
Beam .... 13' 10"
Telescoped Width ...... 7' 11½"
Set Up Time .... 1 hr
Draft .... 9" board up
                    4' board down

Sail Area:
Main .... 230 sq. ft. (fully battened)
Jib .... 106 sq. ft.
Genoa .... 159 sq. ft.
Reacher/Drifter ...... 265 sq. ft.
Spinnaker .... 750 sq. ft.

Hull: Aircraft epoxy/fiberglass and honeycomb composite
Weight: 1,100 lbs. Std. Stiletto; 1,200 lbs. Championship
    Edition; 1,265 lbs. Special Edition
Design Speed: 22 MPH +
Mast: Polyurethane coated aluminum extrusion
    (rotating airfoil design)
Bridgedeck: Fiberglass with molded seats
Daggerboard: Centerline mounted
Rudders: Automatic kick-up and return
Standing Rigging: Stainless steel
Running Rigging: Harken blocks throughout, Internal
    halyards, Full length traveler
Misc. Hardware: Custom stainless steel
Auxiliary: Custom bracket for up to 15 h.p. outboard

Manufactured by
FORCE ENGINEERING
5329 Ashton Ct., Sarasota, FL 33583 (813) 923-1857

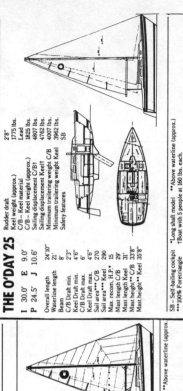

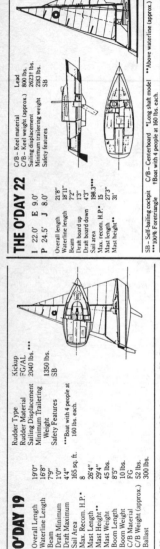

O'DAY 19

Rudder Type	Kickup	
Rudder Material	FG/AL ***	
Sailing Displacement	2040 lbs. ***	
Minimum Trailering Weight	1350 lbs.	
Safety Features	SB	

Overall Length	19'0"
Waterline Length	16'8"
Beam	7'9"
Draft Minimum	1'0"
Draft Maximum	4'4"
Sail Area	165 sq. ft.
Max. Recom. H.P.	8
Mast Length	26'4"
Mast Height**	29'4"
Mast Weight	45 lbs.
Boom Length	8'5"
Boom Weight	10 lbs.
C/B Material	FG
C/B Weight (approx.)	52 lbs.
Ballast	300 lbs.

SR – Self-rescuing   SB – Self-bailing cockpit   C/B – Centerboard   FG – Fiberglass
AL – Aluminum   *Long shaft model   **Above waterline (approx.)

THE O'DAY 23

I¹ 28.0' E 9.0'
P 23.5' J 10.0'

C/B – Keel material	Lead
C/B – Keel weight (approx.)	1200 lbs.
Sailing displacement	3725† lbs.
Minimum trailering weight	3085 lbs.
Safety features	SB

Overall length	22'9"
Waterline length	19'6"
Beam	7'11"
Draft minimum	2'3"
Draft maximum	5'4"
Sail area	246"***
Max. recom. H.P.	15
Mast length	27'
Mast height**	32'

FG – Fiberglass   SB – Self-bailing cockpit   C/B – Centerboard   *Long shaft model   **Above waterline (approx.)
***100% Foretriangle   †Boat with 4 people at 160 lbs. each.   M.O.R.C. 17.9 on design waterline at a weight of 3,425 lbs.

THE O'DAY 22

I 22.0' E 9.0'
P 24.5' J 8.0'

C/B – Keel material	Lead	
C/B – Keel weight (approx.)	800 lbs.	
Sailing displacement	26231 lbs.	
Minimum trailering weight	2183 lbs.	
Safety features	SB	

Overall length	21'8"
Waterline length	18'11"
Beam	7'2"
Draft board up	1'3"
Draft board down	4'3"
Sail area	198.3"***
Max. recom. H.P.	15
Mast length	27'3"
Mast height**	31'

SB – Self-bailing cockpit   C/B – Centerboard   *Long shaft model   **Above waterline (approx.)
***100% Foretriangle   †Boat with 4 people at 160 lbs. each.

THE O'DAY 25

I 30.0' E 9.0'
P 24.5' J 10.6'

Rudder draft	2'8"	
Keel weight (approx.)	1775 lbs.	
C/B – Keel material	Lead	
C/B – Keel weight (approx.)	1825 lbs.	
Sailing displacement C/B†	4807 lbs.	
Sailing displacement Keel†	4762 lbs.	
Minimum trailering weight C/B	4007 lbs.	
Minimum trailering weight Keel	3962 lbs.	
Safety features	SB	

Overall length	24'10"
Waterline length	21'
Beam	8'
C/B Draft min.	2'3"
Keel Draft min.	4'6"
C/B Draft max.	6'
Keel Draft max.	4'6"
Sail area*** C/B	270
Sail area*** Keel	290
Max. recom. H.P.	15
Mast length C/B	29'
Mast length Keel	31'
Mast height** C/B	33'8"
Mast height** Keel	35'8"

SB – Self-bailing cockpit   *Long shaft model   **Above waterline (approx.)
***100% Foretriangle   †Boat with 5 people at 160 lbs. each.

BANGOR PUNTA MARINE 848 AIRPORT ROAD P.O. BOX 991 FALL RIVER MA 02722 (617) 678-5291

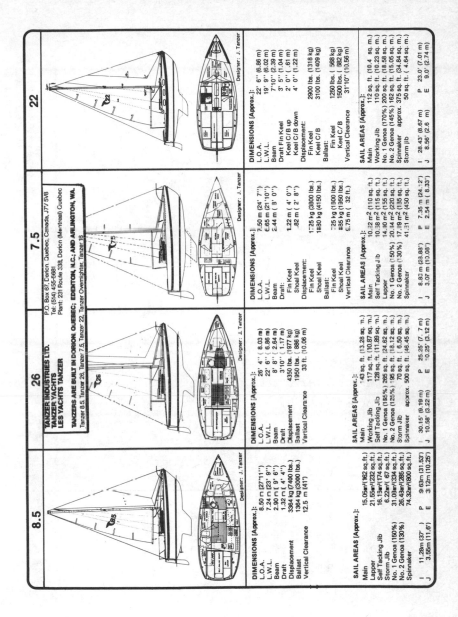

8.5 — Designer: J. Tanzer

DIMENSIONS [Approx.]:
L.O.A. 8.50 m (27'11")
L.W.L. 7.24 m (23' 9")
Beam 2.90 m (9' 6")
Draft 1.32 m (4' 4")
Displacement 3364 kg (7400 lbs.)
Ballast 1364 kg (3000 lbs.)
Vertical Clearance 12.5 m (41')

SAIL AREAS [Approx.]:
Main 15.05 m² (162 sq.ft.)
Lapper 21.55 m² (232 sq.ft.)
Self Tacking Jib 16.13 m² (174 sq.ft.)
Storm Jib 6.22 m² (67 sq.ft.)
No. 1 Genoa (150%) 31.03 m² (334 sq.ft.)
No. 2 Genoa (130%) 26.43 m² (285 sq.ft.)
Spinnaker 74.32 m² (800 sq.ft.)
J 11.28 m (37')   P 9.63 m (31.53')
  3.55 m (11.6')   E 3.12 m (10.25')

26 — Designer: J. Tanzer

TANZER INDUSTRIES LTD.
TANZER YACHTS
LES YACHTS TANZER
P.O. Box 67, Dorion, Quebec, Canada, J7V 5V8
Tel: (514) 455-6681
Plant: 231 Route 338, Dorion (Montreal) Quebec

TANZERS ARE BUILT IN DORION QUEBEC; EDENTON, N.C.; AND ARLINGTON, WA.
Tanzer 8.5, Tanzer 26, Tanzer 7.5, Tanzer 22, Tanzer Overnighter, Tanzer 16

DIMENSIONS [Approx.]:
L.O.A. 26' 4" (8.03 m)
L.W.L. 22' 6" (6.86 m)
Beam 8' 8" (2.64 m)
Draft 3'10" (1.17 m)
Displacement 4350 lbs. (1977 kg)
Ballast 1950 lbs. (886 kg)
Vertical Clearance 33 ft. (10.06 m)

SAIL AREAS [Approx.]:
Main 143 sq. ft. (13.28 sq. m.)
Working Jib 117 sq. ft. (10.87 sq. m.)
Self Tacking Jib 128 sq. ft. (11.89 sq. m.)
No. 1 Genoa (185%) 265 sq. ft. (24.62 sq. m.)
No. 2 Genoa (125%) 195 sq. ft. (18.12 sq. m.)
Storm Jib 70 sq. ft. (6.50 sq. m.)
Spinnaker approx. 500 sq. ft. (46.45 sq. m.)
J 30.15' (9.19 m)   P 25.25' (7.7 m)
  10.58' (3.22 m)   E 10.25' (3.12 m)

7.5 — Designer: J. Tanzer

DIMENSIONS [Approx.]:
L.O.A. 7.50 m (24' 7")
L.W.L. 6.65 m (21'10")
Beam 2.44 m (8' 0")
Draft:
Fin Keel 1.22 m (4' 0")
Shoal Keel .82 m (2' 8")
Displacement:
Fin Keel 1725 kg (3800 lbs.)
Shoal Keel 1830 kg (4150 lbs.)
Ballast:
Fin Keel 725 kg (1600 lbs.)
Shoal Keel 885 kg (1950 lbs.)
Vertical Clearance 9.75 m (32 ft.)

SAIL AREAS [Approx.]:
Main 10.22 m² (110 sq. ft.)
Self Tacking Jib 10.38 m² (115 sq. ft.)
Lapper 14.10 m² (155 sq. ft.)
No. 1 Genoa (150%) 20.44 m² (220 sq. ft.)
No. 2 Genoa (130%) 17.19 m² (185 sq. ft.)
Spinnaker 41.31 m² (450 sq. ft.)
J 8.83 m (28.88')   P 7.35 m (24.12')
  3.07 m (10.08')   E 2.54 m (8.33')

22 — Designer: J. Tanzer

DIMENSIONS [Approx.]:
L.O.A. 22' 6" (6.86 m)
L.W.L. 19' 9" (6.02 m)
Beam 7'10" (2.39 m)
Draft Fin Keel 3' 5" (1.04 m)
Keel C/B up 2' 0" (.61 m)
Keel C/B down 4' 0" (1.22 m)
Displacement:
Fin Keel 2900 lbs. (1318 kg)
Keel C/B 3100 lbs. (1409 kg)
Ballast:
Fin Keel 1250 lbs. (568 kg)
Keel C/B 1500 lbs. (682 kg)
Vertical Clearance 31'10" (10.56 m)

SAIL AREAS [Approx.]:
Main 112 sq. ft. (10.4 sq. m.)
Working Jib 110 sq. ft. (10.23 sq. m.)
No. 1 Genoa (170%) 200 sq. ft. (18.58 sq. m.)
No. 2 Genoa (145%) 162 sq. ft. (15.05 sq. m.)
Spinnaker approx. 375 sq. ft. (34.84 sq. m.)
Storm Jib 50 sq. ft. (4.64 sq. m.)
J 28.43' (8.67 m)   P 23.0' (7.01 m)
  8.56' (2.6 m)   E 9.0' (2.74 m)

SeaPearl 21

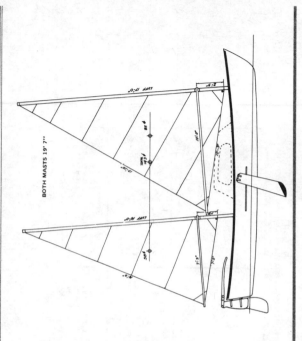

BOTH MASTS 19' 7"

Adventure in exploring
Adventure in sailing
Ease in adventure

Tow her with your sub-compact and launch her anywhere, she only weighs 550 lbs. Sail her right onto a beach and winch her on the trailer. Stow your gear and still have plenty of room to sleep two below deck in an area kept dry by either tonneau cover (standard) or convertable top (optional). Your feet stay dry as well in SeaPearl's self-bailing cockpit with its drain plug above the water line. Free standing mast, kick up lee boards and rudder, wishbone rig, no centerboard trunk, all these features plus her price make her easy to own.

General Specifications

L.O.A.	21'-0"
D.W.L.	19'-0"
Beam	5'-6"
Draft Loaded	6"
Board Down	2'-6"
Trailing Weight	550 Lbs (Approx.)
Sail Area (Lug Rig)	138 Sq. Ft.
Sail Area (Wishbone Rig)	143 Sq. Ft.
Cockpit Length	6'-6"
Headroom-under Conv. Top	3'-6"
Mast Height Above D.W.L.	
Wishbone Rig	19'-8"
Lug Rig	14'-4"

MARINE CONCEPTS

159 Oakwood Street East
Tarpon Springs, Florida 33589
Telephone: (813) 937-0166

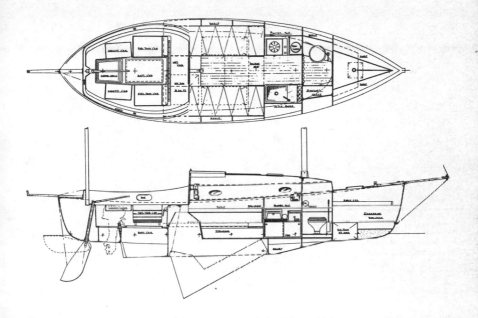

THE ROB ROY · 23 YAWL

Length overall		29'8"
Length on the deck		22'8"
Length on the waterline		20'10"
Beam		6'11"
Draft	(Board up)	1'6"
	(Board down)	4'3"
Displacement		2200 lbs
Displacement/length ratio		108.6
Ballast including centerboard		650 lbs
Sail area		264 square feet
Sail area/Displacement ratio		24.8
Construction		balsa-cored fiberglass
Spars		anodized aluminum

Index